LIBRARY OF NEW TESTAMENT STUDIES

381

formerly the Journal for the Study of the New Testament Supplement series

Editor
Mark Goodacre

Editorial Board
John M. G. Barclay, Craig Blomberg, Kathleen E. Corley, R. Alan Culpepper,
James D. G. Dunn, Craig A. Evans, Stephen Fowl, Robert Fowler,
Simon J. Gathercole, John S. Kloppenborg, Michael Labahn, Robert Wall,
Steve Walton, Robert L. Webb, Catrin H. Williams

PERSPECTIVES ON THE PASSION: ENCOUNTERING THE BIBLE THROUGH THE ARTS

EDITED BY CHRISTINE E. JOYNES

ASSISTANT EDITOR, NANCY MACKY

t&t clark

Copyright © Christine E. Joynes, Nancy Macky and contributors, 2007

Published by T&T Clark International
A Continuum imprint
The Tower Building, 11 York Road, London SE1 7NX
80 Maiden Lane, Suite 704, New York, NY 10038

www.tandtclark.com

British Library Cataloguing-in-Publication Data
A catalogue record for this book is available from the British Library

ISBN-13: HB: 978–0-567–03362-8
ISBN-10: HB: 0–567-03362–7

Typeset by Data Standards Limited, Frome, Somerset, UK.
Printed on acid-free paper in Great Britain by
Cromwell Press Ltd, Trowbridge, Wiltshire.

CONTENTS

ACKNOWLEDGEMENTS

The following sources are gratefully acknowledged for permission to reproduce copyright material:

Chapter 2
Denise Levertov's 'Salvator Mundi. Via Crucis' from *Evening Train* is reprinted by permission of New Directions Publishing Corp.

Chapter 7
Lines from 'Jesus in the olive grove' are reproduced from *The Hymns and Ballads of Fred Pratt Green* (1982), by kind permission of Stainer & Bell Ltd., London, England.

Chapter 10
Sara Maitland's short story 'Bad Friday' is reprinted from *Angel and Me: Short Stories for Holy Week* (1995) courtesy of Mowbray.

Thanks are also due to all those mentioned in the list of illustrations for granting permission to reproduce the images in this volume.

ILLUSTRATIONS

Chapter 1
Figure 1. Edvard Munch, *Golgotha*, 1900, oil on canvas. Munch Museum, Oslo. (Photo: © Munch Museum, Oslo/DACS, London, 2007)

Figure 2. Herbert Falken, *Laughing Double Cross*, 1969. (Photo: © Suermondt Ludwig Museum, Aachen)

Figure 3. Janusz Szpyt, *Family Remembrance*, 1984. (Photo:By kind permission, © Andreas Würbel, Thomas-Morus-Akademie Bensberg, Bergisch Gladbach)

Figure 4. The Crucifixion, from the Rabbula Gospels, Florence, Biblioteca Laurenziana. (Photo: © 1990 Scala, Florence, courtesy of the Ministero Beni e Att. Culturali)

Figure 5. Leonardo da Vinci, *Head of Judas, c. 1495. (Photo: The Royal Collection © 2007 Her Majesty Queen Elizabeth II)*

Figure 6. Guido Rocha, *The Tormented Christ*, 1975, All Africa Conference of Churches Training Center, Nairobi. (Photo: WCC, Geneva)

Figure 7. Rembrandt, *Eli, eli lama sabachthani, c.* 1656. (Photo: © Stiftung Weimarer Klassik und Kunstsammlungen)

Figure 8. Giotto, *The Kiss of Judas, c.* 1305, Scrovegni Chapel, Padua. (Photo: © Scala, Florence)

Figure 9. Piotr Naliwajko, *Pilate I*, 1990. (Photo: By kind permission, © Andreas Würbel, Thomas-Morus-Akademie Bensberg, Bergisch Gladbach)

Figure 10. Marc Chagall, *White Crucifixion*, 1938, oil on canvas, 154.3 x 139.7 cm, Gift of Alfred S. Alschuler, 1946.925, The Art Institute of Chicago. (Photo: © The Art Institute of Chicago/DACS, London, 2007)

Figure 11. Engelbert Mveng, *Crucifixion*, Chapel of the Libermann College, Douala, Cameroon. (Photo: WCC, Geneva)

Chapter 3
Figure 1. Francesco Goya, *Christ on the Cross*, Museo del Prado, Madrid. (Photo: © akg-images/Erich Lessing)

Figure 2. Francesco Goya, *The Third of May 1808*, Museo del Prado, Madrid. (Photo: © akg-images/Erich Lessing)

Chapter 4
Figure 1. Second- or third-century graffito, 'Alexamenos worships his god', Palatine Museum, Rome. (Photo: author)

Figure 2. Crucifixion on a gem (carnelian), *c*. 300 CE. The British Museum, London. (Photo: Jeffrey Spier)

Figure 3. Crucifixion from wooden panel of the doors of Sta. Sabina, Rome, *c*. 435 CE. (Photo: Lee Jefferson)

Figure 4. Crucifixion, side of an ivory casket *c*. 420–30 CE. © The British Museum, London (Photo: © The Trustees of the British Museum, London)

Figure 5. The Crucifixion and Resurrection, from the Rabbula Gospels, Florence, Biblioteca Laurenziana. (Photo: © 1990 Scala, Florence, courtesy of the Ministero Benie Att. Culturali)

Figure 6. Crucifixion, eighth-century fresco from church of Sta. Maria Antiqua, Rome. (Photo: author)

Figure 7. Crucifixion, ivory plaque, tenth century. Metz. Victoria and Albert Museum, London. (Photo: author)

Figure 8. Offering of Isaac on a fourth-century sarcophagus in the Museo Pio Cristiano, Vatican. (Photo: author)

Figure 9. Fourth-century sarcophagus with scenes from the Passion, Museo Pio Cristiano, Vatican. (Photo: author)

Figure 7. Crucifix, mid-sixteenth century, with a corpus made of corn paste, Tlaxcala cathedral. (Photo: author)

Figure 8. Detail from the *Codex Tlaltelolco* (1549). (With permission of the Biblioteca Nacional de Antropología e Historia, Mexico City)

Figure 9. Drawing of the Franciscan catechetical centre at Izamal. From Lara, *City, Temple, Stage.*

Figure 10. Atrial cross with heart and severed aorta on an altar base with four 'horns' at Yecapixtla. (Photo: author)

Figure 11. Detail of a stational chapel in the atrium at San Andrés, Calpan. Decorative pattern with dissected human hearts and conch shells. (Photo: author)

Figure 12. Aztec human sacrifice on cactus plants. Redrawn from the *Codex Boturini*, Biblioteca Nacional de Antropología e Historia, Mexico City.

Figure 13. Atrial cross and altar base at Nonoalco. (Photo: author)

Figure 14. Atrial cross and base with *cuauhxicalli* heart-box (letter 'c') at Cuernavaca. (Photo: author)

Figure 15. Atrial cross with embedded obsidian mirror at Ciudad Hidalgo. (Photo: author)

Figure 16. Atrial cross with carvings of the Aztec deity Xipe Totec at Topiltepec. (Photo courtesy of Prof. Edward Pepe)

Figure 17. Typical colonial eucharistic monstrance. (Photo: author)

Figure 18. Processional image of Christ with moveable limbs, Tlaxcala. (Photo: author)

Figure 19. Processional image of Christ with inserted ribs, Guanajuato. (Photo: author)

Figure 20. Holy Sepulchre Chapel and casket with 'puppet Christ' for Good Friday, Puebla cathedral. (Photo: author)

PREFACE

This volume is the outcome of collaboration which began in March 2005 at an interdisciplinary conference in Oxford entitled 'Perspectives on the Passion'. The aim of the conference, sponsored by The British Academy and hosted by the Centre for the Reception History of the Bible (www.crhb.org), was to bring together scholars from across the Humanities to explore the use, influence and impact of the passion narratives in art, music, literature and theology. Our engagement with this theme incorporated a variety of media, including a concert by the chamber choir *A Capella Portuguesa*, an art exhibition ('Bandages, Cuts and Piercings') by Cambridge artist Kip Gresham, and a dramatic reading ('Bad Friday') by the writer Sara Maitland.

It has been a pleasure to continue in conversation about the reception history of the passion with some of the participants in that conference during the process of compiling this collection of essays. Indeed, many striking resonances appear between the essays from scholars working in very different areas of expertise. By presenting these essays together in one volume, we hope to extend our exploration of the use, influence and impact of the passion narratives to those who were not able to attend the conference, and to encourage further interdisciplinary engagement with this fascinating theme.

In addition to thanking the contributors for bringing this volume into being, I would also like to thank the following people for their invaluable assistance in enabling this project to reach completion: Graham, Elizabeth and John Cairns, who in different ways have all played significant roles in the emergence of this book; Elaine Joynes, for reading the book in its entirety and providing much constructive feedback; Christopher Rowland, especially for help in the planning and organization of the conference; and Nancy Macky, whose editorial assistance has been greatly appreciated.

This volume is dedicated to the memory of Wiard Popkes. He had intended to contribute to the book, but his death prevented this from being fulfilled. His seminar presentation on the theme 'Dying with and in Christ: Passion and Requiem' reflected his growing interest in pursuing the interpretation of the Bible beyond narrow disciplinary boundaries.

The following collection of essays illustrates the rich and varied insights that emerge when interdisciplinary dialogue takes place.

Christine Joynes
Trinity College, Oxford
September 2007

ABBREVIATIONS

ACIAC	*Congresso Internazionale di Archaeologia Cristiana – Atti*
ANF	Ante-Nicene Fathers
Byz.	*Byzantion. Revue internationale des études byzantines*
CCCM	*Corpus Christianorum: Continuatio mediaevalis*. Turnhout 1969–
CCSL	*Corpus Christianorum: Series Latina*. Turnhout, 1953–
DACL	*Dictionnaire d'archéologie chrétienne et de liturgie*
DOP	*Dumbarton Oaks Papers*
DS	H. Denzinger and A. Schönmetzer, *Enchiridion Symbolorum: Definitionum et Declarationum de Rebus Fidei et Morum* (Barcinone: Herder, 36th edn, 1976)
GMO	Grove Music Online
JAAR	*Journal of the American Academy of Religion*
JAC	*Jahrbuch für Antike und Christentum*
JR	*Journal of Religion*
LCL	*Loeb Classical Library*
NPNF	*Nicene and Post-Nicene Fathers*
PEQ	*Palestine Exploration Quarterly*
PG	*Patrologia cursus completus, series Graeca* (ed. Migne)
PL	*Patrologia cursus completus, series Latina* (ed. Migne)
RHR	*Revue de l'histoire des religions*
RivAC	*Rivista di archaeologia cristiana*
SC	*Sources chrétiennes*
ZTK	*Zeitschrift für Theologie und Kirche*

Ancient Sources

Acts John	*Acts of John*
Acts Pil.	*Acts of Pilate*
Ambrose, *Ob. Theo.*	*De obitu Theodosii*
Arnobius, *Nat.*	*Adrerous Nationes*
Augustine, *C. Jul.*	*Contra Julianum*
Augustine, *Serm.*	*Sermones*
Barn.	*Barnabas*

Basil of Caesarea, *Laud. Theo.*	*Laudatio S. Theodori*
Bruno of Würzburg, *Expositio*	*Expositio psalmorum*
Clement of Alexandria, *Paed.*	*Paedagogus*
Clement of Alexandria, *Protr.*	*Protrepticus*
Cyprian, *Ep.*	*Epistulae*
Cyril of Jerusalem, *Myst. cat.*	*Mystagogicae Catecheses*
Egeria, *Peregr.*	*Peregrinatio*
Epiphanius, *Haer.*	*Adversus Haereses*
Eusebius, *Hist.*	*Historia ecclesiastica*
Eusebius, *Vita Const.*	*Vita Constantini*
Gregory of Tours, *Glor. Mart.*	*De gloria martyrum*
Gregory the Great, *Ep.*	*Epistulae*
Hippolytus, *Antichr.*	*De antichristo*
Ignatius of Antioch, *Eph.*	*Epistula ad Ephesios*
Ignatius of Antioch, *Rom.*	*Epistula ad Romanos*
Irenaeus, *Haer.*	*Adversus Haereses*
Jerome, *Epist.*	*Epistulae*
John Chrysostom, *Hom. Jo.*	*Homiliae in Joannem*
John of Damascus, *De imag. or.*	*De imaginibus oratio*
Josephus, *Apion*	*Against Apion*
Justin Martyr, *1 Apol.*	*First Apology*
Justin Martyr, *Dial.*	*Dialogue with Trypho*
Lucian, *Peregr.*	*De morte Peregrini*
Melito of Sardis, *Pasch.*	*Peri Pascha*
Minucius Felix, *Oct.*	*Octavius*
Origen, *Cels.*	*Contra Celsum*
Passio. Perpetua and Felicity	*Passio Perpetuae et Felicitatis*
Paulinus of Nola, *Eps.*	*Epistulae*
Plato, *Polit.*	*Politicus*
Plutarch, *Is. Os.*	*De Iside et Osiride*
Prudentius, *Peri.*	*Peristephanon*
Pseudo-Basil, *Hom.*	*Homilae*
Rufinus, *Hist.*	*Eusebii Historia ecclesiastica a Rufino translata et continuata*
Socrates, *Hist.*	*Historia Ecclesiastica*
Sozomen, *Hist.*	*Historia Ecclesiastica*
Tacitus, *Hist.*	*Historiae*
Tertullian, *Apol.*	*Apologeticus*
Tertullian, *Adv. Jud.*	*Adversus Judaeos*
Tertullian, *Bapt.*	*De baptismo*
Tertullian, *Marc.*	*Adversus Marcionem*
Tertullian, *Nat.*	*Ad nationes*
Tertullian, *Orat.*	*De oratione*
Theodoret, *Hist.*	*Historia Ecclesiastica*

CONTRIBUTORS

William Flynn is Lecturer at the University of Leeds, Institute for Medieval Studies. He is the author of *Medieval Music as Medieval Exegesis. Studies in Liturgical Musicology 9* (1999), which investigates the cross-fertilization of the elementary study of grammar, rhetoric, music and liturgy, and its effects on the production and interpretation of biblical commentary in the eleventh-century church. He participates in the study group Sapientia-Eloquentia based at the University of Stockholm, which is investigating developments in the repertories of liturgical poetry and music from the eleventh to the twelfth centuries.

Timothy Gorringe is Professor of Theological Studies at Exeter University. He has published on many aspects of theology and culture and his most recent book, *Furthering Humanity: A Theology of Culture* (2004), was shortlisted for the Michael Ramsey Prize.

Peter S. Hawkins is Professor of Religion at Boston University, where he is also Director of the Luce Program in Scripture and Literary Arts. Formerly on the faculty of Yale Divinity School, his work has centred on Dante: *Dante's Testaments: Essays in Scriptural Imagination* (1999), *The Poets' Dante: Twentieth-Century Reflections* (2001), and now *A Brief History of Dante* (Blackwell, 2006). He has also published on contemporary American fiction, first in *The Language of Grace* (1983) and, with Paula J. Carlson, in a series of books entitled *Listening for God: Contemporary Literature and the Life of Faith* (forthcoming from Augsburg Fortress).

Emma Hornby is Lecturer in Music at the University of Bristol. A mediaeval musicologist, she uses analysis of formulaic chant to explore questions of chant transmission and composition in early-mediaeval Rome and northern Europe. Her first book, *Gregorian and Old Roman Eighth-Mode Tracts*, was published by Ashgate (2002) and she has published articles in *The Journal of Musicology* and *Plainsong and Medieval Music*. From 2003 to 2007 she was assistant editor to Professor J. R. Watson on a *New Dictionary of Hymnology* and she is currently completing a book entitled *Grammar, Rhetoric and Exegesis in the Second-Mode Tracts*.

Robin Jensen is Luce Chancellor's Professor of the History of Christian Art and Worship at Vanderbilt University. She is the author of numerous articles that range from specific studies of early Christian iconography to various aspects of early Christian liturgical practice in ancient North Africa. Her books include *Understanding Early Christian Art* (Routledge, 2000) and *Face to Face: The Portrait of the Divine in Early Christianity* (Fortress, 2004). She is currently completing a book on the architecture and iconography of early Christian baptism and is co-authoring another with her husband, J. Patout Burns, on the practice of Christianity in Roman Africa.

Christine Joynes is Associate Director of the Centre for the Reception History of the Bible at the University of Oxford. One of her current research interests is the reception history of Mark's Gospel and she is presently writing the Blackwell Bible Commentary, *Mark's Gospel through the Centuries*. She is also coordinating a project entitled *Biblical Women and their Afterlives*. She has written a number of articles exploring the impact of the Bible on art, music and literature.

Jaime Lara is Professor of Christian Art & Architecture and chair of the Program in Religion and the Arts at Yale University. He received his doctorate in the History of Religion and Art from the Graduate Theological Union and the University of California, Berkeley. His book *City, Temple, Stage: Eschatological Architecture and Liturgical Theatrics in New Spain* was published in 2004 by the University of Notre Dame Press. He is presently working on a sequel entitled *Christian Texts for Aztecs: The Liturgical Conquest of Mexico*. His study of liturgy in Latin America in the *Oxford Dictionary of Christian Worship* is forthcoming.

Ulrich Luz is Emeritus Professor of New Testament at the University of Bern, Switzerland, where he taught from 1980 until his retirement in 2003. He also taught at the International Christian University in Tokyo (1970–71) and at the University of Göttingen (1972–80). His publications in English include *Matthew in History: Interpretation, Influence and Effects* (1994), *The Theology of Matthew* (1995), *Studies in Matthew* (2005) and the three-volume commentary on Matthew in the Hermeneia series, published by Fortress Press.

Sara Maitland was born in 1950 and read English at St Anne's College, Oxford. In 1978 her first novel – *Daughter of Jerusalem* – won the Somerset Maugham Award and she has been a freelance writer ever since. She has published a wide variety of books and articles, fiction and non-fiction, including (in both) some theology (*A Big Enough God*; *Angel and Me*; *Virtuous Magic* etc.); and has also written for BBC Radio and worked with Stanley Kubrick on his AI project (now a Spielberg film). She lives in southwest Scotland and is presently working on a cultural history of silence.

Nancy Macky is Associate Professor of English, Emerita, at Westminster College, New Wilmington, Pennsylvania, where she won its prestigious Henderson Lecturer Award. She is the author of several articles on W. B. Yeats, literary reviews for reference works, as well as publications on teaching writing and literature. She was twice Visiting Scholar at Wolfson College, Oxford, collaborating with Professor Jon Stallworthy, most recently on his *Survivors' Songs*, forthcoming at Cambridge University Press. Reader at the Huntington Library in San Marino, California, she has edited books of essays on theology, has taught Literature, Film, and Sacredness seminars at Princeton Theological Seminary, and has conducted writing workshops for faculty at regional colleges.

Regina Schwartz is Professor of English at Northwestern University. Her publications include *Remembering and Repeating: Biblical Creation in Paradise Lost* (1988), which won the James Holly Hanford prize for the best book on Milton; *The Book and the Text: The Bible and Literary Theory* (1990); *Desire in the Renaissance:Psychoanalyis and Literature* (1994); and *The Postmodern Bible* (1995). Her most recent book, *The Curse of Cain: The Violent Legacy of Monotheism* – a study of monotheism, national identity and violence in the Hebrew Bible – was nominated for a Pulitzer Prize. Her current project is a book on the Eucharist in Renaissance literature.

J. R. Watson is Emeritus Professor of English, University of Durham. During his years there (1978–99) his main work was on the Romantic and Victorian periods, with a particular interest in landscape and hymnology. In 1997 he published *The English Hymn* (Clarendon Press, Oxford) subtitled *A Critical and Historical Study*; this was followed by *An Annotated Anthology of Hymns* (Oxford University Press, 2002). With the assistance of Dr Emma Hornby, he is currently attempting to produce a replacement for Julian's *Dictionary of Hymnology* (1892, 1907).

INTRODUCTION

Christine E. Joynes

There is a growing recognition of the importance of investigating the reception history (or 'afterlives') of biblical texts.[1] How people have interpreted and been influenced by the Bible is often as interesting and historically important as what the text may have originally meant. Reception history is interdisciplinary by nature, examining material from a wide variety of contexts and media, and incorporating readings outside the academy, from both church and culture. This is a distinctive feature, broadening the horizons of material traditionally classed as 'biblical interpretation'. So artists, writers and composers are included as biblical interpreters alongside the academic and the religious believer.

The present volume aims to contribute to this broad field of interest by focusing on the theme of the reception history of the passion narratives. The contributions, ranging from 'Christian Cannibalism and Human(e) Sacrifice: The Passion in the Conversion of the Aztecs' to 'Emblem and Irony: Passion Narrative in Post-Reformation Hymnody', offer just a sample of the extensive impact that the passion narratives have had. From public worship to private devotion, cinema screen to political propaganda, the Gospel passion accounts have been influential in various cultural contexts, with significantly different results.

In the opening chapter, Ulrich Luz offers some methodological reflections upon the role of reception history, and then applies these observations to the reception history of the passion in art. His analysis of artistic representations of the passion narratives extends from well-known images, such as Chagall's *White Crucifixion* and Giotto's *Kiss of Judas*, to lesser-known works by artists Janusz Szpyt, Piotr Naliwajko and Guido Rocha. He uses these images to make a case for the rich potential offered by artistic interpretations of biblical texts. Luz's starting-point is the loss of images in the Protestant churches, which he provocatively argues has led to an intellectualized church, whose literacy 'obstructs an immediate,

---

1   See for example the Blackwell Bible Commentary Series, with its distinctive focus on reception history.

intuitive, visual, sensual and holistic access to biblical texts'. He reflects in his essay upon his own tradition within the Swiss Reformed Church, and concludes that in view of the valuable interpretations of the Bible revealed through the language of images, 'it was wrong in the Reformation to banish images from the Churches. For the sake of the Bible we should try to reintroduce them.'

In the course of his analysis, Luz identifies a characteristic theme in twentieth-century art to be a 'sense of a loss of God'. This viewpoint provokes interesting comparisons when juxtaposed with Peter Hawkins' contribution, which explores the precarious balance between the human and divine natures of Christ through an examination of literary portrayals of the Gethsemane 'Moment'. 'Jesus' vulnerability in this scene', Hawkins notes, 'is consistently downplayed in commentaries both ancient and modern.' In this essay he attempts to redress the balance, by drawing our attention to features which highlight Jesus' humanity, suggesting 'resolution belongs to the Lord; he who hesitates is human'.

Hawkins' analysis of the Gethsemane moment in the twentieth century includes discussion of Nikos Kazantzakis' *The Last Temptation of Christ*, José Luis Saramago's *The Gospel According to Jesus Christ*, and Rainer-Maria Rilke's poem 'The Olive-Garden'. The latter clearly illustrates the theme of abandonment, alluded to also by Luz, which leads Hawkins to conclude, 'The twentieth century seems to have turned its back on the balancing act with which we began: the both/and mystery of the Word made flesh affirmed by orthodox Christianity.' Nevertheless, Hawkins manages to find some evidence of continuing attempts to retain the dynamic tension between Christ's humanity and divinity, notably in the poem 'Salvator Mundi. Via Crucis' by Denise Levertov. His detailed exposition of Levertov's poem reminds us of the rich contribution literature can offer to biblical interpretation.

Levertov's poem draws heavily upon visual art. In her imaginative engagement with the passion she suggests, 'That face, in extremis, would have clenched its teeth/in a grimace not shown in even the great crucifixions'. Representations of the crucifixion by great artists, notably Francesco de Goya, are the subject of Tim Gorringe's contribution. Gorringe begins by highlighting Andrew Ure's claim that the passion of Christ was used to discipline the workforce in the early nineteenth century, and he asks whether there might be evidence for this in art. His contrast between Goya's pious and political art provides a clear affirmative to his question.

Gorringe finds evidence for his view that the symbol of the cross has been used as a 'disguised legitimation of social abuses' in the passion mysticism of the fourteenth century, which he contrasts with Lollardy's aniconic reading of the passion. He discovers notable parallels to the perspectives of liberation theology, including a common emphasis on

Christ's poverty, and an *imitatio Christi* that does not concentrate on Christ's suffering but rather on reform of the church and a 'gospel of freedom'. However, in contrast to the aniconic tendency of Lollardy, Gorringe concludes by returning to artistic representations of the passion and drawing our attention to some examples which do not make a virtue out of 'suffering of itself'. Here he highlights Otto Dix's *War* and Chagall's *White Crucifixion*, both of which foreground the political significance of the crucifixion. Such examples, Gorringe argues, alert the viewer to the crucial importance of a political reading of the Gospel texts.

Robin Jensen's essay explores the passion in art from a different angle, examining reasons for the late emergence of the crucifixion image in early Christian art. She notes the enigmatic nature of the first passion images, highlighting their depiction of Christ as physically alive and not visibly suffering on the cross. The wide range of evidence discussed – from satirical graffito to church doors – illustrates the diverse contexts in which the passion narratives had an impact.

Jensen offers five possible reasons for the absence of crucifixion imagery: (i) no precedent existed as a model; (ii) once-existing images were lost or destroyed; (iii) the scandal of crucifixion led to inhibitions about its depiction; (iv) the crucifixion was not a central aspect of early Christian dogma; (v) the crucifixion was a subject too sacred to allow direct depiction. She concludes by suggesting that the 'socio-political transformation of the Christian community' from a persecuted minority to a powerful, protected and significant community is the best explanation for the change in attitude towards depicting the crucifixion. In addition, she suggests:

> The question of the suffering of the divine in the incarnate person of Jesus was a central one from the early fifth century on, and perhaps the greatest impetus for the arrival of the crucifix as a pictorial theme at this time. As the image develops through the subsequent centuries, it has been shown to be similarly adapted according to theological, social, and even political events and concerns.

Jensen's concluding emphasis on the connection between artistic developments and theological discourse bears striking resemblance to the position of Emma Hornby, whose contribution draws our attention to the way in which unique musical phrases were used to highlight key textual phrases in the mediaeval liturgy. She takes as her examples the Good Friday chants *Domine audiui* and *Qui habitat*. Hornby notes that 'while music has no semantic content, the portions of text emphasized musically can reflect the focus of the exegetical literature'.

Hornby points out striking melodic material in the chant *Domine audiui* on the phrase 'in medio duorum animalium innotesceris' ('in the middle of two living creatures you will be known'; Hab. 3.2 Septuagint version); she also notes a musical connection to the Christmas Day alleluia *Dies sanctificatus* in the phrase '*operuit celos*', which establishes a clear association between the events of the passion and the incarnation.

Hornby's analysis of *Qui habitat* highlights its musical emphasis upon the theme that 'God will protect the faithful man in his time of trouble, when he is openly tempted'. Here she notes the unusual melodic flourish on 'a latere' and related phrases; rare cadencing on 'a negotio' and related phrases; striking verse endings in verses 2 and 12 of *Qui habitat*; and use of the 'Cadent melisma'. Musically, she argues, this suggests that the passion is to be understood as 'the climax of the battle between Christ and the Devil'.

William Flynn also highlights the connections between music and biblical exegesis in his essay, illustrating how the late-mediaeval office for the Compassion of Mary was derived from a tradition of creative allegorical interpretation of the Song of Songs. In addition to his assessment of the musical connections between the *Stabat mater* sequence and mediaeval exegesis of the Song of Songs, Flynn also emphasizes the different personae a singer was invited to adopt when performing the service, offering multiple perspectives on the passion. He notes:

> The multivalency of the quoted Scripture (provided by allegorical exegesis) is an important feature of the service for the Feast of the Compassion of Mary, since it underwrote the practice of singing the words both as one's own and in the personae of the various putative speakers assigned within the text itself (or within traditional interpretations). The singers of this service were thus aware of a complex set of relationships they might take to the texts they sang.

Flynn suggests that the goal of the service was for the singers to 'participate actively in Mary's suffering', and concludes, 'The allegorical, literal and tropological modes of response to the passion narrative can thus be seen to be carefully and artfully manipulated, allowing the singers to move easily from Mary's persona to their own personae, and to experience a biblical narration of her experience (in the Song of Songs) as their own.'

Flynn's emphasis on the singer's active participation in the events of the passion foreshadows a theme to emerge prominently in church music after the Reformation, as illustrated in J. R. Watson's essay on post-Reformation hymnody. Indeed, Flynn's analysis supports Watson's suggestion that the hymns of the post-Reformation period reflect both continuity and change. However, Watson also charts a significant shift in emphasis after the Reformation: 'The driving force of post-Reformation hymns is an interest in the self: the question uppermost in the mind is "what does this event mean for me, and for my fellow human beings?" Thus the hymns reflect a Protestant concern with grace: in particular, with the extraordinary nature of grace, and the wonder of it.' In addition,

Watson notes a transition to seeing the cross as emblem, in which it is regarded as sublime. Shame and death become life and health. Interesting connections emerge at this point between Jensen's discussion of the place of shame and scandal in the context of the passion in the early church, and the subsequent emergence of this theme in post-Reformation hymnody on the passion, highlighted by Watson.

Watson's essay illustrates the web of thematic connections between post-Reformation hymns (numerous examples are included – too many to be adequately summarized here, though the themes of 'blood' and 'amazement' feature prominently); he also emphasizes the connection between literature and music, as demonstrated by the influence of poems such as Herbert's 'The Sacrifice'. Notably, Watson concludes by focusing on the 'transformation of the self that takes place through contemplation of the passion' as a central theme reflected in the hymnody.

Whilst there is some chronological overlap between the essays of Watson and Jaime Lara, Lara provides insights into the cross-cultural interpretation of passion imagery in a very different, Latin American, context.[2] He highlights how the central element of the new religion brought by the Europeans to the New World – the passion of Christ – was perfectly understandable and acceptable to a people accustomed to sacred violence. 'The metaphors surrounding pre-Columbian human sacrifice (body, heart, blood, sun, food) were reused as a way of explaining and celebrating the saving mystery of Christianity in the new hybrid culture.'[3] Lara's illustrations reveal this daring reuse of the symbols and concepts of Mesoamerican religion: 'temples, mirrors, dances, metaphoric expressions – even eucharistic tortillas with feather headresses – were reworked to accommodate them to the new religion ... Christianity was both literally and metaphorically built up on top of the materials and symbols of the old religion.'

Lara's essay provides an important reminder of the varying cultural contexts in which the passion narratives were encountered. He gives detailed insights into the alien cultural worldview which the first Christian missionaries met when they sought to convert the Aztecs in the sixteenth century, and he charts the cultural and religious convergence that eventually took place in New Spain.

A different understanding of sacrifice is presented by Regina Schwartz in her essay, which explores the relationship between sacrifice, murder and justice in Shakespeare's *Othello* and the passion narratives. Schwartz asks

2 As Lara points out, 'the evangelization of the New World coincided with the same years in which Luther, Calvin, and others were separating themselves from the Roman Church on important issues like the sacrificial aspect of the Mass and the transubstantiation of the communion elements'.

3 Jaime Lara, unpublished abstract, *Perspectives on the Passion* conference, 2005.

whether Christ suffers as a murder victim or a sacrificial offering, and suggests that Shakespeare challenges us to rethink the differences between sacrifice and murder in his tragedies. In *Othello*, she argues, Shakespeare teases his audience about the possibility of redemption, using numerous perversions and inversions of the passion accounts:

> an aborted mass ministered by a demented priest, a communion cup turned into a vessel of drunken disorderliness and bestiality, a prayer ('Lord, have mercy on me') that is really a plea for life from the hands of a murderer, a vow that is really a curse, a sacrifice that is really a murder, a death that does not make the earth quake or the sun stand still, a light that, once put out, will not rekindle.

Schwartz concludes that all these features leave the audience with a craving for justice, yet 'point beyond the terrors of plot and experience to another vision of human possibility'.

Schwartz's essay addresses the relationship between theatre and the church, arguing that, as a result of the Reformation, the theatre came to replace various ritual functions previously offered by the church. Here again we see important connections between theological controversy and literary developments being proposed, alerting us to the extensive use, influence and impact of the passion narratives.

Our investigation of the reception history of the passion concludes with Sara Maitland's fictional contribution to the volume, 'Bad Friday' from her collection *Angel and Me*. Specially commissioned by BBC Radio 4 for Holy Week, Maitland's story provides a reminder of the continuing need for imaginative, creative engagement with the biblical text.[4] Her essay was performed as a dramatic reading by the author at our 2005 conference, provoking interesting questions about authorial intentionality and meaning in the subsequent discussion. Maitland's 'hermeneutic of the imagination' provides new interpretative possibilities for the reader or listener, but her story also highlights themes which have emerged throughout this volume, most notably challenging us to reflect on how to respond to the accounts of Jesus' suffering in the passion narratives.

Encountering the passion narratives through the arts broadens the interpreter's horizons and may even lead to a changed understanding of the biblical texts. It is our hope that this collection of essays will offer this enlarged vision, and in some cases perhaps even a revised critical approach towards the passion narratives. The essays included, in different ways, provide clear evidence for the importance of interdisciplinary dialogue concerning biblical texts; they also give support to Ulrich Luz's plea for a holistic reading of the Bible, which engages all the senses and offers a whole new realm of interpretative possibilities.

---

4   Sara Maitland, *Angel and Me: Short Stories for Holy Week* (London: Mowbray, 1995).

Chapter 1

'Effective History' and Art: A Hermeneutical Study with Examples from the Passion Narrative

Ulrich Luz

1. *Goals of my hermeneutic of 'effective history'*

My interest in reception history, or as I call it, giving my tribute to Hans-Georg Gadamer, 'effective history',[1] is a hermeneutical one. I take 'reception history' and 'effective history' as synonyms, whereby the first term emphasizes primarily the activity of the recipient, the other primarily the formative power of the texts themselves. In the first section of this essay I will make a few brief remarks on my view of a hermeneutic of effective history.

Like Gadamer, I think that history is never a mere object of our studies, but that we are indebted to history; and we owe to history almost everything that we are: our culture, our language, our worldview, our questions, our biases. History is like a stream which carries the boat of our lives. What Gadamer shows is that there is no 'independent' modern subject above, beyond or outside history. Understanding a text of the past always means understanding our relatedness to our past.

I differ from Gadamer in thinking that we should not be afraid of treating the effective history of biblical texts, that is their reception history, as an 'independent discipline ancillary to the human sciences'.[2] Our culture and our education system have become to a large extent a-historical; we have widely forgotten where we come from. Therefore, in my

---

1 The English translation of the German term 'Wirkungsgeschichte' poses problems. William Glen Doepel, the first translator of Gadamer's *Wahrheit und Methode* (Hans-Georg Gadamer, *Truth and Method* [London: Sheed and Ward, 1975]) chose the term 'effective history'. Joel Weinsheimer and Donald G. Marshall, the new translators (Hans-Georg Gadamer, *Truth and Method* [London: Continuum, 2003]), prefer 'history of effects'. Each translation emphasizes one aspect of the German term, namely 'effective history' the formative, 'productive' power of history, and 'history of effects' its results, the effects 'produced' by history. In the following essay I am more interested in the former aspect and shall use in most cases the term 'effective history'.

2 Gadamer, *Truth and Method* (2003), p. 301.

commentary on Matthew[3] the reception history of biblical texts became an important instrument to regain a 'historically effected consciousness'. We have to remember and to retell the reception history of the biblical texts, because otherwise it will drop out of our cultural memory. Remembering and retelling it, we learn why we interpret a biblical text like this or that, how it has shaped us and what we owe to this text.

Retelling the main types of the reception history of biblical texts in a commentary has for me a twofold goal:

1. The study of reception history shows 'what we have become because of the texts'.[4] Through them, we have become Orthodox, Catholics or Protestants. Through them, we have become European or African Christians. Biblical texts have contributed immensely to our personal, ecclesiastical and cultural identity. Studying the effective history of the biblical texts *illuminates our own hermeneutical situation vis-à-vis the texts*. It helps us to learn that interpreting the texts means also understanding who and what we are through them. It is not possible to exclude the interpreters from the process of interpretation. Only when we become aware of our own personal, religious and cultural identity and of our hermeneutical situation can we avoid the pseudo-neutrality and the widespread a-contextuality of interpretations which make most scholarly commentaries on the Bible so limited and boring. For this the study of the effective history of the Bible is a great help.

2. The second hermeneutic goal of studying reception history is to learn what *others* have become through the effects of the biblical texts. It shows us Protestants what Roman Catholics or Orthodox, Pentecostals, secular people, African women, mediaeval monks or Anabaptist farmers in the time of the Reformation, or what musicians, artists or so-called 'ordinary people' owe to the texts, and how *they* became through them what they were or are. In this way, the study of the reception history of the Bible opens the possibility for an ecumenical dialogue between members of different churches, or an intercultural dialogue, or a dialogue of theologians with artists or poets. *In this way, effective history widens our horizon, by opening us up to other people's horizons.* Studying effective history provides correctives to our own readings. It shows in an exemplary manner what we *could* become by means of the texts, by showing what others have become through them.

These are the two main goals of my hermeneutic of effective history. I will now try to apply these goals to the field of art, concentrating on paintings.

---

3   Ulrich Luz, *Matthew 1–7* (trans. James E. Crouch; Hermeneia; Minneapolis: Fortress, 2007); *Matthew 8–20* (trans. James E. Crouch; Hermeneia; Minneapolis: Fortress, 2001); *Matthew 21–28* (trans. James E. Crouch; Hermeneia; Minneapolis: Fortress, 2005).

4   Luz, *Matthew 1–7*, p. 63.

2. *Effective history and our hermeneutical situation*

How does the reception history of biblical texts in paintings show what we have become through the texts? For me, as a Presbyterian and European theologian, three points are important.

1. I am a member of the Swiss Reformed Church, a church affected by the iconoclasm of the Reformation in the most drastic possible way. Studying the effective history of the Bible in paintings *leads me to realize fully how great our poverty is through the loss of images and paintings* in my church. As is well known, there were two main traditional arguments in favour of images in the church: first, images were interpreted as visible representations of the invisible Divine, made possible through the incarnation. While this argument was important mainly in the Eastern Church,[5] in the Western Church it was complemented by a second argument, formulated pointedly by Gregory the Great: paintings are the Bible for the illiterate.[6] The Reformation was an iconoclastic movement, for which the Word of God was the sole centre and basis of all piety. Zwingli and Luther both rejected any kind of veneration of visual representations of the Divine in paintings or statues. However, only in the Reformed tradition did the iconoclastic tendency become a fundamental theological principle: Zwingli's – and later Calvin's – Christology was basically Antiochene. They tended towards a separation of Christ's human and divine natures. This made visual representations of Christ unnecessary, because the human nature of Christ *should not* be venerated and his divine nature *cannot* be represented through external things.[7] Beyond this, the Old Testament prohibition of idol-making (Exod. 20.4) was a fundamental commandment for both Zwingli and Calvin.[8] Therefore, the rupture with the iconic tradition of the Middle Ages was particularly drastic in the tradition of the Reformed and Calvinistic churches.

The loss of images and visual representations has left an intellectualized church with little possibility of experiencing grace. It has contributed to alienating the Reformed and Presbyterian churches from the illiterate people whose Bible the images were, according to Gregory the Great. It has also contributed significantly to the character of many Presbyterian churches as language- and teaching-oriented middle-class churches. This is particularly visible in Africa and North America. They became intellectual

---

5 E.g. *Concilium Oecumenicum* VII, actio VII (*DS* 36, nr. 601); John of Damascus, *De imaginibus oratio* II.8 (*PG* 94, p. 1328).

6 Gregory the Great, *Ep.* 9.209 (*CCSL* 140A, p. 768).

7 Cf. Hans von Campenhausen, 'Die Bilderfrage in der Reformation', in *idem*, *Tradition und Leben. Kräfte der Kirchengeschichte* (Tübingen: Mohr-Siebeck, 1960), p. 373.

8 This was different for Luther, who took Exod. 20.4-6 as an appendix to the first commandment of the decalogue, not as an independent commandment.

and moralist churches, where much is taught, but little experienced. In contrast, paintings and other visual representations of Christ and biblical scenes are expressions of the wholeness of human beings whose religion is much more than an intellectual conviction and moral life.

2. The effective history of visual representations of biblical scenes and persons shows how *religious art has widely lost its contexts in modern Western culture*. Paintings inspired by the Bible were originally part of an altar or an iconostasis in order to represent the presence of the Divine. Or they were parts of church walls in order to teach the illiterate. Single paintings, of the Crucified for example, were used in monks' cells in the late Middle Ages and later in private homes for contemplation and compassion. Hans Belting has shown, in an impressive monograph, how the context of icons changed on their way from the East to the West during the high and late Middle Ages and in the modern age. Their context was originally church worship, then it became more and more for private individual veneration, then as decoration in the palaces of rich people or as part of royal collections. Finally, in our age these collections became museums.[9]

The Renaissance was the age when a painting's religious values were gradually surpassed by their aesthetic values. If we understand 'art' in the way of modern European thinking as something purely aesthetic, whose only purpose is to be beautiful,[10] abstract from life, as 'art pour l'art', then only in the sixteenth century did something like 'art' come into existence. Naturally, the Reformation, purging churches from all kind of images, accelerated this development. What other context remained now for symbolic religious paintings of earlier ages except to become 'art' and to be evaluated by connoisseurs of the beautiful according to their judgements of taste?

Studying this part of the effective history of the Bible, I realized that in my part of the world it is the history of a total decontextualization of the religious image. In Gadamer's words, 'Detaching all art from its connections with life ... we frame it like a picture and hang it up.'[11] Art has become a field of life which is independent from religion, like science or economics. Thus it has become difficult if not impossible for most people to understand visible images as representations of the invisible God, which was so important for theologians of icons, such as John of Damascus and others. The museum is for many of my Western

---

9 Hans Belting, *Bild und Kult: eine Geschichte des Bildes vor dem Zeitalter der Kunst* (München: C. H. Beck, 1990); cf. *idem*, 'Das Werk im Kontext', in Hans Belting *et al.* (eds), *Kunstgeschichte. Eine Einführung* (Berlin: D. Reimer, 1986), pp. 186–202.

10 Kant's *Critique of Judgment* is a key text for this 'abstract' concept of art; cf. Gadamer, *Truth and Method* (2003), pp. 42–100.

11 *Truth and Method* (2003), p. 135.

European contemporaries the most important, maybe even the only, place where they encounter biblical stories like the life or the passion of Jesus. This decontextualization is part of the autonomy of modern humans which makes it so difficult to connect life with God and images with transcendence. This is an important part of the context in which I had to write my commentary.

3. With my last point I turn to the passion narrative in visual arts. My goal was to learn something about our specific hermeneutical situation vis-à-vis the biblical passion narrative. For this I used paintings (and also literary texts) of the twentieth century as my sources, because they are little influenced by exegesis and theology. My impression was that *the loss of God and the anonymity of transcendence has become a key experience in the twentieth century*. In the eighteenth and nineteenth centuries the exemplary humanity of Jesus was the main focus of interpretations and representations of the passion. The crisis of belief in humanity through the disasters of the twentieth century found its expression in very different interpretations of Jesus' passion in both literature and art. In the twentieth century, Jesus became representative of humanity not in his noble, but in his miserable death. The suffering Jesus became a symbol of all exploited, suffering, tortured and killed human beings of our time who felt left alone both by humanity and God. In many artistic representations of the crucifixion the absence of God seems to be the main feature.

The first of my three examples is a painting by Edvard Munch, from around 1900 (Fig. 1). The Crucified is not its centre, but the people under the cross. Some are laughing, some are indifferent, others do not take any notice. The women are in deep sorrow; an old scribe in the right corner gives his comments; in the left corner we see the face of a laughing man, who seemingly does not notice the event at all. In the middle, the face of an old man with wide-open eyes is visible. His big face is nothing but a great, unanswered question. A second example is the initial painting of the cycle 'scandalum crucis' (1969) by the Roman Catholic priest-artist Herbert Falken (Fig. 2): a bewildering, puzzling double cross.[12] Even Jesus has lost his identity here. He is laughing, shockingly, an expression of the madness not only of the crucifixion but of the whole world. The third example is a painting by the Polish artist Janusz Szpyt of 1984 (Fig. 3).[13] It shows a photograph of an average family: father, mother, son (quite like his father), daughter (quite like her mother). The younger son, still a child, is the only one who is aware of the dead body lying in front of him. Above them is the crucified Christ, leaning over the family, so that

---

12 See Philipp Boonen (ed.), *Herbert Falken. Christusbilder* (Aachener Beiträge zur Pastoral- und Bildungsfragen; Aachen: Einhard, 1986), p. 51.

13 Reproduced in Annette Krauss (ed.), *Unter die Menschen gefallen. Polnische Christusbilder* (München: Claudius, 1991), p. 32.

Figure 1. Edvard Munch, *Golgotha*, 1900, oil on canvas. Munch Museum, Oslo. (Photo: © Munch Museum, Oslo/DACS, London, 2007)

the jacket of the father is full of his blood. Death and murder – of Jesus, of the Jews in the Holocaust, of numerous other innocents. Who is guilty? Who is innocent spectator? Who is involved? Who is only standing by? This painting is a symbol of the tragedy of the twentieth century, frightening, shocking, with a black sky as background and no hope for any kind of resurrection.

The effective history of the passion narrative in the twentieth century, particularly in paintings, helped me to see how important the experience of the 'loss of God' is as a basic characteristic of our hermeneutical situation – the situation in which I have to interpret the passion narrative.

3. *Widening horizons: The 'language' of paintings*

Studying the effective history of the Bible widens the horizon of the interpreter; it provides insights into what *others* have become through the biblical texts and leads into an ecumenical or intercultural dialogue. This was the second dimension of my hermeneutic of effective history.

When I now apply this to the interpretation of the passion narrative in visual arts, I want to limit my field of interest. My interest in this essay is not an iconological one: my question is not what paintings of the passion disclose about the cultural, ecclesial or historical situation of interpretations in other traditions. Rather, I am interested in the process of interpretation of narratives through paintings as such. The interpretation,

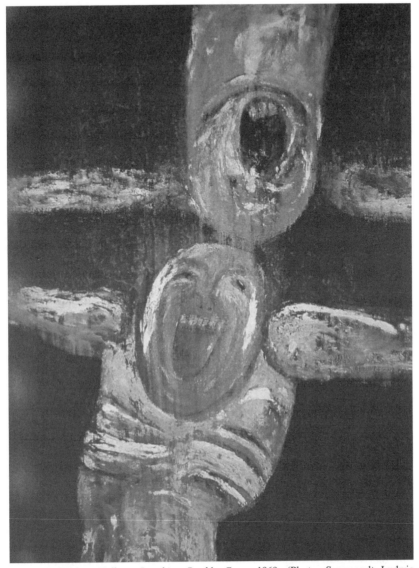

Figure 2. Herbert Falken, *Laughing Double Cross*, 1969. (Photo: Suermondt Ludwig Museum, Aachen)

or better the 'realization' of biblical texts through paintings is a 'non-verbal' interpretation, which is of particular interest for a 'theologian of the word'. What are the characteristics, the possibilities and the strengths of this 'non-verbal' interpretation of biblical narratives? With this question I want to enter into dialogue with a hermeneutic of history of art.

Figure 3. Janusz Szpyt, *Family Remembrance*, 1984. (Photo: By kind permission, Andreas Würbel, Thomas-Morus-Akademie Bensberg, Bergisch Gladbach)

Before entering it, I have to clarify my premises, because my own understanding of what an image is, is not a neutral one. I am not an advocate of a Platonic view of images, according to which paintings are merely imitations of reality and accordingly 'far away from truth'.[14] Paintings are more than photographs; they *create* a world. Nor can I adhere exclusively to Erwin Panofsky's view of iconology. His concept of 'meaning' interprets a painting merely as 'symptom of something else',[15] as a document of an epoch, of a personality or of a religious attitude.[16] And naturally I cannot advocate a view of art as 'pure art', open only to aesthetical 'judgement' in the sense of Immanuel Kant, but not to a rational analysis. This concept separates art ultimately both from the possibility of representing any kind of truth and from the possibility of having effects in society. Rather, I am interested in concepts which analyse the specific character of a painting *as painting*, i.e. its powers, possibilities and its reception strategies. I am interested in what Gottfried Boehm calls the 'iconic plus' of a painting compared with written or spoken

14   Plato, *Polit.* X, 603A.
15   Erwin Panofsky, 'Iconography and Iconology: An Introduction to the Study of Renaissance Art', in *idem, Meaning in the Visual Arts* (Garden City: Doubleday, 1955), p. 31.
16   According to Panofsky iconological interpretation is concerned with, 'those underlying principles which reveal the basic attitude of a nation, a period, a class, a religious or philosophical persuasion – qualified by one personality and condensed into one work' ('Iconography and Iconology', p. 30).

language.[17] I am interested in what Oskar Bätschmann calls 'process effected by a painting' (in German, *Bildprozess*), namely in the 'specific productivity of paintings'.[18] In summary, I am interested in the interpretation of the *paintings* and not in the interpretation of contents or texts or ideas which are behind them. Only then can I realize how the given biblical texts are interpreted *specifically and differently* through their representations in paintings.

Painting a biblical story means a *transformation of its language* into something new, for which even a word in our language is missing. Paintings and sculptures 'speak', metaphorically, their own 'language'. What are the characteristics of this 'language' – or better perhaps the 'image-character' – of visual arts?[19]

1. My first point concerns *space as basic dimension* of the 'language' of images. This is particularly important for the reception of narrative texts. Texts narrate a temporal sequence of events, whereas painters fill a given space. Therefore *simultaneity* of temporal sequences is a characteristic of the 'image-character' of paintings. Simultaneity is even greater when we overcome the decontextualization of many paintings through their transfer into museums. In their original context, on an altar for instance, different paintings can be looked at simultaneously, so that, for example, crucifixion *and* resurrection and sometimes also other events of Christ's life can be looked at together. Duccio's *Maesta*, whose separated fragments we admire today in the Museo dell' Opera del Duomo in Siena, is one example of this. In a wider sense the space of a church enables simultaneity, for example spatial correspondence of Old Testament 'types' and New Testament 'antitypes' on corresponding places of the walls of a church. An example of simultaneity in a painting is the representation of the crucifixion in the famous Syrian Rabbula codex (Fig. 4). In this painting everything is simultaneous: Mary and the Beloved Disciple, the soldiers throwing the dice for Jesus' garment, the three women looking from a distance to the cross, the soldier offering Jesus the vinegar-sponge on his cane and the other soldier, named Longinus here for the first time, who stabbed Jesus' side with his lance. All is simultaneous, so that the view of the painting is entirely synchronic. Moreover, events that happened before the death of Jesus and after his death are simultaneous. Is Jesus dead or not yet dead in this painting? The

17   Gottfried Boehm, 'Zu einer Hermeneutik des Bildes', in Hans-Georg Gadamer *et al.* (eds.), *Seminar. Die Hermeneutik und die Wissenschaften* (Frankfurt: Suhrkamp, 1978), p. 462.

18   Oskar Bätschmann, *Einführung in die kunstgeschichtliche Hermeneutik. Die Auslegung von Bildern* (Darmstadt: Wissenschaftliche Buchgesellschaft, 5th edn, 2001), pp. 131–55.

19   'Image-character' is an attempt to translate Gottfried Boehm's term *Bildlichkeit* – a rather artificial and not colloquial expression – into English. (Boehm, 'Zu einer Hermeneutik', p. 465.)

Figure 4. The Crucifixion, from the Rabbula Gospels, Florence, Biblioteca Laurenziana. (Photo: © 1990 Scala, Florence, courtesy of the Ministero Beni e Att. Culturali)

question cannot be decided but it does not need to be decided, because the Crucified is the living risen Lord, the king of heaven and earth in his purple robe.

2. My second point is the *concreteness* of the 'language of images'. All written or spoken language is conceptualizing. One speaks about a tree or a face but means the concept of a tree or a face. However, a painter cannot paint concepts. He or she has to paint either an olive tree or an oak, either an ugly or a nice-looking, a sympathetic or repelling face. A wonderful example is the face of Judas sketched by Leonardo da Vinci as a preparation for his Last Supper (Fig. 5).[20] This face is sympathetic, individual, reflecting and still full of will and decision. None of the typical characteristics of Judas are to be found: no huge nose, no blubber-lips, no ugly beard. For Leonardo's contemporaries with traditional prejudices of their time, this Judas with his individual, even beautiful face must have indicated a complete turnaround. The concreteness of the image-character of a painting can be very strong, innovative and effective, more than any spoken or written language.

3. Together with this, paintings require a *holistic reception*, not only by

20   See further Bernhard Dieckmann, *Judas als Sündenbock* (München: Kösel 1991), p. 135.

Figure 5. Leonardo da Vinci, *Head of Judas*, c. 1495. (Photo: The Royal Collection © 2007 Her Majesty Queen Elizabeth II)

the intellect, but also by feelings. In the reception of art the whole person is involved; the reception of paintings is an act of 'primary identification'.[21] This has to do with their affinity to the concrete human body: because they do not conceptualize the human body, but paint or represent it as a concrete, beautiful, ugly, young or old body, they can stimulate concrete human imagination, while conceptualizing language only

21 Hans Robert Jauss, *Kleine Apologie der ästhetischen Erfahrung* (Konstanzer Universitätsreden 59; Konstanz: Universitätsverlag, 1972), p. 38.

delineates the field of possible imaginations. A good example is the statue
of the crucified Christ (1975) by the Brazilian artist Guido Rocha (Fig.
6).[22] This Crucified is a black man, one of the poorest of the poor, hungry,
not much more than bones. His cry is full of suffering and protest.
Spectators will be shocked and full of emotions. They have to react. This
Christ is crying for action! This *crucifixus* is a good example to illustrate
the thesis of Jauss, that 'primary identification' includes also the
dimension of action. It is a piece of art which is a cry from the midst of
our antagonistic society.

Figure 6. Guido Rocha, *The Tormented Christ*, 1975, All Africa Conference of Churches
Training Center, Nairobi. (Photo: WCC, Geneva)

22   Reproduced in Hans-Ruedi Weber, *Und kreuzigten ihn* (Göttingen: Vandenhoeck, 2nd
edn, 1982), p. 41. The statue is at the All Africa Conference of Churches Training Center,
Nairobi.

In European art, the examples of the late Middle Ages with its piety of compassion are particularly striking. A well-known example is the *crucifixus* of the Dom of Naumburg, one of the most wonderful examples of early Gothic art. His place is at the entrance of the West Choir, so that everybody who enters there passes under the stretched arms of the crucified Christ and receives his blessing. The sculpture and the space of the Church form a complete unity. The Crucified can be experienced in a very concrete way, even bodily with the feet. No text can provoke such a holistic reception, which includes intellect, feelings and the body, like these paintings and sculptures.

4. The fourth point I want to mention is the *openness* of paintings. Reception aesthetics and reader-response theory have rediscovered the openness of texts. It is not by chance that reader-response has been received readily by art historians.[23] Despite many of the so-called 'voids' of a narrative having to be filled by an artist-interpreter – the face of Judas has or has not to be ugly, Mary and the Beloved Disciple have to stand on the left or on the right side of the cross, the Crucified has or has not to be naked etc. – paintings are very open in their own way. Colours, for instance, almost always resist interpretation by language. The 'invention', that is the composition of a painting, allows only limited possibilities of unambiguous interpretations. A painting offers, like a text, potential roles for readers, whom we could call 'implicit spectators' analogous to the 'implicit readers' in literary criticism. Wolfgang Kemp has edited an excellent book with the title *The Spectator is in the Painting*.[24] What he means can be illustrated by the above painting by Edvard Munch (Fig. 1). The numerous spectators of the crucifixion in this painting reflect the various possibilities of its 'implicit spectator'. They offer possibilities of identification or non-identification to the real spectator outside the painting. Which one we should adopt is only indirectly indicated by the artist.

Even real 'voids' play a role in many paintings. Rembrandt was a master of 'voids'. One impressive example is his last sketch of the crucifixion (Fig. 7).[25] Above the silhouette of the city of Jerusalem is just nothing. Only a thin, hardly visible diagonal line leads up to heaven. What does it mean? How does it interpret the text, 'My God, my God, why hast

---

23   Cf. Wolfgang Kemp, 'Kunstwissenschaft und Rezeptionsästhethik', in *idem* (ed.), *Der Betrachter ist im Bild. Kunstwissenschaft und Rezeptionsästhetik* (Berlin: D. Reimer, 2nd edn, 1992), pp. 7–29; *idem*, 'Kunstwerk und Betrachter: Der rezeptionsästhetische Ansatz', in Hans Belting *et al.* (eds), *Kunstgeschichte. Eine Einführung* (Berlin: D. Reimer, 1986), pp. 203–21.

24   See above, footnote 23.

25   Reproduced in Hans Martin Rotermund (ed.), *Rembrandt's Handzeichnungen und Radierungen zur Bibel* (Zürich: Zwingli Verlag, 1963), p. 231.

Figure 7. Rembrandt, *Eli, eli lama sabachthani, c.* 1656. (Photo: © Stiftung Weimarer Klassik und Kunstsammlungen)

thou forsaken me?' (Mt. 27.46)? It is the spectator who has to work on this. In this respect, Rembrandt's drawing remains open.

5. This leads me to the next point, the *iconic density* of paintings, illustrated by the arrest of Jesus painted by Giotto in the Arena chapel in Padova (Fig. 8).[26] I follow the well-known interpretation of Max Imdahl, who has taken this painting as one example for his 'iconic' interpretation of the painting as painting.[27] Jesus and Judas are in the middle; the hand of the priest is on the right, the weapon in the hand of the servant on the left and all torches point to their heads. Jesus is the dominating figure; he is the tallest of all. But he is almost invisible, because he is covered by Judas with his cloth. It is as if Judas would swallow him up with his cloth. But still Jesus is the dominating figure. He looks at Judas, and it is as if Judas has to stop shortly before he reaches Jesus' lips. Jesus is absolutely powerless and seized by Judas, while at the same time he is absolutely

26 See further Luciano Belloso, *Giotto. Das malerische Gesamtwerk* (Firenze: Scala, 1981), p. 47.

27 Max Imdahl, *Giotto. Arenafresken, Ikonographie, Ikonologie, Ikonik* (Theorie und Geschichte der Literatur und schönen Künste 60; München: W. Fink, 1980), pp. 93–5; *idem*, 'Ikonik. Bilder und ihre Anschauung', in Gottfried Boehm (ed.), *Was ist ein Bild?* (München: W. Fink, 1994), pp. 310–13.

Figure 8. Giotto, *The Kiss of Judas, c.* 1305, Scrovegni Chapel, Padua. (Photo: © 1990 Scala, Florence)

powerful, so that he remains master over Judas and functions as coordinating reference point of the whole painting. Imdahl concludes that this 'iconic density of meaning' is possible only in a painting.[28] The iconic density makes it possible to express what conceptual language can express only in paradoxes.

However, narrative language too can express the same ambiguity, as for instance the Johannine passion narrative shows in comparison with the various scholarly attempts to interpret it conceptually either from the viewpoint of a theology of the cross or from a viewpoint of proto-docetism, or from a dialectical point of view. A close affinity exists between narrative language and the 'language of images', compared to conceptual language.

6. My sixth point is the *contemporaneity* of iconographical paintings.

---

28 Cf. Imdahl, *Giotto*, p. 95.

Contemporaneity refers to the spectator and is something different from 'simultaneity' within the painting. Contemporaneity was self-evident in Eastern iconography, where icons were interpreted in Platonic categories as visible representations of the eternal.[29] But it was not self-evident in the West, where iconography was much more closely related to biblical history and to the biblical stories, and where its purpose was primarily to function as a painted Bible for teaching the illiterate. Particularly in the late Middle Ages when the suffering of Christ – together with his humanity and his history – were emphasized more strongly, and where the reception process became more conscious, the contemporaneity had to be made explicit. This happened in different ways,[30] for example through a contemporary setting of Calvary against the background of a mediaeval city,[31] or by including the figures of a painting's donors in a position of prayer or adoration.

In modern paintings contemporaneity is quite normal. An impressive modern example of contemporaneity is the 1990 painting of Pilate's handwashing by the Polish artist Piotr Naliwajko (Fig. 9).[32] Pilate is a so-called 'innocent bourgeois' of today; Jesus, visible only from his back, is a 'hippie' or other type of 'flipped out' youngster.

Contemporaneity is also a basic concept of biblical narratives. Many biblical stories, among them the Gospels according to Matthew, Mark and John, are 'transparent' stories which have their reality on two levels: the 'then' of the narrated time and the 'now' of the hearers. These two levels are not separated. Rather, on the narrative level they are inseparably linked with each other, so every narration of a story about Jesus is also a narration about the hearer's own life and leads immediately to application. The same is true for many iconographical representations from the Middle Ages until today. Conceptual language can only analyse this. However, the transformation of biblical stories into paintings makes the same effect possible. Its 'instruments', the language of a narration and the image-character of a painting, are quite different, but they function in the same

29   A good example of contemporaneity in Eastern iconography is the representation of the Lord's Supper as apostles' communion, i.e. not in the setting of a meal, but in the setting of the liturgical celebration of Eucharist. Cf. Gertrud Schiller, *Ikonographie der christlichen Kunst* (vol. 2; Gütersloh: Gütersloher Verlagshaus, 1968), pp. 38–41.

30   One of the early examples of explicit contemporaneity is a new type of representation of the Lord's Supper from the sixth century on, where the position of reclining during the meal was replaced by sitting according to the changed eating-custom of the time.

31   Very well known are the paintings of Calvary in the late Middle Ages, where 'Jerusalem' normally was painted as a mediaeval city, and the people looking at the crucifixion were its contemporary population, the spectators in the painting. Cf. Elisabeth Roth, *Der volkreiche Kalvarienberg in Literatur und Bildkunst des Spätmittelalters* (Philologische Studien und Quellen 2; Berlin:Erich Schmidt, 2nd edn, 1967).

32   Reproduced in Krauss, *Unter die Menschen gefallen*, p. 19.

Figure 9. Piotr Naliwajko, *Pilate I*, 1990. (Photo: By kind permission, Andreas Würbel, Thomas-Morus-Akademie Bensberg, Bergisch Gladbach)

way. Again, transforming narrations into images is an ideal way to experience their efficiency.

7. My seventh and last characteristic is *alienation*. Since the Renaissance, the basic element of every painting is the 'invention' of the artist, the 'disegno interno', the inner vision of the artist, which he or she imprints upon the traditional material. The growing weight of the invention in early modern art goes hand in hand with the artists'

increasing emancipation from their traditional subjects and with the increasing autonomy of art. An artist sees traditional materials in a new way. For the spectators of their paintings this could mean an alienation, sometimes even a shocking alienation. Paintings which concentrate a new vision of a traditional, familiar biblical story into one compact work of art are powerful. Examples are the head of Judas by Leonardo (Fig. 5) or the representation of Pilate by Naliwajko (Fig. 9). This innovating force of paintings is strongly emphasized by Hans Robert Jauss in his splendid essay against the 'pure' aestheticism of bourgeois 'art pour l'art' and against the long familiar separation of aesthetics, truth and society.[33] This innovating and alienating power is a fundamental strength of visual art, and is probably the main instrument for modern art to become socially or politically engaged.

This is also applicable to visual representations of biblical stories. Due to the remnants of Christian socialization and education in our secular society they belong to the long-familiar, seemingly well-known and accordingly less exciting parts of our cultural heritage. Paintings can effectively provide a *new* vision of them through the experience of surprise and the 'space to be used by human freedom',[34] created in the spectator through the new invention of an artist. In this way they have an important cognitive and pragmatic function.

4. *Final reflections*

Our point of departure was the loss of images in the Protestant, mainly Reformed and Presbyterian churches after the Reformation. Churches lost their images and religious images lost their context and their originally intended function. All the specific possibilities of what one could call the 'language of images' which I have mentioned above are to be understood as a plea for the potential of images for interpreting the Bible, in particular biblical narratives. Paintings provide an excellent possibility to interpret many biblical texts in a new and often congenial way. The 'language of images' and narrative language are very close in several respects. In view of the rich potential meaning of the *Bible* it was wrong in the Reformation to banish images from the Churches. For the sake of the *Bible* we should try to reintroduce them. Differing from Gregory the Great I emphasize that the interpretation of the Bible through the medium of images is even more important for today's literates than for illiterates, because it is exactly their literacy that obstructs an immediate, intuitive, visual, sensual and holistic access to biblical texts.

---

33 Jauss, *Kleine Apologie*.
34 Jauss, *Kleine Apologie*, p. 39. In German, *Spielraum menschlicher Freiheit*.

Can the other theological argument for images that was so important for the Eastern Orthodox Church still carry weight for us? Is it still possible for us modern Westerners that images can become representations of invisible transcendent reality? This seems to be very difficult. Too much has happened in the history of Western Europe after the Middle Ages: images have been decontextualized from their religious context. Art has become an independent, autonomous province of human life. The 'subjects' of art have become human and earthly; no more the Divine, but

Figure 10. Marc Chagall, *White Crucifixion*, 1938, oil on canvas, 154.3 × 139.7 cm, Gift of Alfred S. Alschuler, 1946.925, The Art Institute of Chicago. (Photo: © The Art Institute of Chicago/DACS, London, 2007)

humanity and nature are in the foreground. In many twentieth-century images of Jesus' passion, God and transcendence have become totally invisible – only human suffering, hopelessness with no way out, human madness remains visible.

However, I think even for us it is not totally impossible for images to become vessels for experiences of transcendence. Because in our modern and postmodern world all such experiences are ambiguous and subjective in more than one way, it is impossible to go beyond subjective experiences. Therefore, I have chosen two examples with no other claim than that they became particularly important for me. Neither belongs to Western-Christian culture. The first is Marc Chagall's *White Crucifixion* (1938). In this painting (Fig. 10), the Crucified stands in the middle of a Belorussian Jewish village. It anticipates prophetically what happened some years later in the Second World War. Invading soldiers break in; the inhabitants try to save themselves in a ship across the river. The synagogue is in flames; a Jew saves the Torah scroll. In the centre is the Crucified. He is standing in a ray of light beaming from above. It is the Jew 'Jesus the Nazarene, the King of the Jews', as it is written in Hebrew letters. At his feet the seven-armed candelabra can be seen. Indeed, an incarnation of God's light in the Jew Jesus in the middle of the deadly darkness of Israel's imminent annihilation.

My second example is from an African artist, Engelbert Mveng (Fig. 11). It is a painting in the chapel of the Libermann College in Douala, Cameroon.[35] The crucified risen Lord is represented with open eyes as in the church of antiquity, as crucified cosmocrator, with his hands stretched out to heaven in order to bless the world. It shows contemporaneity: Christ blesses the martyrs of Uganda who stand beside the cross and touch it with their hands. The risen cosmocrator is incarnated, shown by the colours. We have only three: red is the colour of life, white is the colour of death, and black is the colour of suffering. This painting is not decontextualized: it is part of the altar from where the blessings of the Crucified are received in the Eucharist. A eucharistic service in this chapel has the chance to become something like a *Gesamtkunstwerk* (complete work of art) celebrating incarnation. These two examples show that we European Christians need the eyes and the 'invention' of others in order to see again what we have widely lost.

---

35   Reproduced in Weber, *Und kreuzigten ihn*, p. 63.

Figure 11. Engelbert Mveng, *Crucifixion*, Chapel of the Libermann College, Douala, Cameroon. (Photo: WCC, Geneva)

References

Bätschmann, Oskar, *Einführung in die kunstgeschichtliche Hermeneutik. Die Auslegung von Bildern* (Darmstadt: Wissenschaftliche Buchgesellschaft, 5th edn, 2001).

Belloso, Luciano, *Giotto. Das malerische Gesamtwerk* (Firenze: Scala, 1981).

Belting, Hans, *Bild und Kult: eine Geschichte des Bildes vor dem Zeitalter der Kunst* (München: C. H. Beck, 1990).

—— 'Das Werk im Kontext', in Hans Belting *et al.* (eds), *Kunstgeschichte. Eine Einführung* (Berlin: D. Reimer, 1986).

Boehm, Gottfried, 'Zu einer Hermeneutik des Bildes', in Hans-Georg Gadamer *et al.* (eds), *Seminar. Die Hermeneutik und die Wissenschaften* (Frankfurt: Suhrkamp, 1978), pp. 444–71.

Boonen, Philipp (ed.), *Herbert Falken. Christusbilder* (Aachener Beiträge zur Pastoral- und Bildungsfragen; Aachen: Einhard, 1986).

von Campenhausen, Hans, 'Die Bilderfrage in der Reformation', in *idem*, *Tradition und Leben. Kräfte der Kirchengeschichte* (Tübingen: Mohr-Siebeck, 1960), pp. 361–407.

Dieckmann, Bernhard, *Judas als Sündenbock* (München: Kösel, 1991).

Gadamer, Hans-Georg, *Truth and Method* (trans. William Glen Doepel; London: Sheed and Ward, 1975).

—— *Truth and Method* (trans. Joel Weinsheimer and Donald G. Marshall; London: Continuum, 2003).

Imdahl, Max, *Giotto. Arenafresken, Ikonographie, Ikonologie, Ikonik* (Theorie und Geschichte der Literatur und schönen Künste 60; München: W. Fink, 1980).

—— 'Ikonik. Bilder und ihre Anschauung', in Gottfried Boehm (ed.), *Was ist ein Bild?* (München: W. Fink, 1994).

Jauss, Hans Robert, *Kleine Apologie der ästhetischen Erfahrung* (Konstanzer Universitätsreden 59; Konstanz: Universitätsverlag, 1972).

Kemp, Wolfgang, 'Kunstwerk und Betrachter: Der rezeptionsästhetische Ansatz', in Hans Belting (ed.), *Kunstgeschichte. Eine Einführung* (Berlin: D. Reimer, 1986), pp. 203–21.

—— 'Kunstwissenschaft und Rezeptionsästhethik', in Wolfgang Kemp (ed.), *Der Betrachter ist im Bild. Kunstwissenschaft und Rezeptionsästhetik* (Berlin: D. Reimer, 2nd edn, 1992), pp. 7–29.

Krauss, Annette (ed.), *Unter die Menschen gefallen. Polnische Christusbilder* (München: Claudius, 1991).

Luz, Ulrich, *Matthew 1–7* (trans. James E. Crouch; Hermeneia; Minneapolis: Fortress, 2007).

—— *Matthew 8–20* (trans. James E. Crouch; Hermeneia; Minneapolis: Fortress, 2001).

—— *Matthew 21–28* (trans. James E. Crouch; Hermeneia; Minneapolis: Fortress, 2005).

Panofsky, Erwin, 'Iconography and Iconology: An Introduction to the Study of Renaissance Art', in *idem, Meaning in the Visual Arts* (Garden City: Doubleday, 1955).

Rotermund, Hans Martin (ed.), *Rembrandt's Handzeichnungen und Radierungen zur Bibel* (Zürich: Zwingli Verlag, 1963).

—— *Marc Chagall und die Bibel* (Lahr: Kaufmann, 1970).

Roth, Elisabeth, *Der volkreiche Kalvarienberg in Literatur und Bildkunst des Spätmittelalters* (Philologische Studien und Quellen 2; Berlin: Erich Schmidt, 2nd edn, 1967).

Schiller, Gertrud, *Ikonographie der christlichen Kunst* (vol. 2; Gütersloh: Gütersloher Verlagshaus, 1968).

Weber, Hans-Ruedi, *Und kreuzigten ihn* (Göttingen: Vandenhoeck, 2nd edn, 1982).

Chapter 2

HE WHO HESITATES IS HUMAN: LITERARY PORTRAYALS OF THE GETHSEMANE 'MOMENT'

Peter S. Hawkins

'But who do you say that I am?' This question, posed by each of the Synoptic Gospels, is central to the whole Gospel enterprise – itself an extended question about one particular 'I am' that requires a personal response. One might say that the same is true of the church's creeds, only in their case the question is suppressed and answer is all. Put crudely, the purpose of a creed is to nail down, be precise, defend the faith against heresy by being as restrictive as possible. Narrative, by contrast, moves in the opposite direction: it opens possibilities rather than closing them; it requires interpretation more than assent; it confuses and complicates rather than clarifies.

For an extreme case of creedal precision, take the approach to Christ's identity in the fifth-century *Quicumque vult*, the so-called 'Athanasian' Creed:

> [Our] Lord Jesus Christ, the Son of God, is God and Man;
> God, of the substance of the Father, begotten before the worlds;
> and Man of the substance of his Mother, born in the world;
> Perfect God and perfect Man,
> of a reasonable soul and human flesh subsisting.
> Equal to the Father, as touching his Godhead; and inferior to the
> Father, as touching his Manhood; Who, although he be God and Man,
> yet he is not two, but one Christ;
> One, not by conversion of the Godhead
> into flesh, but by taking of the Manhood into God;
> One altogether; not by confusion of Substance,
> but by unity of Person. For as the reasonable soul
> and flesh is one man, so God and Man is one Christ [.] [1]

This dense series of theological affirmations amounts to an extended balancing act. God and Man are at two poles brought into perfect

---

1 *The Book of Common Prayer* (New York: Church Hymnal Corporation, 1979), p. 865.

equipoise by repeated assertion. Substance of Father *and* Mother, a begetting before all worlds *and* a birthing in the world, divine *and* human perfection. Here theology eschews the complications of metaphor as much as it can. Yet, when speaking of the Word, it finds itself unable to forgo a figure of speech: the Incarnation took place (in a phrase beloved of Charles Williams) 'not by conversion of the Godhead into flesh but by the taking of the Manhood into God'.

Move from proposition to narrative, however, and problems arise. For how is it possible to represent these clear and distinct ideas; how conceive of two distinct or 'unconfused' substances joined in a single human person? By sheer creedal fiat one might say, 'Let them be not the same but one!' Yet how can we actually see divine and human perfection in simultaneous action? Would it be in rapid-fire alternation, a sequence so blurred to the eye that the two in effect become one? Would one go back and forth, as does the Anglo-Saxon poem, 'The Dream of the Rood', and have the wood of the cross on which Christ suffered, 'covered with blood', celebrate the moment when 'the Young Hero – He was God almighty – firm and unflinching, stripped Himself; he mounted on the high cross, brave in the sight of many'?[2] Or, to put it another way (and in the terms of the Athanasian Creed), how can one represent Christ equal to the Father as 'touching' his Godhead but 'inferior to the Father, as touching his Manhood'?

The passion story itself provides the premier context for exploring such questions. Take Jesus' last spoken words as variously reported in the four Gospels. It might be possible to find one who is equal to the Father in Luke's gracious saviour, who when crucified is merciful to those who mock him ('Father, forgive them, for they know not what they do', 23.34) and promises the 'good' thief an immediate reward for his faithfulness ('Today you will be with me in paradise', 23.43).[3] Likewise, when we turn to the Gospel of John we find a Lamb of God so in control of the horrible scene on Golgotha that he can find his mother another son to look after her (19.26-27). At the end, he announces when enough is enough, 'It is finished' (19.30).

On the other hand, when it comes to finding the Son's inferiority to the Father 'as touching his Manhood', one must go to Matthew and Mark, who have Christ give up the ghost in a cry of dereliction, 'My God, my God, why have you forsaken me?' It is only when the larger context of the text he cites, Psalm 22, is understood to be included within its opening line

---

2   'The Dream of the Rood', in *Anglo-Saxon Poetry* (trans. R. K. Gordon; New York: Dutton, 1967), p. 236.

3   All citations of the Bible are taken from the NRSV in the *New Oxford Annotated Bible* (New York: Oxford University Press, 3rd edn, 2001).

that these last words can be seen to span the gap between death and resurrection, mortal despair and trust in divine certainty.

These quite different presentations of the God-man on the cross are lost when the four Gospels are merged – not (as might actually have been the case) into a single 'harmonized' text that makes the rough places plain, but in the living practice of the church during Holy Week when it presents the passion in preaching and liturgy. The Good Friday tradition of the Seven Last Words, for instance, joins the six 'comfortable' sayings found in Luke and John to the single *un*comfortable word of Matthew and Mark: 'Eloi, Eloi, lama sabachthani?' In the tally of final sayings, therefore, numbers talk: six to one reveal that the saviour knows what he is doing and where he is going. The Manhood is effectively taken into God – at least if you manage to keep the cry of dereliction out of your head.

But then there is the particular passion scene that I want to focus on here: the Garden of Gethsemane. It comes as no surprise that the Gospel of John barely enters it: John places Jesus in an olive grove across the Kidron Valley (18.1) but only for the barest moment, and then only as the backdrop for his arrest. The tortuous experience of the Garden is bypassed altogether; the closest thing we get to it is a rhetorical question in ch. 12 that gives way immediately to a robust affirmation. 'Now my heart is troubled, and what shall I say? "Father, save me from this hour?" No, it was for this reason I came to this hour. Father, glorify your name' (12.27-28). Jesus need not wait but a minute for what amounts to a clear 'I do': 'Then a voice came from heaven, "I have glorified it, and I will glorify it again"' (12.28).

Gethsemane as a scene in Christ's life occurs in all three of the Synoptics, with Matthew pretty much taking up Mark's account but also clarifying and intensifying his source. The episode is prepared for in Matthew by two events. The first, the Lord's Supper (26.17-30), is when Christ blesses bread and cup before predicting that his betrayer is at hand. Secondly, after master and disciples leave the upper room for the Mount of Olives (26.31-32), Peter twice protests that he will never fall away from his master, even if he is the only one to remain faithful. In the middle of these disclaimers, Christ says, 'This very night, before the cock crows, you will deny me three times' (v. 34). The chapter continues:

> Then Jesus went with them to a place called Gethsemane; and he said to his disciples, 'Sit here while I go over there and pray.' [37]He took with him Peter and the two sons of Zebedee, and began to be grieved and agitated. [38]Then he said to them, 'I am deeply grieved, even to death; remain here, and stay awake with me.' [39]And going a little farther, he threw himself on the ground and prayed, 'My Father, if it is possible, let this cup pass from me; yet not what I want but what you want.' [40]Then he came to the disciples and found them sleeping; and he said to Peter, 'So, could you not stay awake with me one hour? [41]Stay awake and pray

that you may not come into the time of trial; the spirit indeed is willing, but the flesh is weak.' [42]Again he went away for the second time and prayed, 'My Father, if this cannot pass unless I drink it, your will be done.' [43]Again he came and found them sleeping, for their eyes were heavy. [44]So leaving them again, he went away and prayed for the third time, saying the same words. [45]Then he came to the disciples and said to them, 'Are you still sleeping and taking your rest? See, the hour is at hand, and the Son of Man is betrayed into the hands of sinners. [46]Get up, let us be going. See, my betrayer is at hand.'

After reading commentaries on this passage, both ancient and modern, I am struck by the degree to which Jesus' extraordinary vulnerability in this scene is consistently downplayed. The text, however, does not pull back from the brink until the last moment, when Jesus sees that the end is nigh and takes charge: 'Get up'. To begin with, there is the bitter irony of the narrative framing to note: Jesus leaves behind the bulk of the disciples and takes with him to a place apart 'Peter and the two sons of Zebedee' (both of whom are named by Mark as James and John). This trio was last assembled by Jesus on the Mount of Transfiguration, when they beheld the apotheosis of the Lord in a cloud of glory and heard a voice from heaven say, 'This is my Son, the Beloved; with him I am well pleased; listen to him!' (Mt. 17.5). But that was then; here we have a *reversal* of the Transfiguration. No cloud of glory, no voice from heaven, no corroborating presence of Law and Prophets such as had been offered in the figures of Moses and Elijah. Nor does Jesus say anything here about the Son of Man being raised from the dead (Mt. 17.9). Instead of encountering the Father's beloved, theophanic son, on the Mountain, we find a Jesus who is twice said to be in passionate turmoil, once by the narrator ('He was grieved and agitated') and once by Jesus himself ('I am deeply grieved, even to death').

Add to these words dramatic gesture. When Jesus moves spatially further into Gethsemane's 'oil-press' – the etymology of the place name – he also moves more deeply into his grievance-unto-death: 'And going a little farther, he threw himself on the ground'. Again, one recalls by contrast the Transfiguration, when it was the *disciples* who fell to the ground 'overcome by fear', only to have Jesus come to them, touch them by way of comfort, and say, 'Get up and do not be afraid' (17.7). Here it is Jesus who comes to where they are resting, who appeals to them not once but three times, only to find them fast asleep on every occasion. Their oblivion, made especially poignant by Peter's recent assurance, 'Even if all fall away, I will not', then occasions from Jesus what sounds like a put-down on the way to becoming a proverb: he says, 'the spirit indeed is willing, but the flesh is weak'.

It is not the weakness of the disciples' flesh, however, that is at the centre of the story; rather, it is *Jesus'* own humanity: his deep emotion, his need for creature comfort, his dependence on the very same men who until now were his 'little children' and who all along the way have demonstrated their limitations. For the ancient Stoic or indeed for any learned pagan (as we know from Origen's *Contra Celsum*), such behaviour was unthinkable. Sophocles drank his cup of hemlock with dignity; he did not rant and rave. How can one who claims to be divine, asks Celsus, 'mourn and lament and pray to escape the fear of death, expressing himself thus, "O Father, if it be possible, let this cup pass from me"?' (*Contra Celsum* 2.24).[4]

Whereas Peter will not stay awake even one hour, Jesus cannot rest assured for a minute. Instead, he throws himself on the ground (again and once again), praying three times, 'Father, if it is possible, let this cup pass from me; yet not what I want but what you want'. As we have seen, John's Jesus barely raised this possibility before he swept it away – 'no, it was for this very reason I came to this hour' (12.27) – but the Jesus of Matthew and Mark, 'saying the same words', asks for it twice over. Mark further heightens this poignancy by having Jesus call out not only to his Father but (in a sudden move from Greek to Aramaic) to his 'Abba', his Papa – a one-word shift into what linguists call the intimate or 'caritative' mode of address. Well might a beloved son so address his beloved father. But there is no paternal presence here; Jesus is all alone, and the crying out only seems more remarkable given the fact that he has never needed to do so before. He has had no previous experience of being lost.

Jesus prays that the cup before him might be withdrawn from his lips. Because the contents of that cup are not specified, centuries of speculation have stepped into the textual gap. What the cup holds for Jesus is entirely ours to imagine, which only heightens the parity between us and him. Was the drink that he dreaded his imminent death and suffering, or the burden of the sins of the whole world, or the particular pain of abandonment by his disciples? Was it a foretaste of 'Eloi, eloi, lama sabachthani?', the bitterly human experience of being cut off from God?

With the image of the cup, moreover, we are reminded of the challenge which Jesus not long before threw out to his friends when predicting his death: 'Can you drink the cup I am going to drink?' (Mt. 20.22). We also look back on that 'hour' in the Upper Room when Jesus reclined at table with the twelve. At the Last Supper he blesses a cup, speaks of the wine as the blood of a new covenant, looks forward to the day when he would share it with his disciples in the Father's kingdom. Now, in Gethsemane, 'this cup' seems like poison.

---

4 Cited by Raymond E. Brown, *The Death of the Messiah: From Gethsemane to the Grave: A Commentary on the Passion Narratives in the Four Gospels* (vol. 1; Garden City: Doubleday, 1994), p. 218. I am greatly indebted to Brown's magisterial treatment of the Gethsemane episode, pp. 110–310.

Tradition has turned this agonizing prayer, and indeed the whole episode, into a teaching moment, as in the first stanza of James Montgomery's 1820 hymn, 'Go to dark Gethsemane':

Go to dark Gethsemane,
Ye that feel the Tempter's power;
Your Redeemer's conflict see,
Watch with Him one bitter hour;
Turn not from His griefs away,
Learn of Jesus Christ to pray.[5]

The hymn-writer ventures, however, where the Synoptics did not actually go: there is no Tempter in Gethsemane. Instead, Jesus seems to battle with those parts of himself which, although unspecified, are presumably part of his 'flesh', aspects that show him as vulnerable human and therefore vastly 'inferior to the Father as touching his Manhood'. Resolution belongs to the Lord; he who hesitates is human.

This vision of Jesus at a loss is one that Luke simply cannot abide, despite the irrefutable evidence of Jesus' painful hesitation before the cup (Lk. 22.39-46). Luke's Jesus warns his disciples, 'Pray that you will fall not into temptation', which he himself never does. He next withdraws a stone's throw away and then decorously *kneels down* (literally, 'puts the knees down') and prays. His words in Luke are virtually identical to those in Matthew and Mark, and they are prayed (but only one time, not three) so earnestly that 'his sweat was like blood falling to the ground'. According to Raymond Brown in *The Death of the Messiah*, however, this sweat is a sign of Jesus' strength, not his anxiety: he is like the athlete preparing for the monumental feat that will lead to victory.[6]

Furthermore, throughout this *agon*, Jesus is not alone. Although the Father's voice does not comfort him from Heaven, as it had at his baptism and Transfiguration, there is suddenly an angel who descends in order to strengthen him. Luke's Jesus does not thrash on the ground or wake the three disciples so that they can keep watch with him. Instead, he kneels at prayer the way Christians are said to do several times in Luke's Acts of the Apostles (7.60; 9.40; 20.36; 21.5). There is neither fear nor anguish in this scene, but rather a hero valiantly fighting the good fight – a strenuous *agon*, yes, but one with angels on the side.

It is unmistakably Luke's account that stands behind the iconography of a fifteenth-century Catalan painting by Jaime Huguet now in the collection of Oxford's Campion Hall. In it Jesus kneels before the prie-

---

5 'Go to dark Gethsemane', words by James Montgomery (1771–1854), set to the tune 'Petra' by Richard Redhead (1820–1901), in *The Hymnal 1982 according to the use of The Episcopal Church* (New York: The Church Hymnal Corporation, 1985).
6 Brown, *Death of the Messiah*, p. 189.

dieu of a hillock rising up within the enclosure of Gethsemane. To his left and in the foreground Peter, James and John are shown in deep slumber. By contrast, Jesus is wide awake. We see him looking up at an angel who hovers before him at slightly higher than eye-level – a tiny figure, more hummingbird than seraph. This messenger from heaven wears priestly vestments and extends a eucharistic chalice, the host, and a corporal. He is an altar on the wing. The cup that the Jesus of Matthew and Mark attempts to turn away from three times is bestowed here with all the reassurance and ceremony of a sacrament that one takes to one's comfort, as the Book of Common Prayer would have it, 'devoutly kneeling'.

The painter intuits properly, I think, what Luke wants us to see, no matter how anachronistic and ecclesiastical the vision. Gethsemane is a last rite that comes to a Jesus who is fully prepared, who looks beyond the present horror toward a cup of thanksgiving in glory. We behold the viaticum administered from on high, confident that in the night that Jesus was betrayed – and despite the sweat like drops of blood falling to the ground – the saviour made a good Christian death, fortified by the Eucharist and ready for the cross. Gethsemane, therefore, reveals his resolve, his grace under pressure, and thus provides a model for ourselves. As the Montgomery hymn would have it (alluding not to Luke but to John, Luke's partner in a more divinely composed passion), ' "It is finished!" hear Him cry;/ learn of Jesus Christ to die'.

It might go without saying that in twentieth-century literature the dual nature of Christ as presented with such precision in the Athanasian Creed is not to be found in the 'enfleshment' of contemporary narrative; there is also little if any Godhead for the Manhood to be taken up into. In *The Last Temptation of Christ* (1955), for instance, Nikos Kazantzakis presents the whole of Christ's life as a struggle between willing spirit and weak flesh. Gethsemane is the place where he is almost overcome 'by the longing to see men, to hear a human voice, to touch the hands he loved', to find on earth the only paradise anyone could want:' "Father," Jesus murmured, "Father who are in heaven, Father who are on the earth: the world you created is beautiful, and we see it; beautiful is the world which we do not see. I don't know – forgive me – I don't know, Father, which is the more beautiful." '[7]

For José Luis Saramago, in *The Gospel According to Jesus Christ* (1991), Gethsemane turns into the Temptation scene, in which God and the Devil, revealed to be two sides of the same divine coin, present Jesus with the 'cup' of the future. They predict the hideous deaths of the disciples, give a lengthy alphabetical procession of subsequent martyrs, foretell the Crusades, and the Inquisition. This vision of constant suffering

---

7 *The Last Temptation of Christ* (trans. P. Bien; New York: Simon & Schuster, 1960), p. 443, p. 440.

finally provokes a confrontation between Son and Father wherein the biblical Gethsemane's one-way communication – the Son's anguished prayer – becomes a dialogue:

> And all this is my fault. You are not to blame. Your cause
> demands it. Father, take away from me this cup. My power
> and glory demand that you drink it to the last drop. I don't want
> the glory. But I want the power.

This version of Gethsemane ends with the Devil's observation, 'One has to be God to countenance so much blood.'[8] Jesus is a dupe, his Father a vampire.

In Rainer-Maria Rilke's 'The Olive-Garden' ('*Der Ölbaum-Garten*'), first published in his 1907 *New Poems* (*Neue Gedichte*), there is neither Devil nor Father to contend with in Gethsemane.[9] 'I am alone', says Rilke's Jesus, 'I am alone with all of human grief,/ which I undertook through You to soothe,/ You who are not' (lines 11–14). The poet makes his point about Jesus' utter solitude by having him deny the angel that Luke and later iconography have introduced into the scene:

> Later they would say: an angel came –
>
> Why an angel? It was the night that came,
> and leafed indifferently through the trees.
> The disciples stirred in their dreams.
> Why an angel? It was the night that came. (lines 15–19)

Against the softening effect of Christian tradition, with its heavenly intermediary and assurance that the saviour was never truly abandoned in his grief, Rilke refuses a divine intervention. There is no heavenly Father, so 'Why ... Why an angel?' Furthermore, he insists that Jesus' aloneness in Gethsemane links him to the human plight of everyone else. 'The night that came was no uncommon one;/ hundreds like it pass men by':

> For angels don't answer the prayers of such men
> and the nights don't expand around them.
> Those who lose themselves are let go by everything,
> and are abandoned by their fathers
> and excluded from their mothers' wombs. (lines 25–9)

Rilke's Jesus is a motherless as well as a fatherless child – 'let go', 'abandoned', 'excluded'. 'Why an angel?' indeed.

---

8 *The Gospel According to Jesus Christ* (trans. from the Portuguese by Giovanni Pontiero; San Diego: Harcourt Brace & Company, 1994, p. 330.).

9 *New Poems (1907)* (trans. Edward Snow; San Francisco: North Point Press, 1984, pp. 38–41).

The twentieth century seems to have turned its back on the balancing act with which we began: the both/and mystery of the Word made flesh affirmed by orthodox Christianity. Yet not entirely. I want to close with a poem from Denise Levertov's 1992 collection, *Evening Train*, that is an unusual representation not only of the 'Athanasian' equipoise of Christ's two natures but also of the dynamic tension between them – the give and take of divine and human.[10] It is entitled '*Salvator mundi: Via Crucis*':

Maybe He looked indeed
much as Rembrandt envisioned Him
in those small heads that seem in fact
portraits of more than a model.
A dark, still young, very intelligent face,
a soul-mirror gaze of deep understanding, unjudging.
That face, in extremis, would have clenched its teeth
in a grimace not shown in even the great crucifixions.
The burden of humanness (I begin to see) exacted from Him
that He taste also the humiliation of dread,
cold sweat of wanting to let the whole thing go,
like any mortal hero out of his depth,
like anyone who has taken a step too far
and wants herself back.
The painters, even the greatest, don't show how,
in the midnight Garden,
or staggering uphill under the weight of the Cross,
He went through with even the human longing
to simply cease, to not be.
Not torture of body,
not the hideous betrayals humans commit
nor the faithless weakness of friends, and surely
not the anticipation of death (not then, in agony's grip)
was Incarnation's heaviest weight,
but this sickened desire to renege,
to step back from what He, Who was God,
had promised Himself, and had entered
time and flesh to enact.
Sublime acceptance, to be absolute, had to have welled
Up from those depths where purpose
Drifted for mortal moments.

The double title of the poem, itself a play of duality, places the text in the Latin world of the Roman-Catholic West, as well as literally and figuratively in Jerusalem. We are asked to behold the saviour of the world as he is to be found on the Way of the Cross. But 'Salvator mundi' also

---

10 *Evening Train* (New York: New Directions, 1992), p. 144. Copyright © by Denice Levertov. Reprinted by permission of New Directions Publishing Corp.

indicates a traditional iconographic pose, in which Christ (holding a globe or some other accoutrement of authority) looks straight into the eyes of the viewer, as in the Albrecht Dürer painting of this name.

Levertov depends heavily on visual art, but it is no Christus Rex that she conjures up, despite her title; rather, she alludes to two very different portrayals of the saviour of the world – each of which offers us a 'Maybe' (the poem's opening word) of what he looked like. On the one hand, she names Rembrandt and refers generally to several portraits of unnamed Semitic-looking young men taken to be a 'Christus tronie nae't leven' – 'a Christ head after life' – whose models were all Amsterdam Jews.[11] Levertov does not allude to Rembrandt's Philosemitism or to her own Jewish ancestry through her Anglican priest-father. Rather, she concentrates on the vivid, welcoming humanity of an unhaloed Christ – the accessible thirty-something rabbi, the itinerant healer, or perhaps the word-playing stranger who engaged the much-married Samaritan woman at her village well in Jn 4.7-30:

> Maybe He looked indeed
> much as Rembrandt envisioned Him
> in those small heads that seem in fact
> portraits of more than a model.
> A dark, still young, very intelligent face,
> a soul-mirror gaze of deep understanding, unjudging

In contrast to this gentle, serene visage – this portrait of the saviour as a young Jew – she then conjures 'that face, in extremis', and therefore moves us from the day-to-day life of Christ to the terrible end-game of his passion. But whereas Rembrandt could give a probable likeness of the young Jew, not even the Old Masters could convey in line or paint what the tortured man might have looked like in his agony. 'That face, in extremis, would have clenched its teeth/ in a grimace not shown in even the great crucifixions.'

The rest of the poem takes us along the Via Crucis – the second part of the poem's title – from the Garden of Gethsemane to Golgotha, by means of an imaginative exploration of the saviour's interior life. Levertov signals Christ's divinity not only by referring to him as 'He' and 'Himself' in the reverential upper case, but also by the quasi-creedal language used to express the God's-eye view of the incarnation. The descent into human vulnerability was 'what He, Who was God,/ had promised Himself, and had entered/ time and flesh to enact'. Here we have one who is 'Equal to the Father, as touching his Godhead'.

The bulk of the text, however, explores what Levertov refers to as 'the

11   Michael Zell, *Reframing Rembrandt: Jews and the Christian Image in Seventeenth-Century Amsterdam* (Berkeley: University of California Press, *c.* 2002), pp. 56–7.

burden of humanness', that is, the weight of being human, which she
enters by means of an extended investigation of the mind of Gethsemane
as it might be understood by a poet steeped in the passion accounts of
Matthew and Mark. This Jesus is 'like any mortal hero out of his depth'.
He tastes 'the humiliation of dread'; he experiences 'the cold sweat of
wanting to let the whole thing go'. In a show of personal empathy and
identification with the male Christ, she likens him to 'anyone who has
taken a step too far/ and wants *herself* back', (emphasis mine). She also
suggests what the final refusal of the cup might have meant:

> Not torture of body,
> not the hideous betrayals humans commit
> nor the faithless weakness of friends, and surely
> not the anticipation of death (not then, in agony's grip)
> was Incarnation's heaviest weight,
> but this sickened desire to renege,
> to step back from what He, Who was God,
> had promised Himself, and had entered
> time and flesh to enact.

'Maybe'. The poem begins in surmise, and uses the resources of art
history, *lectio divina*, and the work of sympathetic imagination to give us a
keener sense of the God-Man. It draws to a close, moreover, in a flourish
of the indicative, with the repeated assertion of what is (or rather, is *not*)
the case: not, not, nor, nor, but. We approach the mystery of Christ's
anguish by eliminating the likely possibilities. Yet in her final lines,
Levertov moves very subtly away from assertion and back into surmise.
She cannot presume to fathom the saviour's heart and mind any more
than Rembrandt or the 'greatest painters' could capture his likeness,
either as a young Jewish man in repose or as someone on the cross 'in a
grimace'. She has only the fervour of her own conviction to go on.

> Sublime acceptance, to be absolute, had to have welled
> Up from those depths where purpose
> Drifted for mortal moments.

In these, her poem's 'last words', Levertov brings together the passion
accounts of Matthew and Mark with those of Luke and John, but without
erasing their differences; there is 'not two, but one Christ' presented in her
alternation between christologies. The 'sublime acceptance' of the passion
we find in Luke and John, in order to be 'absolute' as well as true, *had to
have*, *could only have* 'welled up' from the depths we witness on the bare
ground of Gethsemane. For the God-Man to have been human indeed,
and not a god merely playing at humanity, he *would have* (and repeatedly)
threw himself on the earth, his soul 'deeply grieved, even unto death'.
For before the Manhood could be taken into God it must have returned

to the dirt from which Adam was moulded. *Contra* Celsus, scandal is an inevitable burden of the Incarnation.

In '*Salvator mundi. Via Crucis*', Levertov works valiantly to maintain the precarious balance of the creed but with an obvious tip of the scale in our human direction. She upholds the 'purpose' of the Incarnation with orthodox conviction; she gives us the saviour of the World. Yet her poem both lingers and terminates where it must, in the drift of those very 'mortal moments' which link us to the God-Man, and which are all that 'mortal us' – absent an angel – are likely to know.

References

The Book of Common Prayer (New York: Church Hymnal Corporation, 1979).

Brown, Raymond E., *The Death of the Messiah:From Gethsemane to the Grave: A Commentary on the Passion Narratives in the Four Gospels* (vol. 1; Garden City: Doubleday, 1994).

'The Dream of the Rood', in *Anglo-Saxon Poetry* (trans. R. K. Gordon; New York: Dutton, 1967).

The Hymnal 1982 according to the use of The Episcopal Church (New York: The Church Hymnal Corporation, 1985).

Kazantzakis, Nikos, *The Last Temptation of Christ* (trans. P. Bien; New York: Simon & Schuster, 1960).

Levertov, Denise, *Evening Train* (New York: New Directions, 1992).

New Oxford Annotated Bible (New York: Oxford University Press, 3rd edn, 2001).

Rilke, Rainer-Maria, *New Poems (1907)* (trans. Edward Snow; San Francisco: North Point Press, 1984).

Saramago, José Luis, *The Gospel According to Jesus Christ* (trans. from the Portuguese by Giovanni Pontiero; San Diego: Harcourt Brace & Company, 1994).

Zell, Michael, *Reframing Rembrandt: Jews and the Christian Image in Seventeenth-Century Amsterdam.* (Berkeley: University of California Press, c. 2002).

Chapter 3

THE TRANSFORMING POWER OF THE CROSS

Timothy Gorringe

In a notorious passage in his *Philosophy of Manufactures*, published in 1835, Andrew Ure appeals to the transforming power of the cross of Christ as that which fits a workforce for discipline:

> It is the sacrifice which removes the guilt of sin: it is the motive which removes the love of sin: it mortifies sin by showing its turpitude to be indelible except by such an awful expiation; it atones for disobedience; it excites to obedience; it purchases strength for obedience; it makes obedience practicable; it makes it acceptable; it makes it in a manner unavoidable, for it constrains to it; it is, finally, not only the motive to obedience, but the pattern of it.[1]

Ure's book was familiar to Marx, and certainly confirmed, if it did not suggest, his view of Christianity as an opiate. Ure's rhetoric in this passage is impeccably orthodox, drawing not only on Methodism, its immediate origin, but beyond that on the passion mysticism of the Middle Ages which was mediated to Wesley through Moravianism. The cynical use to which passion mysticism is here put, however, illustrates its problematic nature. As Schillebeeckx puts it, 'the Christian interpretation of suffering enters a phase in which the symbol of the cross becomes a disguised legitimation of social abuses ... 'Suffering in itself', no longer suffering through and for others, took on a mystical and positive significance so that instead of having a critical power it really acquired a reactionary significance. Suffering in itself became a "symbol".'[2]

In his great, early book on Picasso, John Berger reminds us not to be mystified by Picasso's reputation. Much of what Picasso created, he is unafraid to say, was trash.[3] Some of us are prepared to dismiss some religious art as kitsch, but most of us fall solemnly silent before depictions

---

1 A. Ure, *Philosophy of Manufactures* (1835), pp. 423–5. Cited in E. P. Thompson, *The Making of the English Working Class* (Harmondsworth: Penguin, 1980), p. 398.

2 E. Schillebeeckx, *Christ: The Experience of Jesus as Lord* (New York: Crossroad, 1990), p. 699.

3 J. Berger, *Success and Failure of Picasso* (Harmondsworth: Penguin, 1965).

of the passion. But might some depictions constitute a 'disguised legitimation of social abuses' – and is there evidence that the greatest artists realized this and sought ways in which to deal with it? The answer, I think, is 'yes' in both cases. Consider, first, two examples from one of Ure's contemporaries, Francesco Goya.

Goya's one study of a crucifixion (Fig. 1) is an insipid piece, painted to gain academy membership. Robert Hughes's judgement on it is severe:

> It is without doubt the worst painting he ever did. How could the man who would emerge, some thirty years later, as the most powerful reporter of human anguish in all of Western art have produced this soapy piece of *bondieuserie*? The ladylike body, unmarked by torment; the absence of any kind of empathy with what real bodies underwent in the course of flogging and crucifixion; the enervated 'correctness' of the pose – all this combines to convey a sort of sickly, moaning piety that, if it were not for the relative liveliness of the paint and its impeccable provenance, would make you doubt it was by Goya at all.[4]

Contrast this with one of Goya's most famous images, *The Third of May* (Fig. 2), in which Goya uses the image of crucifixion to depict the only too commonplace occurrence of the murder of insurgents by occupying forces – exactly what the original crucifixion was, of course. *The Third of May* is a protest against occupation and military brutality, against arbitrary power and inhumanity. Goya invokes the crucified Christ in this image, even alluding to the marks of the nails in the central character's left hand. He understands crucifixion within its political context. Listen to the Salvadorean theologian, Jon Sobrino: 'In Latin America the concrete mediation of the "death of God" has been the "death of the other human being" – that is, the death of the peasantry, the native Indian, and so forth … In historical terms God is to be found in the crosses of the oppressed rather than in beauty, power, or wisdom.'[5] This, I would argue, could be read as a commentary on these two paintings of Goya. On the one hand a conventional and vapid passion icon; on the other a depiction of a political passion. Goya depicts crucifixion with tremendous power, but when he comes to *Christ on the Cross* centuries of conventional religious piety prevent him saying anything important. The image evokes no spark. It is opiate for the people for whom it was painted, the pious upper class, locked into a piety which knew nothing of social justice, and which Goya savagely derided in some of his royal paintings. *The Third of May*, on the other hand, is a revolutionary painting and understands crucifixion as a revolutionary act. Sobrino again: 'The cross is not the result of some divine decision independent of history; it is the outcome of the basic

---

4   R. Hughes, *Goya* (London: The Harvill Press, 2003), p. 99.
5   J. Sobrino, *Christology at the Crossroads* (London: SCM, 1978), p. 201.

Figure 1. Francesco Goya, *Christ on the Cross*, Museo del Prado, Madrid. (Photo: © akg-images/Erich Lessing)

Figure 2. Francesco Goya, *The Third of May 1808 (Execution of the ensurgents on the Montana del Principe Pio*, Museo del Prado, Madrid. (Photo: © akg-images/Erich Lessing)

option for incarnation in a given situation. That entails conflict because sin holds power in history and takes the triumphant form of religious and political oppression.'[6] The cross, Sobrino insists, challenges both the idolatrous use of power to oppress people, and the idolatrous conception of God that justified that use. *The Third of May* savages that idolatrous use of power. It could at once be objected that this is to reduce the significance of the crucifixion to martyrdom, but here, too, we can appeal to the Salvadorean theologians, who speak of 'the crucified peoples' and understand the crucifixion primarily through Isaiah 53.[7] This gives us a different account of the redemptive significance of the cross than much Western theology, but not an illegitimate one.

Perhaps something similar is going on in Goya's contemporary, William Blake. He executed various studies of the crucifixion for Thomas Butts, which seem to me almost entirely conventional. Since Blake is incapable of being conventional, something odd must be going on here, and indeed it was. Blake loathed the conventional theology of atonement of his day, describing it to Crabbe Robinson as 'a horrible

6 Sobrino, *Christology*, p. 214.
7 J. Sobrino, *Witnesses to the Kingdom* (New York: Orbis, 2003), p. 70.

doctrine'.[8] For Blake, Christ's death is the perpetual example of that self-sacrifice by which alone human beings can live. What threatens human life, 'Satan', is 'the Great Selfhood', man's self-righteous pride:

> In Hell all is Self Righteousness; there is no such thing there as Forgiveness of Sin; he who does Forgive Sin is Crucified as an Abettor of Criminals, & he who performs Works of Mercy in Any Shape whatever is punished &, if possible, destroy'd, not thro' envy or Hatred or Malice, but thro' Self-Righteousness that thinks it does God service, which God is Satan.[9]

Blake reads the crucifixion, therefore, primarily through Lk. 23.34 ('Father, forgive them'). More than anyone in his day he had an understanding of 'the powers' that oppress people, the idols of death, and to symbolize these he created his own mythological world. This understanding is the reason that the real energy of Blake's art is not in depictions of the crucifixion but, for example, in the image of Michael binding Satan, an image of an older atonement theology in terms of conflict with the powers of darkness. Like Goya, Blake has needed to find an alternative language to speak of what the Gospels depict as the significance of the crucifixion. The actual image has become too clichéd for use.

Let me turn now to a great period of passion mysticism, and of depictions of the passion in art: the late fourteenth century. The growing emphasis on the suffering of Christ from the eleventh century on is a commonplace of art criticism. As James Marrow puts it in his great study of passion iconography:

> By the fourteenth century a concerted effort was under way in northern Europe to add to the narrative of the passion recounted by the Evangelists all those details and incidents of cruelty that were not reported in the Gospels ... incidents of generalized torment as hair-pulling, and treading underfoot were now liberally sprinkled through the narrative of the passion ... writers on the passion began to take steps to provide accounts of the previously unknown torments undergone by Christ.[10]

The humiliated and tortured Christ was the dominant icon of the late mediaeval church. This makes it especially interesting that in Lollardy,

---

8   E. J. Morley (ed.), *Blake, Coleridge, Wordsworth, Lamb etc. Being Selections from the Remains of Henry Crabbe Robinson* (Manchester: Manchester University Press, 1922), p. 26.

9   'A Vision of the Last Judgement', in Geoffrey Keynes, *The Writings of William Blake* (vol. 3; London, 1925), p. 160.

10   J. H. Marrow, *Passion Iconography in Northern European Art of the Late Middle Ages and Early Renaissance* (Kortrijk: Van Ghemmert, 1979), p. 95.

and the writing around Wycliffe, there is both opposition to the art of the cross and a distinctly different reading of the passion.

Margaret Aston has documented the aniconic tendencies of Lollardy, which, whatever the relation between Lollardy and Wycliffe, already finds indignant expression in Wycliffe's *Treatise on Papal Power*. Various priests and lay people were brought before the courts for failing to venerate the cross, including Sir John Oldcastle who, when challenged on veneration of the cross, spread his arms wide and said, 'This is the cross.' In 1429 a housewife called Margery Baxter of Martham told a friend that she would show her the true cross there in her house. When her friend said she would love to see it she replied, 'Look, this is the true cross of Christ, and you can and ought to see and worship this cross everyday here in your own home, and you're labouring in vain when you go to church to worship or pray to other images and dead crosses.' Aston comments, 'That was Oldcastle's message – that man was the true image of God. The ancient figure of the *orans*, the priest standing *in modum crucis*, was the only true representation of the crucifixion.'[11] Much of the debate about veneration of the cross at this period seems to have been cast in terms of *dulia* and *latria*, the adoration reserved for God and the respect due to the image, which was familiar to the Middle Ages from the twelfth-century translation of John of Damascus. There is, however, some indication that it went further.

David Aers, for instance, has challenged the view, advanced by Caroline Bynum, that the bleeding or lactating Christ was the centre of late-mediaeval piety, to be imitated in a praxis of suffering. On the contrary, he argues that the perspectives of liberation theology would not have been utterly foreign to believers in the later fourteenth century. He points, for example, to Wycliffe's insistence that 'Christ, our God, was during the time of his pilgrimage, the poorest man'.[12] He taught an *imitatio Christi* that did not involve intense concentration on Christ's suffering so much as a reform of the church which involved challenges to the existing church's power and theology all along the line. Were Christ to come on earth again, Wycliffe argues (as both Blake and Dostoevsky were to argue later), the church would crucify him. As Aers puts it:

> Wycliffe's representation of Christ's humanity does not negate the Crucifixion nor occlude his suffering. What it does do is refuse to split these off from Christ's prophetic ministry, its transgressions of existing

11 M. Aston, 'Lollards and the Cross', in F. Somerset *et al.*, *Lollards and their Influence in Late Medieval England* (Woodbridge: The Boydell Press, 2003), pp. 99–114.

12 Wyclif, *Opera Minora* (ed. J. Loserth; London: Wyclif Society, 1913), p. 19. Cited by D. Aers, 'The Humanity of Christ: Representations in Wycliffite Texts and Piers Plowman', in D. Aers and L. Staley, *The Powers of the Holy: Religion, Politics and Gender in Late Medieval English Culture* (Pennsylvania:Pennsylvania State University Press, 1996), p. 46.

powers and its political communitarian dimensions. It becomes very difficult to abstract cross and suffering from contingent particularities of human power, authority, justice and self-legitimating ideologies. The imperative 'to perform an imitatio Christi, to become what Wycliffe termed a Christicola, a dweller in Christ in whom Christ himself is to be found', might well lead to persecution under the present church.[13]

The *imitatio Christi* of Lollardy was not a call to follow the tortured bleeding body of so much art, but rather to follow the preacher of Nazareth who moved around Galilee preaching the gospel of freedom. So the Lollard priest William Thorpe defended himself in his interrogation before the archbishop in 1407. When charged with causing a commotion, Thorpe reminded his archbishop of Luke chapter 4, and insisted that both Jerusalem and Nazareth had cast Christ out after his preaching. A Wycliffite sermon on Good Friday goes in for none of the elaborations of the violence of the scene with which we are so familiar, but instead focuses on Pilate's injustice and on Christ's trial for heresy. Similarly, Aers argues, Langland also fails to elaborate on the tortures Christ suffers but, 'integrates Crucifixion with creation, harrowing of hell, and the power displayed in and through the resurrection. The emphasis is on the way divine power, through the incarnation, is identified with the cause of humankind (5.477–505).'[14] In the first Passus of *Piers Plowman* 'love of neighbour in social practice is given a Christological basis and given as the way humans may move toward God, an ethical disposition which becomes the path of salvation'.[15] In Passus 16 the passion and crucifixion have just five lines, in which there are no details of physical suffering:

> Jesus on the Friday following for mankind's sake
> Jousted in Jerusalem, a joy to us all.
> On cross upon Calvary Christ took the battle
> Against death and the devil; destroyed both their mights
> Died and death fordid, and day of night made.[16]

Aers argues that Langland's vision is centred more on the incarnation as a form of solidarity with humans which grounds Christian fraternalism.[17] Compare Sobrino, who argues that what is at stake in the cross is the question of which God we have to deal with:

> What is at stake here is the kind of solidarity that God has with human beings. Does his solidarity with us mean that God himself must go by way of the cross in the midst of countless historical crosses, or in the last

13   Aers, 'Wycliffite Texts', p. 46.
14   Aers, 'Wycliffite Texts', p. 61.
15   Aers, 'Wycliffite Texts', pp. 60–1.
16   *Piers Plowman* 16.162–6.
17   Aers, 'Wycliffite Texts', p. 72.

analysis does God himself remain untouched by the historical cross because he is essentially untouchable? ... At bottom the cross challenges us to say what sort of God we believe in. Insofar as salvation is concerned, it does not simply ask how people are saved passively; it also asks how God saves people in a world where there is no salvation.[18]

To say the least, setting this reading of the passion and a hostility to images of the cross side by side is suggestive. Coming from a different theological position, and lacking an alternative pictorial tradition, perhaps the Lollards had no option but to be aniconic. It could, of course, be argued that the mediaeval nativities, equally as popular as depictions of the passion, formed a dialectical counterpoint to portrayals of the passion. They were a perfect opportunity to show the priority of the poor, in the presence of the shepherds, which, as Michel Mollat has shown, was such a consistent theme in mediaeval rhetoric.[19] Alternatively it might be argued, as Archbishop Arundel argued, that the Lollards had misunderstood the heart of their faith, or perhaps that there are alternative ways of construing the centrality of 'the man of sorrows'. In the case of the Grünewald triptych, for example, beneath a reproduction of which Karl Barth sat for the whole of his working life, it seems right to understand it as a representation of divine solidarity with the patients for whom it was painted, who, in virtue of their terrible illness, were necessarily marginalized. It is a profound meditation on Isaiah 53, and it needs to be understood, of course, with the resurrection image painted on the reverse, so that it insists on reading death and resurrection together just as the liberation theologians do.

   Are there representations of the passion which break the mould of the man of sorrows and which do not make a virtue out of suffering of itself? We could begin with a painting which alludes to Grünewald, namely Otto Dix's *War*, painted in 1932. The left-hand panel, with soldiers marching off to the front, corresponds with the way of the cross. The right-hand panel (as we look at it) corresponds to the Deposition. The predella unmistakeably echoes Holbein's *Dead Christ*, depicting soldiers trying to sleep in their dugout. In the central panel, Grünewald's 'pointing finger of John the Baptist' is replaced by the outstretched arm of the corpse impaled on mangled iron pointing to a crucified figure blown to pieces and upside down. In the background, beyond the mangled bodies, a series of uprights, which may be burned trees, suggest crosses. The unmistakable allusion to Grünewald marks this out as a way of talking of the continuing crucifixion brought about by human wickedness. In the right-hand panel the Joseph of Arimathea character, carrying his wounded comrade, is

18   Sobrino, *Christology*, p. 190.
19   Michel Mollat, *The Poor in the Middle Ages: An Essay in Social History* (trans. A. Goldhammer; New Haven: Yale, 1986).

given Dix's own features. Unlike the Grünewald, there is no resurrection in this painting, only the affirmation of continuing human decency amidst absolute horror.

Another painting which certainly makes no virtue of suffering is Chagall's *White Crucifixion*, painted in 1938, a tremendous protest against both Fascist and Russian pogroms and more pointedly still a protest against the Kristallnacht.[20] Here the political significance of the crucifixion is absolutely foregrounded. The crucified Christ is the crucified Jew, wearing his prayer shawl as a loincloth, the titulus in Hebrew alone, torah scrolls either blazing or clasped in the hands of fleeing Jews. Some embark in small and inadequate boats for Israel. What appear to be the souls of dead rabbis hover above both the destruction and the crucifixion which sums it all up. The crucifixion of Jesus becomes an icon for the attack on Jews throughout European history. As a political painting this invites comparison with Picasso's *Guernica* and it is specifically the Jewishness of Jesus which has allowed Chagall to use the cross in this way. *Guernica*, of course, also includes an allusion to *The Third of May*, and to that extent also an allusion to the crucifixion.[21]

In the earlier tradition both Bosch and Rembrandt offer us political readings of the passion. In his account of *The Crowning with Thorns* Bosch puts Christ in the hands of power, and more especially of the mailed fist. It is impossible to understand this painting abstractly. Anybody who had any experience of the School of the Americas would understand this painting at once. Bosch's image was, it seems to me, later picked up by Stanley Spencer who, however, generalizes the cruelty into a comment on the human condition, telling the shocked audience at Aldenham school, for which this crucifixion was painted, that it was they and the governors who were crucifying Christ.

Rembrandt painted an image of Christ alone, enveloped in darkness, in 1631, as did many other seventeenth-century artists, and as we have seen so did Goya. Such images correspond, in my view, with an abstract theology of the atonement. To quote Sobrino:

> It is not just that they tend to centre salvation around the individual, nor is that the main problem. The real problem is that they tend to treat salvation in terms of inner life, explaining how the cross can bring forgiveness for one's sins, while neglecting to treat of salvation in relationship to the world outside and the problems of externalised injustice and sinfulness.[22]

20   See above, p. 25 for a reproduction of this image.
21   This allusion is strengthened by the way in which Picasso echoes *Guernica* in his one account of the crucifixion.
22   Sobrino, *Christology*, p. 190.

The Elevation of the Cross, painted later, perhaps in 1633, is quite different. A richly costumed turbaned man, perhaps Pilate, his hand raised in command, fixes us from near the centre of the picture.[23] We are all familiar with that gaze: Your country needs you! A soldier doing his bidding strains to bring the cross upright, an effort in which he is helped by the artist Rembrandt and by a proletarian figure behind. Just in front of the cross a gravedigger's spade, which has dug a hole to receive the cross, also catches the light. To the left of the picture a priestly figure seems to be saying, 'There! Now we've dealt with that problem.' In the background another guerrilla is being nailed to his cross. It is, of course, a picture of human complicity in the death of Christ, but the armour of the soldier, and the rider in his conventionally military pose, put this complicity in an inescapably political context. The same is true, it seems to me, of the two etchings made twenty years later, in which the soldiery plays an inescapable part and in which the thieves crucified along with Christ look like political victims from Spartacus onwards.

The Lollards, in 1395, referred back to the Roman martyr Laurence in speaking of 'pore men, tresoreris of Cryst and his apostlis'.[24] They represent a tradition which distrusted abstraction. They contested the doctrine which, 'instead of viewing the cross in all its irrepeatable and scandalous uniqueness' understood it rather in terms of a cultic sacrifice.

> More and more the cross took on a 'religious' character. It became the factor that made possible a Christian cult with sacrifice understood along the lines of other religions. Once the cross was translated into cultic terms of that sort, the danger increased that it would end up as a 'de-historicised' cross and that 'worship' would end up replacing the real following of Jesus.[25]

Whether in hymnology or art this dehistoricized cross could function more or less as Andrew Ure wished and was certainly deprived of critical power. Many artists, like many theologians, expressed precisely such a version of the atonement. The way to avoid it, it seems, is through a political hermeneutic which many would argue is crucial to a proper reading of the Gospels themselves. Displaced by piety, or the rather gloomy Platonism of Augustine or Anselm, such a hermeneutic has nevertheless made itself felt at different stages of the church's history and today is found most strongly in the tradition of liberation theology. As we have seen, it has a certain anticipation in parts of the artistic and literary tradition.

23   It is true, of course, that this figure is most obviously read as the centurion, but the turban inescapably recalls Pilate in Rembrandt's *Ecce Rex Vester*.

24   H. S. Cronin, 'The Twelve Conclusions of the Lollards', *The English Historical Review* 22 (1907), 29.

25   Sobrino, *Christology*, p. 194.

References

Aers, D., 'The Humanity of Christ: Representations in Wycliffite Texts and *Piers Plowman*', in D. Aers and L. Staley, *The Powers of the Holy: Religion, Politics and Gender in Late Medieval English Culture* (Pennsylvania: Pennsylvania University Press, 1996), pp. 43–76.

Aston, M., 'Lollards and the Cross', in F. Somerset *et al.*, *Lollards and their Influence in Late Medieval England* (Woodbridge: The Boydell Press, 2003), pp. 99–114.

Berger, J., *Success and Failure of Picasso* (Harmondsworth: Penguin, 1965).

Cronin, H. S., 'The Twelve Conclusions of the Lollards', *The English Historical Review* 22 (1907), 292–304.

Hughes, R., *Goya* (London: The Harvill Press, 2003).

Keynes, G., *The Writings of William Blake* (vol. 3; London, 1925).

Marrow, J. H., *Passion Iconography in Northern European Art of the Late Middle Ages and Early Renaissance* (Kortrijk: Van Ghemmert, 1979).

Mollat, M., *The Poor in the Middle Ages: An Essay in Social History* (trans. A. Goldhammer; New Haven: Yale, 1986).

Morley, E. J. (ed.), *Blake, Coleridge, Wordsworth, Lamb etc. Being Selections from the Remains of Henry Crabbe Robinson* (Manchester: Manchester University Press, 1922).

Schillebeeckx, E., *Christ: The Experience of Jesus as Lord* (New York: Crossroad, 1990).

Sobrino, J., *Christology at the Crossroads* (London: SCM, 1978).

—— *Witnesses to the Kingdom* (New York: Orbis, 2003).

Thompson, E. P., *The Making of the English Working Class* (Harmondsworth: Penguin, 1980).

Chapter 4

The Passion in Early Christian Art

Robin M. Jensen

Introduction

In 2004, at the beginning of Lent, Mel Gibson's film *The Passion of the Christ* stimulated an emotionally charged debate about the merits (or morality) of a protracted and exceedingly violent portrayal of Christ's scourging and crucifixion in full colour and close-up. Some viewers testified that the gruesome depiction was powerfully affecting, that they were moved to tears and had their faith profoundly strengthened by seeing Christ's agony projected on a big screen. Others were offended by what they saw to be overlong and unnecessary (and unscriptural) emphasis on Jesus' physical suffering, and charged that Gibson's R-rated (for its violence) film contained strong elements of anti-Semitism. Gibson, in answer to these criticisms, reported that he had been inspired by late-mediaeval representations of the crucifixion, the visions of a nineteenth-century German nun and mystic (Anne Catherine Emmerich), and by certain aspects of traditional Roman Catholic piety.

Similar graphic portrayals of a suffering Christ on the cross are, of course, often seen in churches, museums, or art history classes. Being accustomed to these images, however, did not numb audiences to Gibson's interpretation, since the medium of film engages a viewer in a different way. Contemplation of a single image is impossible when watching a movie; and the difference between art and reality is blurred in that kind of theatrical presentation. Gibson's film, more than most other cinematic renderings of the passion, did not allow a kind of safe distance between image and viewer, and was undeniably hard to watch. In addition, Gibson's use of Aramaic and Latin undermined the function of dialogue and forced the observer to pay even more attention to the visual images. At the same time, given the flurry of publicity around the movie, those almost taken-for-granted crucifixes on altars and in reproductions of great paintings came back into focus; they received renewed attention, their power acknowledged.

Given the acknowledged centrality of this visual image in the history of

Christian art, one might assume that it existed in Christian art from the beginning, along with the equally universal portrayal of the Madonna and child. But art historians have long known that apart from a small group of rather ambiguous or enigmatic exceptions (such as the Palatine graffito discussed below), the earliest examples of actual depictions of Jesus' crucifixion cannot be dated before the fifth century and are rare before the seventh or eighth century CE. Furthermore, these early figural images have little in common with later representations of the crucifixion since they do not show Christ as suffering or dying, but rather as physically alive, alert and vigorous. Emphasizing Christ's anguish by showing his wounds, blood, and sagging belly was not common before the twelfth century in the West. Thus the art of the *early* church had little in common with the iconography of Mel Gibson.

The first images

Arguably the earliest known visual depiction of Christ crucified dates from the second or third century. Coming from what is almost certainly a non-Christian source, the so-called 'Palatine graffito' is a scratched, satirical figure discovered on a plaster wall of a military barracks or the servants' quarters of the Imperial Palace near the Circus Maximus on the Palatine Hill. In this image the figure of a young man (a soldier?) salutes a naked, donkey-headed figure tied to a cross (Fig. 1).[1] The Greek legend, '*Alexamenos sebete theon*' translated as 'Alexamenos worships his God' or 'Alexamenos, worship God!' may refer to the rumour that Christians worshipped a donkey-headed god. Such a rumour is noted as slanderous by several early Christian writers. Tertullian claims its source was the historian Tacitus, who not only erroneously stated that Jews had worshipped the head of an ass but mistakenly conflated Judaism with Christianity, and moreover forgot to mention that when Pompey the Great entered the temple in Jerusalem, he found no figural images at all.[2] A little further on, Tertullian accuses a Carthaginian Jew of publicly displaying a caricature of a man with the ears of an ass, one hoofed foot, carrying a book and wearing a toga. The caption below this figure read,

---

1 Different descriptions of the original context of this object suggest some confusion about its original provenance. See Graydon F. Snyder, *Ante Pacem: Archaeological Evidence of Church Life before Constantine* (Macon, Ga: Mercer University Press, 2nd edn, 2003), pp. 60–2; Everett Ferguson, *Backgrounds of Early Christianity* (Grand Rapids: Eerdmans, 2nd edn, 1993), pp. 550–61; Erich Dinkler, 'Das Kreuz als Siegeszeichen', in *idem*, *Signum Crucis* (Tübingen: J.C.B. Mohr, 1967), pp. 150–2; Marja Itkonen-Kaila and Heikki Solin in *Graffiti del Palatino: vol. 1 Paedagogium* (ed. Veikko Väänänen; Acta Instituti Romani Finlandiae 3, Helsinki, 1966), pp. 40–1, fig. 35 and pp. 209–12, no. 246; and Henri Leclercq, 'Croix et crucifix', *DACL* 3.2, pp. 3050–6.

2 Tertullian, *Apol.* 16; *Nat.* 1.11; Tacitus, *Hist.* 5.304. See also Minucius Felix, *Oct.* 9.3.

Figure 1. Second- or third-century graffito, 'Alexamenos worships his god', Palatine Museum, Rome. (Photo: author)

'The God of the Christians, offspring of an ass'.[3] Interestingly, Josephus reports a similar accusation against the Jews by the Egyptian, Apion, and (like Tertullian) argues that the Jews have always been obedient to divinely sanctioned laws against idolatry.[4]

3 The last word is Greek – deus christianorum ὀνοκοίτης. *Apol.* 16.12 (*CCSL* 1, p. 116, author's translation); see also *Nat.* 1.14.

4 Josephus, *Apion* 2.7.80–8; see also Plutarch *Is. Os.* 31 (363C–D). Thomas Mathews argues, however, that some Christians did venerate the ass, noting amulets and gold glass bowls of the early Christian era with asses labelled 'Jesus Christ' and suggesting that the Palatine graffito might have been Alexamenos's own profession of faith. See Mathews, *The*

Quite different from this satirical graffito is a small group of rare gems with crucifixion scenes, two of them now in the British Museum. Rarely published, scholars have dated them to different periods and origins, and interpreted them in various ways. However, more recent work has dated one of them, a magical amulet, to the third century, and the others to the early fourth.[5] The first, a bloodstone, portrays Jesus, nude on the cross and is inscribed on both sides with Greek magical formulae. The second, a carnelian, shows Christ as a large naked figure in front of a cross, flanked by six figures (apostles?) on either side (Fig. 2). His arms are slightly bent and seem to float below the horizontal arm of the cross, rather than being nailed to it. The Greek word ΙΧΘΥΣ (icthus, fish) is engraved in reverse over his head. A third gem (once in the collection of Revd G. F. Nott) survives only as a cast impression and is similar in its composition to the carnelian, except that it has a lamb in the lower field, and the legend ΕΗΣΟ ΧΡΕΣΤΟΣ (a variant spelling of 'Jesus Christ') divided between the upper and lower sections of the field.[6]

The nudity of Christ may be important in these examples, because it is otherwise almost unknown in crucifixion iconography. The normal Roman custom would have been to crucify the condemned naked, but there is some speculation that a concession would have been made to Jews, considering their horror of nudity.[7] On the other hand, early texts presume that Jesus was crucified nude, the soldiers having taken all his clothing to divide among themselves (Jn 19.23-24 and parallels).[8]

Because one of the British Musem gems shows a nude and limp image of a crucified Jesus surrounded by a Greek magical inscription, some

---

Clash of Gods: A Reinterpretation of Early Christian Art (Princeton: Princeton University Press, rev. edn, 1993), pp. 48–50. As background to this argument is the somewhat dubious evidence, mainly drawn from the imaginative heresiologist Epiphanius (*Haer.* 39.1), that a certain Egyptian gnostic sect (the Sethians) identified Seth (an ass-headed god) with Jesus. See also Morton Smith, *Jesus the Magician* (San Francisco: Harper & Row, 1978), pp. 62–3, and Max Sulzberger, 'Le Symbole de la Croix et les Monogrammes de Jésus chez les premiers Chrétiens', *Byz.* 2 (1925), 337–448, esp. pp. 388–91. On the other side of the argument, see Lukas Vischer, 'Le prétendu "culte de l'âne" dans l'église primitive', *RHR* 139 (1951), 14–35.

5   On these gems see the recent work of Jeffrey Spier, *Late Antique and Early Christian Gems* (Wiesbaden: Reichert, 2007), pp. 73–5. Felicity Harley's dissertation also offers very helpful discussion of these objects: 'Images of the Crucifixion in Late Antiquity: The Testimony of Engraved Gems' (unpublished doctoral dissertation, Adelaide University, 2001).

6   See Spier, *Late Antique and Early Christian Gems*, cat. no. 445, pp. 73–4.

7   See Jub. 3.30-31; 7.20. For more discussion and rabbinic sources see Raymond E. Brown, *The Death of the Messiah: From Gethsemane to the Grave. A Commentary on the Passion Narratives in the Four Gospels* (vol. 2; New York: Doubleday, 1994), pp. 952–3.

8   This is a citation, also, of Ps. 22.18. Melito of Sardis, *Pasch.* 97 describes Jesus as naked on the cross and says that the heavenly lights were darkened in order to protect Jesus' modesty.

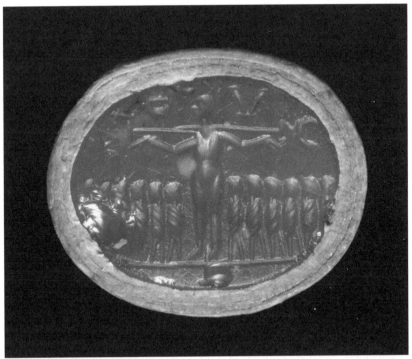

Figure 2. Crucifixion on a gem (carnelian), *c.* 300 CE. The British Museum, London. (Photo: Jeffrey Spier)

historians have suggested that these gems may have been amulets produced for a Christian sectarian (perhaps gnostic) or even for a non-Christian patron.[9] Irenaeus's claim that certain gnostics – Carpocratians – possessed images of Christ gives slim documentary evidence for this.[10] Other scholars date these objects much later, and are less certain about their association with specific 'heretical circles'. If these gems were made for non-Christian patrons, they (like the graffito) testify to an awareness of the signal importance of Christian devotion to the crucifixion in the wider culture.

Two identifiably Christian examples are easier to date – both to the early fifth century. One comes from the wooden doors of Rome's ancient basilica of Sta. Sabina, which are assumed to be contemporary with the consecration of the church (432–40 CE). Far from monumental, this carving (Fig. 3) is one of the smallest of the doors' variously-sized carved

9   Spier, *Late Antique and Early Christian Gems*, pp. 74–5, who cites R. Kotansky, *Greek Magical Amulets* (Papyrologica coliensia, 22.1; Opladen: Westdeutscher Verlag, 1994), p. 335.

10   Irenaeus, *Haer.* 1.25.6.

Figure 3. Crucifixion from wooden panel of the doors of Sta. Sabina, Rome, *c.* 435 CE. (Photo: Lee Jefferson)

wood panels, in a group of an original 28 (18 still existing). The panels make a complicated composition of Old and New Testament scenes, including Elijah's ascension, Moses' miracles, the magi adoring the infant Jesus, Christ before Pilate, as well as the crucifixion. Since the panels have been restored and probably rearranged over the years, it is not clear that the crucifixion was originally placed where it is today (in the upper left corner).[11]

In any case, this small, unprecedented crucifixion image is unique. Christ appears between the two thieves, his body almost twice their size, his hair and beard longer as well. The three figures are wearing simple loincloths (*subligacula*), which distinguishes the image from the graffito and gems described above, possibly aligning this iconography with later apocryphal documents.[12] Behind them a three-gabled brick structure (the one on the left has a window) may represent the city wall of Jerusalem. The crosses are barely apparent and none of the figures is visibly suffering, even though their hands are nailed to the horizontal beam. Their eyes are still open and their bodies look strong and alive. Their poses all mimic the

11   See the discussion of these doors by E. Lucchesi Palli in the exhibition catalogue *Age of Spirituality, Late Antique and Early Christian Art, Third to Seventh Century* (ed. Kurt Weitzmann; New York: Metropolitan Museum of Art, 1979), cat. # 438, pp. 486–90 (with bibliography).

12   *Acts Pil.* 1.10 claims that Jesus was given a loincloth.

posture of prayer – the *orans* position.[13] No nails are to be seen in the feet or ankles; the three figures seem almost to be standing on the ground.

The other image, a small ivory relief, known as the Maskell ivory, is roughly contemporary with the Sta. Sabina panel, and also quite small. It is one of a set of four, now in the British Museum. Together they form the sides of a casket that was probably used as a reliquary.[14] The presumed date and provenance – a fifth-century product of a Roman workshop – are based on stylistic evidence. However, size, date and geographical origin are the only common characteristics of these two objects (the wood carving and this ivory): they are quite different in style, material, artistic quality and iconography. The ivory piece has nearly three-dimensional carving, beautifully modelled figures, and compact but sophisticated composition. By contrast, the wood carving seems cruder, its composition simpler.

All four panels of this casket ivory portray episodes from the passion and resurrection narratives. The first of the four scenes shows Pilate washing his hands, while Christ carries away his cross and Peter denies him. The third plaque shows the women arriving at the tomb, guarded by two sleeping soldiers (note the raising of Lazarus on the door of the tomb). The fourth illustrates a post-resurrection appearance of Christ to the disciples and the doubting Thomas. The second panel shows the death of Judas juxtaposed with the crucifixion of Christ (Fig. 4). Judas hangs from a tree which arches over his head, his money bag spilling out coins at his feet. The figure of Christ on the cross is slightly off-centre and rather than the two thieves, the downcast figures of Mary and the Beloved Disciple stand on Christ's right, while a Roman soldier thrusts a (now lost) spear into Christ's left side.

The composition of this panel contains several interesting features, including effective use of curving lines to draw the viewer's eye to the central figure of Christ, which is only slightly elevated and (in this case) not significantly larger than the other figures in the panel. Despite their comparable size, Christ's face and nearly nude body command the viewer's attention. He wears the same type of minimal loincloth as in the Sta. Sabina carving and his body appears similarly vital. His wide-open eyes stare straight ahead. His body weight seems to be supported by the foot rest (*suppedaneum*). This gloriously alive and almost nude Christ strikingly contrasts to the dead, clothed, and limply hanging Judas.

---

13 Perhaps significantly, the *orans* position was compared to the crucifix as well, by Tertullian, *Orat.* 14; and Minucius Felix, *Oct.* 29.8.

14 Bibliography on this object includes L. Kötzsche, 'Die trauernden Frauen, Zum Londoner Passionskätschen', in David Buckton and Thomas A. Heslop (eds), *Studies in Medieval Art and Architecture Presented to Peter Lasko* (London: Trustees of the British Museum, 1994); *idem*, cat. # 452 in Weitzmann (ed.), *Age of Spirituality*, pp. 502–4.

Figure 4. Crucifixion, side of an ivory casket *c.* 420–30 CE. The British Museum, London
(Photo: © The trustees of the British Museum, London)

Christ's halo and the plaque (*REX IUD[aeorum]*) also occur in this
composition, along with a leafy branch on which a bird sits, just to the
right of Christ's head. The coin purse below Judas's feet adds an
interesting iconographical detail, as its drawstring seems to evoke the
serpent of evil, overcome by the crucified Messiah.

Different as they are from one another, neither of these two objects
bears much resemblance to the next oldest surviving example – a full page
miniature from a sixth-century illuminated manuscript (*c.* 586 CE) from
Mesopotamia – the Syriac Rabbula Gospels (Fig. 5).[15] This leaf shows
Jesus clothed in a long sleeveless royal purple robe (*colobium*), decorated
with two gold stripes (*clavi*). He has a gold halo, banded with blue.
Although his eyes are open (as in the previous two images), his head
inclines slightly to his right and his face wears an expression of grief or
sorrow. The two thieves are placed on either side of and slightly lower
than Christ; the horizontal beams of their crosses fit neatly in the space
below Christ's arms. They wear fuller knotted undergarments (*perizo-
mata/succintoria*) and their bare chests are bound to their crosses with

15   The main work on these Gospels is that of Carlo Cecchelli, Giuseppe Furlani and
Mario Salmi, *The Rabbula Gospels: Facsimile Edition of the Miniatures of the Syria
Manuscript Plut. I, 56 in the Medicaean-Laurentian Library* (Olten: Urs Graf-Verlag, 1959).

Figure 5. The Crucifixion and Resurrection, from the Rabbula Gospels, Florence, Biblioteca Laurenziana. (Photo: © 1990 Scala, Florence; courtesy of the Ministero Beni e Att. Cullturali)

ropes. All three figures are crucified through the palms of their hands, and in both feet at the ankles. No foot supports are visible.

The portrayal here has added significant narrative elements, not found in the others. Just below Christ stand two figures: on one side a Roman soldier (identified by his tunic and greaves and the name 'Longinus') holds a lance to Christ's side; an unidentified male stands on the other side. He wears a white tunic, and holds a bucket in one hand, a stick with a sponge in the other. Beneath Christ's cross three figures cast lots for his garments. To the left stand Jesus' mother and the Beloved Disciple. Mary's halo is identical to Christ's. The Beloved Disciple holds a book in one hand and touches his face with the other in an expression of fear or awe. On the far right are three other women – the bystanders mentioned in the Gospel narratives. The landscape behind shows the two hills of Jerusalem (Agra and Gareb), and both sun and moon can be seen on either side of the cross. Below the crucifixion, in a separate panel, the women (Mary Magdalene and the other Mary) arrive at the empty tomb to be greeted by the angel on one side. Christ appears to them on the other. The resurrection scene follows the narrative in Matthew's Gospel, while the crucifixion scene more closely represents John's version.

The composition here is especially notable, compared to the image on the Sta. Sabina door or even the ivory in the British Museum, because of certain standard elements common to passion iconography from the sixth to ninth centuries, in particular Christ's long purple *colobium*. Showing Christ in such a garment might be a reference to Herod or the Roman soldiers clothing him in rich robes (Lk. 23.11; Jn 19.3),[16] or to his enthronement as heavenly king. Important iconographic parallels to this miniature imply the existence of an influential (but lost) sixth-century prototype, perhaps another manuscript illumination, a monumental painting, or an apsidal mosaic. Such parallels include a crucifixion scene on the lid of a seventh- (or eighth-) century Palestinian reliquary now in the Vatican Museum. This shows significant similarities to the Rabbula illumination, including the purple tunic with its two stripes, two hills in the background, and the knotted loincloths of the two thieves. In this example, Mary and the Beloved Disciple stand on either side of the cross. An eighth-century fresco from Rome's church of Sta. Maria Antiqua is a Western example of this type, though without the two thieves (Fig. 6).

Christ wears a similar purple *colobium* on an eighth- or ninth-century enamel reliquary box now in the Metropolitan Museum in New York, which may have been produced in Constantinople; in another Syriac manuscript now in the Bibliothèque Nationale, Paris; and on an eighth-century icon at the monastery of St Catherine in Sinai. This movement toward a common type corresponds, also, with the crucifixion figures found on small lead *ampullae* brought back by pilgrims to the Holy Land, many now housed in the cathedral in Monza, Italy. These have common details, although in some cases they show only the two thieves actually

16 Cf. Mt. 27.31 and Mk 15.20, where Jesus is later stripped of the robe, exchanged for his own clothes.

Figure 6. Crucifixion, eighth-century fresco from church of Sta. Maria Antiqua, Rome. (Photo: author)

crucified, while a bust of Christ hovers above a central cross. Christ also wears the *colobium* on a group of sixth-century Syrian pectoral crosses.[17]

Christ's being garbed in a robe rather than shown as nude is important, both for dating and interpretation of these images. The only surviving textual reference to a depiction of the crucifixion comes from a treatise of Gregory of Tours, probably written around the same time as the painting of the Rabbula miniature (*c.* 580 CE). In this work, *The Glory of the Martyrs*, Gregory recounts an incident in the cathedral of Narbonne, where a much 'observed' picture of 'our Lord on a cross, girded with a

17   On these objects and their relationship to developing crucifixion iconography see A. Grabar, *Ampoules de Terre Sainte (Monza, Bobbio)* (Paris: Klincksieck, 1958); and Kurt Weitzmann, 'Loca Sancta and the Representational Arts of Palestine', *DOP* 28 (1974), 33–55.

linen loincloth' was prominently displayed.[18] One of the cathedral's priests had a series of visions in which a man instructed him to 'cover with a linen cloth the picture in which I appear on the cross; otherwise a quick death might befall you'. These terrifying messages prompted the clergy to cover the picture with a curtain that could be occasionally lowered for viewing.

Thus, both textual and visual evidence suggest that during the sixth century portrayals of Christ on the cross began to be more common, but also began to present Jesus robed, rather than as partially nude. Significantly, however, the purple *colobium* begins to disappear from art works that date after the iconoclastic era (beginning in the tenth century), and Christ appears again wearing the knotted apron-like *perizoma* similar to those worn by the thieves in the Rabbula Gospels. This return to a nearly naked figure may have been intended to allow the iconography to less modestly (and less regally) emphasize the human flesh of Christ, subject to death and then victoriously returned to life. Simultaneously, these images begin to show Christ with his head bowed, eyes closed, and body sagging, a reference to his physical suffering and death not overtly depicted in the earlier images (cf. Fig. 7). In the intervening centuries, however, crucifixion portrayals varied. During the ninth century some representations showed either a dead or a still-alive Christ wearing a *colobium*, but for the first time others portrayed a dead Christ wearing the loincloth.[19] Very possibly, the *kind* of loincloth (*perizoma*) depicted in these representations alludes to the 'aprons' that Adam and Eve made for themselves in the Garden, since both Greek and Latin Bibles use that word for the garments described in Gen. 3.7.[20]

This summary of the emergence and evolution of the crucifixion image does not explain, however, why it took so long to appear. On the other hand, one might ask why it appeared *at all* – when, where, and how it did. Answers to these questions require some context as well as caveats.

18 Gregory of Tours, *Glor. Mart.* 1.22; see edition and translation of Raymond Van Dam, *Gregory of Tours, Glory of the Martyrs* (Liverpool: Liverpool University Press, 1988), p. 41.

19 See Anna Kartsonis, *Anastasis: The Making of an Image* (Princeton: Princeton University Press, 1986), p. 127. Also, Celia Chazelle, *The Crucified God in the Carolingian Era: Theology and Art of Christ's Passion* (Cambridge: Cambridge University Press, 2001), especially chapter 7, 'Three Later Carolingian Crucifixion Images', pp. 439–99.

20 See Augustine's use of the Latinized form 'perizoma' in *C. Jul.* 4.82, 5.5, 5.7, for example.

Figure 7. Crucifixion, ivory plaque, tenth century Metz. Victoria and Albert Museum, London. (Photo: author)

Context and Caveats

First, the crucifixion is not the only theme prevalent in later Christian art but 'missing' from the catalogue of early Christian iconography. The oldest known Christian art objects, including the frescoes in the Christian catacombs in Rome, carved stone sarcophagi, and small private or domestic objects (bowls, lamps, glass or gems), show certain common stock figures or symbols (e.g. the shepherd, praying figure, dove, peacock, fish, anchor). These almost generic types were relatively soon followed by abbreviated narrative images based upon the Hebrew Scriptures (e.g. Jonah, Daniel, Noah and Moses), and then by scenes from the Gospels, including depictions of Jesus healing and working wonders (the paralytic, man born blind, multiplying the loaves and fishes, changing water to wine, etc.). Scenes of the adoration of the magi and of John baptizing Jesus also occur around the late third or early fourth century. Meanwhile, apart from unique and difficult-to-identify paintings in the third-century Roman Catacomb of Priscilla, representations of the Annunciation to Mary, or the Holy Family with the infant Jesus are virtually absent prior to the turn of the fifth century. The same is true for pre-fifth-century portrayals of the Last Supper, the Resurrection, the Ascension, or the descent of the Holy Spirit at Pentecost.

Putting the crucifixion into this context gives some perspective, but a caveat must be added. Conclusions about iconographic themes that did or did not exist sometimes need revising following new discoveries. The surviving material data from this early period thus cannot be deemed reliably to represent all that there *was*. Undoubtedly an enormous amount of evidence, some of it certainly exceptional and even contradictory, has been lost to the wrecking balls of history – urban renewal, deliberate destruction, and the ash heap. It sometimes takes only one discovery to demolish a long-held viewpoint or scholarly hypothesis.[21]

Second, although pre-fifth-century depictions of *crucifixion* are rare, several different kinds of early *cross* figures, *tau*-crosses, and *staurograms* as well as possible cross symbols do exist.[22] Although scholars differ on the dating, identification, and meaning of many of these figures and symbols (e.g. an anchor, axe, ship's mast, etc.), most agree that *some*

---

21 For example, the discovery of the lavishly decorated synagogue at Dura Europos caused much scholarly rethinking (and debate) about Jewish attitudes toward figurative art in late antiquity.

22 See *Barn.* 9.8 on the letter *tau* as a cross sign. Also, Larry Hurtado, 'The Staurogram in Early Christian Manuscripts: The Earliest Visual Reference to the Crucified Jesus?', in Thomas J. Kraus and Tobias Nicklas (eds), *New Testament Manuscripts: Their Text and Their World* (Leiden: Brill, 2006), pp. 207–26; also Larry Hurtado and Matthew Black, 'The Chi-Rho Sign: Christogram and/or Staurogram', in W. Ward Gasque and R. P. Martin (eds), *Apostolic History and the Gospel* (Grand Rapids: Eerdmans, 1970), pp. 319–27.

crosses come from the third, and even more from the early fourth century.[23] However, the degree to which all or even any of them refer explicitly to the crucifixion is unclear. A few of these purported crosses have turned out to be mere masons' marks or wall brackets.[24] Documentary evidence suggests that others *should* be seen as crosses or references to the cross. The *staurogram* may even be more than a mere cross-reference, but a more graphic reference to the crucifix since the loop of the *rho* superimposed on the vertical stroke of the *tau* gives the appearance of a figure on a cross.

Justin Martyr, in the mid-second century, as well as Minucius Felix and Hippolytus at the beginning of the third, interpreted almost any cross-shaped object as a symbol of the crucifixion, including a ship's mast, a plough, and even military banners.[25] Tertullian proclaimed that Christianity could be called a 'priesthood of the cross' because of the veneration Christians showed to that symbol. For Tertullian, this reverence for the cross contrasted with the pagan veneration of idols.[26] Tertullian's statement also suggests that a cult of the cross may have existed quite early and could have been the impetus for the tradition of Helena's 'discovery' of the true cross at Calvary in the early fourth century.

Third, other known images clearly allude to the crucifixion even if they do not physically depict it. A number of early Christian texts demonstrate that several Old Testament figures were understood as adumbrations of the crucifixion, including Moses raising the brazen serpent aloft on a pole and Abraham's offering of his son Isaac.[27] For example, according to Tertullian, 'Isaac, being led by his father to be a victim, and carrying the firewood himself, at that moment indicated Christ's death, submitting himself to his father as a victim and bearing the wood of his own

23 See Robin Jensen, *Understanding Early Christian Art* (London: Routledge, 2000), pp. 130–41; Jack Finegan, *Archaeology of the New Testament* (Princeton: Princeton University Press, 1969), pp. 220–60; and Erich Dinkler, 'Zur Geschichte des Kreuzsymbols', *ZTK* 48 (1951), 148–72.

24 For instance, see R. Houston Smith, 'The Cross Marks on Jewish Ossuaries', *PEQ* (1974), 53–75; regarding the famous case of a supposed cross at Herculaneum see Lucien de Bruyne, 'La "crux interpretum" di Ercolano', *RivAC* 21 (1944/5), 281–309; and Snyder, *Ante Pacem*, pp. 60–1.

25 Justin Martyr, *1 Apol.* 55, and *Dial.* 86, 90, and 97; Minucius Felix, *Oct.* 26.6; Hippolytus, *Antichr.* 59. See also *Barn.* 9.8. Paulinus of Nola continues this tradition citing a plough and a boat's mast, *Eps.* 9.4 and 23.30.

26 Tertullian, *Nat.* 1.12; *Apol.* 16.

27 For Moses and the serpent see Justin Martyr, *Dial.* 91; Tertullian, *Jud.* 10. For Abraham and Isaac see *Barn.* 7.3; Melito of Sardis, *Pasch.* 9–11; Irenaeus, *Haer.* 4.10.1; and Clement of Alexandria, *Paed.* 1.23. Also, Jensen, *Understanding Early Christian Art*, pp. 143–50 (with bibliography).

passion.'[28] The depiction of Abraham, his arm raised to slaughter his son, made an early and prominent appearance in Christian iconography, perhaps as a substitute for the crucifixion (Fig. 8). The lamb, of course, was (among other things) a metaphorical allusion to Christ's passion (cf. Rev. 5.6), as he was often depicted as the paschal lamb or '*agnus deï*'.[29] According to his own account, Paulinus of Nola decorated the apse of his church with a visual representation of the Trinity which included the lamb, the Father's voice, and the dove. In addition to this he describes a cross surmounted by a gleaming wreath and encircled by the twelve apostles represented as doves. According to him, both the cross and the lamb symbolize the 'holy victim'.[30]

Finally and significantly, toward the end of the fourth century, scenes from the narrative of Christ's passion begin to turn up in extant Christian art with some regularity, most notably on a group of sarcophagi now in the Vatican Museum. Although these monuments do *not* portray the crucifixion *as such*, they do include a number of episodes leading up to the crucifixion, including Jesus' arrest and trial before Pilate. The centrepiece of most of these narrative cycles is the victorious empty cross, usually depicted as surmounted by a *chi rho* within a wreath. Thus the iconography only alludes to Christ's suffering while pointing graphically and insistently to its triumphant conclusion.

For example, the four scenes on one famous fourth-century 'Passion' sarcophagus are connected by alternating gabled and arched niches at the centre of which is a cristogram (*chi rho*) within a wreath, mounted on an empty cross (Fig. 9).[31] On the far left Simon carries the cross to Golgotha, urged on by a Roman soldier. In the next niche another Roman soldier holds a laurel wreath rather than a crown of thorns above Christ's head.

---

28   Tertullian, *Jud.* 10.6 (*CCSL* 2, p. 1376, author's translation).

29   See discussion in Jensen, *Understanding Early Christian Art*, pp. 141–3. Lambs are not always references to the passion, however. They often appear with the Good Shepherd, or are simple allusions to a bucolic or pastoral setting. See Snyder, *Ante Pacem*, pp. 45–7. The lamb was prohibited as a symbol in the 696 Council of Trullo (Quinisext Council, can. 82) on the grounds that it undermined the reality of Christ's human incarnation and redeeming sacrifice.

30   Paulinus, *Ep.* 32.10. Compare the description of the imagery in the basilica at Fundi, later in the letter (32.17): a lamb (for Christ), that is being 'haloed' by a dove (Holy Spirit), and crowned by the 'Father from a reddish cloud'.

31   This sarcophagus, now in the Vatican Museo Pio Cristiano, is described by Friedrich Gerke as the earliest depiction of the passion in Christian art. See Gerke, *Die christliche Sarkophage der vorkonstantinischen Zeit* (Berlin: de Gruyter, 1940), pp. 40–8. The main catalogue descriptions of these sarcophagi (with bibliography) are in Friedrich W. Deichmann, Giuseppe Bovini and Hugo Brandenburg, *Repertorium der christlich-antiken Sarkophage*, i:Rom und Ostia (Wiesbaden: Steiner, 1967). The sarcophagus discussed above is nr. 49. See also Hans von Campenhausen, 'Die Passionssarkophage: Zur Geschichte eines altchristlichen Bildkreises', *Marburger Jahrbuch für Kunstwissenschaft* 5 (1929), 39–68.

Figure 8. Offering of Isaac on a fourth-century sarcophagus in the Museo Pio Cristiano, Vatican. (Photo: author)

In the two right hand niches Christ stands before Pilate, who turns away and is about to wash his hands. Considering the prominence of the Roman soldiers in this composition, the iconography emblematically implies both the cross of Christ and the trophy of military victory. Two soldiers (one sleeping on his shield) sit beneath the horizontal beam, which is the perch for two doves. A simple wreath appears above the niches on

Figure 9. Fourth-century sarcophagus with scenes from the Passion, Museo Pio Cristiano, Vatican. (Photo: author)

the far right and left, parallel to the one being placed on Christ's head. The instrument of Christ's passion is here transformed into the sign of victory, bracketed by the arrest and trial. The imagery omits the humiliation and suffering, and points directly to the glory of the resurrection.

A similar pattern of moving the viewer directly from the episodes of Christ's arrest and trial to the resurrection (bypassing the crucifixion) occurs in the early-sixth-century mosaic programme of Ravenna's basilica of S. Apollinare Nuovo. On the right-hand wall, moving from the altar area toward the entrance door, the passion story is represented in a sequenced narrative programme, beginning with the Last Supper, through the scene in the Garden, the arrest, trial, the road to Golgotha, continuing to the empty tomb and Christ's post-resurrectional appearances.

In summary, although Christian art in the first four centuries predominantly portrayed episodes of Christ healing or working wonders, the inclusion of crosses, typological references to Christ's passion, and the emergence of these fourth-century passion narratives demonstrate that Christ's crucifixion is far from outside the visual imagination of early Christians. Instead, the crucifixion is *referenced* in the art as much as in the theological writings, even though it is not *concretely* portrayed in a historical or narrative image. Nevertheless, the question of *why* this is so – why the art is so indirect – may by answered by one or more of the following five possibilities.

Possible Reasons for Lack of Crucifixion Imagery

1. No precedent existed as a model

The absence of a crucifixion image cannot be explained by the simple lack of any precedent for it in Roman or earlier classical art. First, it should be noted that other Christian images exist without any obvious pagan precedent, including scenes of baptism and the three youths in the fiery furnace. Second, Roman art of the first three centuries is not characterized by any reluctance to show human brutality, tragedy, or violent death. Portrayals of the sacrifice of Iphigenia and the flaying of Marsyas were widely distributed, the former having some similarities to representations of Abraham's offering of Isaac and the latter showing surprising resonance with later crucifixes (Fig. 10). Scenes of gladiatorial contests and even the feeding of victims to the beasts in the arena decorated the floors of grand Roman houses. One scholar recently speculated that Paul's question in Gal. 3.1 ('who has bewitched you, before whose eyes Jesus

Figure 10. Marsyas, first or second century CE, found in Rome. Louvre Museum, Paris. (Photo: author)

Christ was publicly portrayed as crucified?') may have referred to certain wall paintings in early Christian house churches.[32]

Nevertheless, definitively *Christian* visual representations of suffering are rare. Art historians have noted the near non-existence of extant martyrdom scenes, despite the widespread popularity of the accounts (*acta*) of the martyrs' heroic actions in documentary sources and the almost sudden appearance of martyrs' portraits in the early fifth century. Two well-known exceptions are worth noting, however. One, a late fourth- or early fifth-century fresco on the wall of a small *confessio* adjacent to the ancient basilica of Ss. Giovanni and Paolo in Rome, shows the beheadings of three saints. The other, a relief of the beheading of S. Achilleus, comes from one of two small ciborium columns in the fourth-century church of Ss. Nereus and Achilleus, built over the catacomb of Domitilla. The absence of scenes of human brutality, torment or agony may be explained by context as much as sensibility. Funerary settings are more likely to focus on images of consolation and reassurance.

2. Once-existing images were lost or destroyed

These rare exceptions do not actually prove the rule that Christians did not have numerous other such images. Documentary evidence indicates that such iconography existed, and may have been both monumental and extensive. A homily delivered at Antioch (probably by John Chrysostom) referred to a painted image of the martyrdom of St Barlaam.[33] Basil of Caesarea similarly told of a representation of St Theodore's martyrdom, and praised the artist for including the saint's resistance, torments and death.[34] Asterius of Amaseia claimed to have been captivated by a painting of St Euphemia's martyrdom, which included a number of episodic scenes of her torture, imprisonment and execution by fire.[35]

The most extensive verbal record of these scenes comes from the writings of Prudentius, a fourth- and early fifth-century Spanish ascetic, whose cycle of martyr poems, the *Peristephanon*, both recounts the deeds of renowned saints and describes a cycle of paintings (for which the poems may have been intended as accompanying inscriptions) that portrayed them in graphic and gory detail. One of those poems in fact describes an image of the crucifixion, in which Christ's pierced side brings forth both

32   David Balch, 'The Suffering of Isis/Io and Paul's Portrait of Christ Crucified (Gal. 3.1): Frescoes in Pompeian and Roman Houses and in the Temple of Isis in Pompeii', *JR* 83 (2002), 24–55.

33   Ps. Basil, *Hom.* 17 (*PG* 31, col. 489), trans. in C. Mango, *The Art of the Byzantine Empire 312–1453: Sources and Documents* (Toronto: University of Toronto Press, 1986), p. 37.

34   *Laud Theo* (*PG* 46).

35   Included in Mango, *Art of the Byzantine Empire*, pp. 37–8.

water and blood. The two thieves are also depicted, on either hand, one denying God and the other winning the crown of martyrdom.[36] Less than a century later Gregory of Tours told his parable of the 'talking' crucifix (mentioned above).

The images described by these documents have never been discovered. If they were as widely known as the texts imply, they represent only a fraction of those that existed at the time. Iconoclasm undoubtedly destroyed much of the earliest evidence of Christian art in the East, and much of the rest was lost through the renovation of church buildings in later centuries.

Apart from a few exceptions such as the house church at Dura Europos or the chapel at Hinton St Mary's in Dorset, most examples of pre-fifth-century Christian art come from sepulchral contexts (tombs and sarcophagi), which survive in large part because they were underground. Each of these monuments, furthermore, contains images that are otherwise unique for their time (e.g. the three women arriving at the tomb in Dura and the portrait of Christ at Hinton St Mary's). And although those above-mentioned exceptions demonstrate that early churches may well have been decorated, they do not establish that churches and funerary monuments would have exhibited the same iconographic motifs, especially in other geographical regions.

3. *The scandal of crucifixion led to inhibitions about its depiction*

Even though they might allude to it indirectly or symbolically in visual art, Christian sensitivity to their non-Christian neighbours' derision may have made them reluctant to render the crucifixion itself realistically. Traditional polytheists might have accepted a dying and rising god, but being executed as a criminal in so degrading and physically painful a manner contradicted their very definition of deity.[37] The proclamation of a crucified god subjected Christians to ridicule, as illustrated by the graffito discovered on the Palatine Hill.[38] As Paul himself admitted, such a death was 'a stumbling block to Jews and folly to Gentiles' (1 Cor. 1.23).

Pagan scorn for this aspect of Christian teaching shows up in a number of early church documents, including Minucius Felix's dialogue, *Octavius*.

---

36 Prudentius, *Peri.* 42 (*CCSL* 126, nr. 42, pp. 390–400). Although roughly contemporary in date to the Sta. Sabina and Maskell ivory images, the iconography described here corresponds closely to neither.

37 On the manner of crucifixion in the ancient world (and the classes of persons most likely to suffer this particular punishment) see Brown, *The Death of the Messiah*, vol. 2, pp. 946–60; and Martin Hengel, *Crucifixion* (Philadelphia: Fortress Press, 1977), chapters 4–8.

38 For discussion of similar examples of this kind of visual ridicule see Harley, 'Images of the Crucifixion', pp. 19–20.

In this work, the pagan interlocutor, Caecilius, claims that according to rumour, Christians venerated both a crucified criminal and the wood of his cross.[39] A half century later Origen of Alexandria summarized the arguments of Celsus, the pagan critic of Christianity. According to Origen, Celsus called the Christian Son of God a 'most degraded man, punished by scourging and crucifixion'.[40] Celsus argues that if he were a real divinity, he would have been able to disappear from the cross unharmed.[41] Origen dodges the issue by explaining that Christians do not regard Jesus as Son of God *because* he was crucified, but because he healed the lame, raised the dead, overcame demons and because he was the saviour of the human race.[42] Here, while not denying the actuality of Christ's death by crucifixion, even Origen seems to want to downplay its relative importance.

On the other hand, even though they are aware of the scandal of crucifixion, most early Christian authors *never* deny its centrality to Christian dogma.[43] Like Paul, they 'knew nothing' apart from Christ – and 'him crucified' (1 Cor. 2.2). Ignatius of Antioch claimed to be 'dedicated to the cross', an 'offence to unbelievers but to Christians salvation and eternal life'.[44] Clement of Alexandria announced that 'Christ transformed the sunset into sunrise, and by his crucifixion, death into life.'[45] Melito of Sardis wrote an entire treatise on the passion of Christ, comparing the sacrifice of Jesus to that of the Passover Lamb.[46] The almost constant treatment of the crucifixion in documentary evidence makes the absence of a visual image even more enigmatic.

The crucifixion did, however, apparently scandalize some groups of Christians as well as pagans. From the second to the fourth centuries, documentary evidence witnesses to several sects who denied that the crucifixion actually took place, or that Christ suffered in the flesh. Perhaps in response to the objections of pagan philosophers and followers of traditional religion, many gnostic groups, followers of Marcion or docetic Christians denied the human birth, agony and death of Christ.[47] The

---

39   Minucius Felix, *Oct.* 9.4. See also 12.4; and 29.6. Tertullian also notes the charge of worshipping a wooden cross: *Nat.* 1.21.1; *Apol.* 16.6.

40   Origen, *Cels.* 2.31 (*ANF* 4, 444).

41   *Cels.* 2.68.

42   *Cels.* 2.47; see also 6.10. For other examples, see Lucian, *Peregr.* 11; Justin, *Apol.* 1.13; Arnobius, *Nat.* 1.36.

43   For a thorough summation of the New Testament and early Christian texts see Sulzberger, 'Le Symbole de la Croix', pp. 337–448.

44   Ignatius of Antioch, *Eph.* 18.1 (LCL, *Apostolic Fathers* 1.216, trans. K. Lake).

45   Clement of Alexandria, *Protr.* 11.114.1 (*SC* 2, 182).

46   Melito, *Pasch., passim.* On these texts see also Hengel, *Crucifixion,* chaps. 1, 10.

47   Such groups were first identified (and attacked) by Ignatius of Antioch who against them insists on Christ's physical suffering and death on the cross. See Ignatius, *Eph.* 1.1 and

second-century apocryphal Acts of John, for example, gives a mystical interpretation of the cross and portrays Jesus as hovering above it, neither suffering nor dying.[48] Some historians have additionally argued that social class discrimination along with political insecurity may have played some role in this move to downplay the crucifixion, since Christians prior to the 'peace of the church' would have felt vulnerable not only to the ridicule and stigmatization of their neighbours but also to exposure to danger from both official and popular anti-Christian hatred and violence.[49]

Although one could argue that residual reticence about this unfathomable, embarrassing, or even repugnant aspect of the Christian *kerygma* should have begun to dissipate after the 'peace of the church' and the patronage of the Roman emperor in the early fourth century, the evidence for crucifixion scenes from that period indicates that they were still rare. Unless a large number of examples have been lost, Christian reluctance to represent the crucifix remained. Presumably, Constantine's banning of crucifixion as a means of execution in 316 CE was intended to suppress a living reminder of Christ's humiliating death.[50] At the beginning of the fifth century, Augustine *still* had to admonish his flock not to be ashamed by taunts that they worship a man who was crucified.[51]

Undoubtedly, Helena's 'discovery' of the True Cross (313–14 CE), the growing 'cult' of the cross, the popularity of pilgrimages to Holy Land, the building of the Church of the Holy Sepulchre (325 CE), and the carrying of cross fragments back to the West helped to dissipate embarrassment about the crucifixion and replace it with an attitude of sanctity or awe.[52] The establishment of the Feast of the *Inventio Crucis* emerged shortly after the dedication of the Constantinian basilica of the Holy Sepulchre at the site of Golgotha. Jerome reports that when his

---

Rom. 6.6. On the gnostic counterpart to this see (for example) Irenaeus, *Haer.* 1.7.2; 1.26.1-7; 3.16.1-5; 3.18.5; 4.33.5. Tertullian describes the followers of Marcion in the same way, see *Marc.* 1.19. See Hengel, *Crucifixion*, chapters 3, 15–21.

48 *Acts John* 97–104.

49 Massey Shepherd made a connection between the legal and social status of Christians and the lack of crucifixion imagery, especially in times of persecution. See his article 'Christology: A Central Problem of Early Christian Theology and Art', in Weitzmann (ed.), *Age of Spirituality*, p. 112. Also Hengel, *Crucifixion*, pp. 2–10, 359–63.

50 *Cod. Theo.* 9.5.1; Sozomen, *Hist.* 1.8.13.

51 Augustine, *Ser.* 279.8; also 174.3.

52 Ambrose is the earliest witness to the story of Helena's discovery (Eusebius makes no mention of it). See his sermon *Ob. Theo.* 46. John Chrysostom mentions the discovery but not Helena's role, *Hom. Jo.* 85.1. See also Rufinus, *Hist. Eccl.* 1.7 and Paulinus, *Ep.* 31.4-6, both of whom cite miraculous cures. Paulinus puts the story within a letter accompanying one of the relics he sent as a gift to his friend Severus. Other accounts include Socrates, *Hist.* 1.17; Sozomen, *Hist.* 2.1; and Theodoret, *Hist.* 1.18. On the tradition of Helena's 'discovery' of the cross see J. W. Drijvers, *Helena Augusta: The Mother of Constantine the Great and the Legend of her Finding of the True Cross* (Leiden: Brill, 1992).

Roman disciple, the wealthy matron Paula, first arrived at the site of the Holy Sepulchre, she prostrated herself before the cross placed there in adoration as if she beheld Christ himself still hanging on it. Pouring forth tears and groaning, she had to tear herself away so that she could continue on to the next holy place.[53] The pilgrim Egeria describes the exhibition of the wood of the cross on Good Friday and the need for deacons to keep close watch, lest someone coming to venerate it try to carry a fragment away.[54] Paulinus, who recounts receiving one such relic from Melania the Elder for his church at Nola, marvels that despite its being constantly divided, the power of the inanimate wood suffers no diminution.[55] We are even tempted to attribute the emergence of crucifixion iconography directly with these events; perhaps even to imagine that the Holy Sepulchre's apse contained the first monumental representation of the crucifix and the model for those sixth-century images of Christ wearing the purple *colobium*.[56] The art on the reliquaries and tourist souvenirs (*ampullae*) may be the link between this sacred site and its developing representative image as pilgrims brought home reminders of the scene.[57]

4. The crucifixion was not a central aspect of early Christian dogma

In the mid-1970s, E. J. Tinsley argued that a particular type of crucifixion image – the dead and naked Christ on the cross, unknown before the ninth or tenth century – emerged as a kind of visual response to a specific Christological development which he described as a 'renewed emphasis' on the humanity of Christ in the early ninth century, in the 'wake' of the iconoclastic controversy in the East. In his view, earlier Christian teachers had worried that the visual representation of Christ's crucifixion might be misunderstood to overemphasize his humanity, rather than attend to his divinity and victory over death.[58] In a reply to Tinsley, Peter G. Moore asserted that the situation was much more complicated than Tinsley had suggested, and proposed that the earliest images of both cross and crucifix

53 Jerome, *Epist.* 108.9.

54 Egeria, *Peregr.* 37.1-3.

55 Paulinus, *Ep.* 31.6. See also *Ep.* 32.11. Compare the hymn by Venantius Fortunatus, composed around 570 to celebrate the receipt of one of the cross fragments by the monastery in Poitiers, France ('*Vexilla regis prodeunt*').

56 This has been suggested before. See Margaret Frazer, 'Holy Sites Representations', in Wietzmann (ed.), *Age of Spirituality*, pp. 564–5. Unfortunately, neither Eusebius nor Egeria describe the iconography in the apse, although Eusebius, *Vita Const.* 3.31, describes other aspects of the building.

57 See Josef Engemann, 'Palastinische Pilgerampullen im F. J. Dölger Institut in Bonn', *JAC* 16 (1973), 5–27; and Gary Vikan, 'Pilgrims in Magi's Clothing: The Impact of Mimesis on Early Byzantine Pilgrimage Art', in Robert Ousterhout (ed.), *The Blessings of Pilgrimage* (Urbana, Ill.: University of Illinois Press, 1990), pp. 97–107.

58 E. J. Tinsley, 'The Coming of a Dead and Naked Christ', *Religion* 2 (1972), 24–36.

be read in light of the resurrection, manifesting Christ's glory according to the theology presented in John's Gospel. For this reason Moore argued that early Christian theology did not *require* the crucifixion, and that its eventual appearance can neither be explained as part of a progressive theological evolution nor evaluated in terms of what contemporary theologians might judge a 'satisfactory' Christology.[59]

These arguments notwithstanding, the issue under consideration is not different kinds of *portrayals*, but the nonappearance of one specific image *entirely*. Attending to the kind of theological questions raised by Tinsley and Moore requires us to ask not just whether a *certain type* of crucifixion image de-emphasizes Christ's human suffering and plays up his glory and triumph, but whether the *lack* of the image actually obscures Christ's death *altogether*. And if one concludes that this is so, the next question is whether early Christian visual art reflects a theology diametrically opposed to what is generally accepted as 'orthodox'. Did the art agree with Celsus – that the Christian saviour *should* have disappeared from the cross, inasmuch as he *could* (and did) disappear from the tomb?[60] Such a theological position does not eliminate the *cross* as a visual motif; but it *does* eliminate the crucifix.

This possibility is problematic, however, because it proposes that among the different sects or groups in early Christianity there were some who commissioned the extant visual art and who denied Christ's death by crucifixion, and others who left the bulk of extant theological treatises (but no art works) who believed the crucifixion to be essential and emphasized it in their doctrinal exposition. To be sure, as noted above, certain sects, among them various gnostic or docetic groups, emphasized the resurrection but denied the crucifixion, but these seem unlikely to have been the prominent (or even exclusive) patrons of artists' workshops as late as the fourth and fifth centuries.[61] A different theory identifies a hypothetical (art-making) community that highlighted the humanity of Jesus and his role as teacher and healer rather than as a suffering, dying and resurrected divine saviour, a view more compatible with the early iconography in general. In this case, the figure of Abraham about to

---

59   Peter G. Moore, 'Cross and Crucifixion in Christian Iconography: A Reply to E.J. Tinsley', *Religion* 4 (1974), 104–13.

60   Origen, *Cels.* 2.68.

61   This is asserted by Ernst Renan who argued that Christian art emerged in docetic groups in *Histoire des origines du christianisme 7: Marc Aurèle et la fin du monde antique* (Paris: Calman Lévy, 6th edn, 1882), pp. 539–46. See also James D. Breckenridge, 'The Reception of Art into the Early Church', *ACIAC* 1975, vol. 1, pp. 361–405; and P. Corby Finney, 'Did Gnostics Make Pictures?', in Bentley Layton (ed.), *The Rediscovery of Gnosticism: Proceedings of the International Conference on Gnosticism at Yale, New Haven, Connecticut, March 28–31, 1978* (vol. 1; Leiden: Brill, 1980), pp. 434–54.

sacrifice Isaac would serve more as a symbol of liberation from danger or social adversity than as a visual allegory for the passion.

According to at least one scholar, the arrival of crucifixion imagery is linked with the iconography of imperial and ecclesial power and thus delayed until the early Byzantine era, coinciding with the political establishment of the church.[62] According to this theory the primitive church was more focused on the earthly ministry of Jesus than on his redemptive sacrifice. Problematically, either of these positions fails to account for the arguably close relationship between church officials and the main extant venue of early Christian paintings, in particular the Catacomb of Callixtus traditionally thought to have been supervised by one of the archdeacons of Rome and to have been the burial place of early Roman bishops.

Although in the past century historians have come to recognize that early Christianity was a complex and diverse phenomenon, an apparent divergence in extant material and textual evidence need not be tied to groups with deviating theological perspectives or different socio-political identities. The stories of Christian martyrs, presumably popular among 'rank and file' Christians, were filled with references to the saints' imitation of Christ's suffering and death on the cross. Ignatius of Antioch understood that his end was to be like Christ's and was eager to be God's sacrifice, suffering and rising just as Jesus did.[63] The second-century Lyons martyr, Blandina, is specifically identified as appearing Christ-like as she hung upon a post in the form of a cross.[64] Perpetua and her companions rejoice that they participate – have their share – in Christ's sufferings as they are scourged, mocked, and finally executed by Roman soldiers.[65]

Early Christian liturgical documents also highlight the centrality of Christ's crucifixion in early Christian church practice among a broad spectrum of the faithful. The Eucharist was fully understood as a representation of Christ's passion by the middle of the third century.[66] Cyprian explicitly affirms that the mixed wine in the eucharistic cup was foretold by the prophets (Prov. 9.5) and accomplished in the passion when the wound from Christ's side gave forth both blood and water. He goes on to assert that because the church re-enacts his passion in the sacrifice, it should perform it exactly as Christ did (cf. 1 Corinthians 11).[67] A half-century earlier, Tertullian had asserted that the baptismal water was

---

62   See for example, Snyder, *Ante Pacem*, p. 64, and pp. 100–1; and Eduard Syndicus, *Early Christian Art* (trans. J. R. Foster; New York: Hawthorn, 1962), p. 103.

63   Ignatius, *Rom.* 4–6.

64   Text found in Eusebius, *Hist.* 5.1.41.

65   *Passio. Perpetua and Felicity*, 20.

66   Some scholars might point to the New Testament Epistle to the Hebrews as earlier evidence.

67   Cyprian, *Ep.* 63.17.1.

shown forth from the cross when Jesus was speared with the soldier's lance.[68] Moreover, the Christian Passover was the right time for baptism since Christians are thus initiated into the Lord's passion.[69] Early baptismal creeds clearly outlined the significance of confessing the suffering and death of Christ. By the mid-fourth century, the ritual of baptism had come to be the primary moment for Christian participation in Christ's death and resurrection (as proclaimed by Paul in Romans 6) and it was typically held on the vigil of Easter. Cyril of Jerusalem reassures his newly baptized that they, of course, did not really die on a cross and rise again, that their 'imitation' was symbolic and without the anguish and sweat of the real thing, but that their nakedness in the font was a reminder of Christ's *nakedness* on the cross.[70] Cruciform baptismal fonts in some places made this connection very concrete.

A study of extant fourth-century Christian homilies also shows that public preaching emphasized that Christ died, that his death was salvific, and that it involved humiliation, bloodshed and torture. Although most of the sermons on the subject do not dwell in extensive detail on the sufferings, they are not passed over or neglected. For example, in one of John Chrysostom's homilies on the Gospel of John he declares, 'We admire him not only on account of the miracles, but also by reason of the sufferings; as that he was nailed upon the cross, that he was scourged, that he was buffeted, that he was spit upon, that he received blows on the cheek from those to whom he had done good.' He then proclaims that, 'For even of those very things which seem to be shameful, it is proper to speak, since he himself called the crucifixion "glory". What took place was proof not only of kindness and love but also of unspeakable power.'[71]

Similarly, Augustine preached a Good Friday sermon in which he reminded his congregation that there were *three* people crucified at Calvary: one died and was condemned, one was saved by his faith, but only one was the Saviour of the world. He insisted, therefore, that Christ's divinity was not established by his suffering or his crucifixion, but by every aspect of his life and ministry, including his human death and glorious resurrection.[72] And perhaps this is the theology reflected by early Christian images. Christ is encountered in catacomb paintings and sarcophagus reliefs first as healer and teacher, and then, in the extant monumental art of the next generation, as the one who *overcomes* suffering and death rather than succumbs to it. The development of this iconography is, perhaps, as much explained by the art's context and the

---

68 Tertullian, *Bapt.* 9.
69 Tertullian, *Bapt.* 19.
70 Cyril of Jerusalem, *Myst. cat.* 2.2, 5.
71 John Chrysostom, *Hom. Jo.* 12.3 (*NPNF*, Ser. 1, vol. 14, 42).
72 Augustine, *Serm.* 327.2. See also *Serm.* 328.7, 335.12, 331.2, 335.2.

church's growth and security as it is by theological divergence. The crucifixion was always central to the storytelling, preaching, catechesis and liturgy of the church, although it may have been fearfully intimidating to depict or observe at first. This only demonstrates the power of the image, not its insignificance.

5. *The crucifixion was a subject too sacred to allow direct depiction*

In contrast to the possibility that shame or scandal associated with the crucifixion might have inhibited Christian depictions is the possibility that the subject was too holy to be allowed visual rendering in a realistic way. This explanation depends on perceiving a difference between the impact of verbal descriptions and visual portrayals – and according the graphic image a kind of power or even danger that surpasses the mental image. The resistance to giving concrete form to this story may be due to awe-filled reverence, almost requiring that it be represented by some 'safer' symbolic or allegorical substitution such as the image of Abraham offering Isaac or the *agnus dei*. Not only are pictorial representations somehow more vulnerable, they are also more likely to be misunderstood or misinterpreted. This may also explain why the first visual references to the passion concentrated more on the victory won on the cross than on Jesus' humiliation, agony and death. Triumph is more positive than pathos as a public image.

Such a possibility raises an additional matter – the fear of idolatry associated with representing the divine subject, in this case in his transition from earthly teacher and healer to glorified saviour (cf. Jn 12.16-36). Visual representations of the works of Christ during his lifetime may not have had the taint of an image designed to be worshipped in an era when Christians still refuted the idol veneration of their pagan neighbours. Just as Moses was not allowed to see God's face (Exod. 3.6), Christians were reluctant to portray Christ's sacrifice. They veiled *this* image from sight, like the holy of holies, from the profane world and the eyes of the non-initiated, in the same way that they kept the liturgical memorials of Christ's sacrifice – the Eucharist and baptism – out of public view (the *disciplina arcani*). Only well after the transition from a persecuted minority cult to a powerful, protected and significant community could fears of idolatry, profanation and potential transgression be sidelined – in other words, when heresy and schism replaced idolatry as the main threat to the faith and when few non-believers would dare to disrespect the sacred image.[73]

---

73 See Robin Jensen, *Face to Face: The Portrait of the Divine in Early Christianity* (Minneapolis: Fortress Press, 2005) for a parallel explanation for the emergence of the portrait of Christ in Christian art.

Conclusion

This socio-political transformation of the Christian community is perhaps the only way to explain a change in attitude about depicting the crucifixion. The scandal of the image was no longer a pertinent issue, nor was the threat of idolatry as paganism seemed to be on the decline. Pilgrimages to the Holy Land undoubtedly began to stimulate interest in the representation of holy sites and the sacred stories along with the need to bring home souvenirs – relics and other objects – that connected the faithful with the reality of Christ's physical, historical existence. Furthermore, what rose to the attention of theologians in the early fifth century was the christological question of Christ's essential nature(s) more than analysis of his earthly works. The question of the suffering of the divine in the incarnate person of Jesus was a central one from the early fifth century on, and perhaps the greatest impetus for the arrival of the crucifix as a pictorial theme at this time. As the image develops through the subsequent centuries, it has been shown to be similarly adapted according to theological, social, and even political events and concerns.

This returns the discussion to the present, and the Gibson film. Gibson's provocative movie included an oddly anticlimactic resurrection scene, but his project was to portray the suffering and not the glory. Although many critics disagree, he and others believe that a graphic portrayal of the violent death of Christ is not only valid and edifying but an aid to devotion, inspiration, compassion, and even to conversion. Perhaps this film was right for its time, insofar as it concentrated on the human suffering of the saviour and the political blundering of the secular powers. Triumph was not the point, but rather the brutality of human pride. In any case, the film's enormous success as well as its provocation of controversy clearly demonstrates the power of the graphic image – and this image in particular. If the image does its work, it should always be so.

References

Balch, David, 'The Suffering of Isis/Io and Paul's Portrait of Christ Crucified (Gal. 3.1): Frescoes in Pompeian and Roman Houses and in the Temple of Isis in Pompeii', *JR* 83 (2002), 24–55.

Breckenridge, James D., 'The Reception of Art into the Early Church', *ACIAC* 1975 (vol. 1), pp. 361–405.

Brown, Raymond E., *The Death of the Messiah: From Gethsemane to the Grave. A Commentary on the Passion Narratives in the Four Gospels* (vol. 2; New York:Doubleday, 1994).

de Bruyne, Lucien, 'La "crux interpretum" di Erculano', *RivAC* 21 (1944/5), 281–309.

von Campenhausen, Hans, 'Die Passionssarkophage: Zur Geschichte eines altchristlichen Bildkreises', *Marburger Jahrbuch für Kunstwissenschaft* 5 (1929), 39–68.

Cecchelli, Carlo, Giuseppe Furlani and Mario Salmi, *The Rabbula Gospels: Facsimile Edition of the Miniatures of the Syria Manuscript Plut. I, 56 in the Medicaean-Laurentian Library* (Olten: Urs Graf-Verlag, 1959).

Chazelle, Celia, *The Crucified God in the Carolingian Era: Theology and Art of Christ's Passion* (Cambridge: Cambridge University Press, 2001).

Deichmann, Friedrich W., Giuseppe Bovini and Hugo Brandenburg, *Repertorium der christliche-antiken Sarkophage*, i: Rom und Ostia (Wiesbaden: Steiner, 1967).

Dinkler, Erich, 'Zur Geschichte des Kreuzsymbols', *ZTK* 48 (1951), 148–72.

——— 'Das Kreuz als Siegeszeichen', in *Signum Crucis* (Tübingen: J.C.B. Mohr, 1967), pp. 150–2.

Drijvers, J. W., *Helena Augusta: The Mother of Constantine the Great and the Legend of her Finding of the True Cross* (Leiden: Brill, 1992).

Engemann, Josef, 'Palastinische Pilgerampullen im F. J. Dölger Institut in Bonn', *JAC* 16 (1973), 5–27.

Ferguson, Everett, *Backgrounds of Early Christianity* (Grand Rapids: Eerdmans, 2nd edn, 1993).

Finegan, Jack, *Archaeology of the New Testament* (Princeton: Princeton University Press, 1969).

Finney, P. Corby, 'Did Gnostics Make Pictures?', in Bentley Layton (ed.), *The Rediscovery of Gnosticism: Proceedings of the International Conference on Gnosticism at Yale, New Haven, Connecticut, March 28–31, 1978* (vol. 1; Leiden: Brill, 1980), pp. 434–54.

Frazer, Margaret, 'Holy Sites Representations', in K. Weitzmann (ed.), *Age of Spirituality, Late Antique and Early Christian Art, Third to Seventh Century* (New York: Metropolitan Museum of Art, 1979), pp. 564–5.

Gerke, Friedrich, *Die christliche Sarkophage der vorkonstantinischen Zeit* (Berlin: de Gruyter, 1940).

Grabar, A., *Ampoules de Terre Sainte (Monza, Bobbio)* (Paris: Klincksieck, 1958).

Gregory of Tours, in *Gregory of Tours, Glory of the Martyrs* (Raymond Van Dam, trans.); (Liverpool: Liverpool University Press, 1988).

Harley, Felicity, 'Images of the Crucifixion in Late Antiquity: The Testimony of Engraved Gems' (unpublished doctoral dissertation, Adelaide University, 2001).

Hengel, Martin, *Crucifixion* (Philadelphia: Fortress Press, 1977).

Hurtado, Larry, 'The Staurogram in Early Christian Manuscripts: The

Earliest Visual Reference to the Crucified Jesus?', in Thomas J. Kraus and Tobias Nicklas (eds), *New Testament Manuscripts: Their Text and Their World* (Leiden: Brill, 2006), pp. 207–26.

Hurtado, Larry and Matthew Black, 'The Chi-Rho Sign: Christogram and/or Staurogram', in W. Ward Gasque and R. P. Martin (eds), *Apostolic History and the Gospel* (Grand Rapids: Eerdmans, 1970), pp. 319–27.

Itkonen-Kaila, Marja and Heikki Solin, in *Graffiti del Palatino, vol. 1 Paedagogium* (ed. Veikko Väänänen: Acta Instituti Romani Finlandiae 3, Helsinki, 1966), pp. 40–1, fig. 35 and pp. 209–12, no. 246.

Jensen, Robin, *Understanding Early Christian Art* (London: Routledge, 2000).

—— *Face to Face: The Portrait of the Divine in Early Christianity* (Minneapolis: Fortress Press, 2005).

Kartsonis, Anna, *Anastasis: The Making of an Image* (Princeton: Princeton University Press, 1986).

Kötzsche, L., 'Die trauernden Frauen, Zum Londoner Passionskätschen', in David Buckton and Thomas A. Heslop (eds), *Studies in Medieval Art and Architecture Presented to Peter Lasko* (London: Trustees of the British Museum, 1994).

Leclercq, Henri, 'Croix et crucifix', *DACL* 3.2, pp. 3050–6.

Mango, C., *The Art of the Byzantine Empire 312–1453: Sources and Documents* (Toronto: University of Toronto, 1986).

Mathews, Thomas, *The Clash of Gods: A Reinterpretation of Early Christian Art* (Princeton: Princeton University Press, rev. edn, 1993).

Moore, Peter G. 'Cross and Crucifixion in Christian Iconography: A Reply to E.J. Tinsley', *Religion* 4 (1974), 104–13.

Palli, E. Lucchesi, in Kurt Weitzmann (ed.), *Age of Spirituality*.

Renan, Ernst, *Histoire des origins du christianisme 7: Marc Aurèle et la fin du monde antique*, (Paris: Calman Lévy, 6th edn, 1882), pp. 539–46.

Shepherd, Massey, 'Christology: A Central Problem of Early Christian Theology and Art', in K. Weitzmann (ed.), *Age of Spirituality*.

Smith, Morton, *Jesus the Magician* (San Francisco: Harper & Row, 1978).

Smith, R. Houston, 'The Cross Marks on Jewish Ossuaries', *PEQ* (1974), 53–75.

Snyder, Graydon F., *Ante Pacem: Archaeological Evidence of Church Life before Constantine* (Macon, Ga: Mercer University Press, 2nd edn, 2003).

Spier, Jeffrey, *Late Antique and Early Christian Gems* (Wiesbaden: Reichert, 2007).

Sulzberger, Max, 'Le Symbole de la Croix et les Monogrammes de Jésus chez les premiers Chrétiens', *Byz.* 2 (1925), 337–448.

Syndicus, Eduard, *Early Christian Art* (trans. J. R. Foster; New York: Hawthorn, 1962).

Tinsley, E. J. 'The Coming of a Dead and Naked Christ', *Religion* 2 (1972), 24–36.

Vikan, Gary, 'Pilgrims in Magi's Clothing: The Impact of Mimesis on Early Byzantine Pilgrimage Art', in Robert Ousterhout (ed.), *The Blessings of Pilgrimage* (Urbana, Ill.: University of Illinois Press, 1990), pp. 97–107.

Vischer, Lukas, 'Le prétendu "culte de l'âne" dans l'église primitive', *Rev. Hist. Rel.* 139 (1951), 14–35.

Weitzmann, Kurt (ed.), 'Loca Sancta and the Representational Arts of Palestine', *DOP* 28 (1974), 33–55.

—— *Age of Spirituality, Late Antique and Early Christian Art, Third to Seventh Century* (New York:Metropolitan Museum of Art, 1979).

Chapter 5

FROM NATIVITY TO RESURRECTION: MUSICAL AND EXEGETICAL RESONANCES IN THE GOOD FRIDAY CHANTS *DOMINE AUDIUI* AND *QUI HABITAT*

Emma Hornby

Introduction

Second-mode tracts were among the longest and most challenging chants in the mediaeval Western liturgy.[1] Each biblical verse usually has four formulaic musical phrases. Phrase 1 appears first in the verse, cadencing on d. Phrase 2 appears second in the verse, ending on c at the half-verse caesura. Phrase 3 begins the second half of the verse and cadences on f. Phrase 4 ends the verse on d. A typical verse therefore has the underlying tonal scaffold d-c-f-d. Different versions of the four basic phrases are used depending on the accent patterns and, within each phrase, melodic shapes are consistently applied either to accented or to unaccented syllables.[2] At first glance, this is a genre that one could 'paint by numbers'.

However, the second-mode tracts are not merely the result of a mechanical application of certain rules. Instead, each melody promotes a particular grammatical and semantic interpretation of its text.[3] The

---

1 Angilram, Bishop of Metz 768–91, included *Qui habitat* (twice), *Deus deus meus* and *Domine exaudi* in his list of *stipendia* as chants so challenging that the singer would receive extra renumeration. Edited with commentary in M. Andrieu, 'Règlement d'Angilramme de Metz (768–91) fixant les honoraires de quelques fonctions liturgiques', *Revue des Sciences Religieuses* 10 (1930), 349–69.

2 See Xavier Kainzbauer, 'Der Tractus Tertrardus—eine centologische Untersuchung', *Beiträge zur Gregorianik* 11 (1991), 1–132, for a detailed exploration of this in the eighth-mode tracts; the same holds for the second-mode tracts.

3 Textual grammar was one of the principal determinants of musical form in mediaeval chant. See Leo Treitler and Ritva Jonsson, 'Medieval Music and Language: A Reconsideration of the Relationship', in Ellen Beebe (ed.), *Music and Language* (Studies in the History of Music, vol. 1; New York: Broude, 1983), pp. 1–23; Calvin Bower, 'The Grammatical Model of Musical Understanding in the Middle Ages', in P. Gallacher and H. Damico (eds), *Hermeneutics and Medieval Culture* (Albany: State University of New York Press, 1989), pp. 133–45; Karen Desmond, '*Sicut in Grammatica*: Analogical Discourse in Chapter 15 of Guido's *Micrologus*', *Journal of Musicology* 16 (1998), pp. 467–93. For

melodies also highlight key moments through the use of unique or striking melodic material which connects texts and ideas within chants, between chants, and between liturgical occasions. Because the second-mode tracts are largely formulaic, such long-range connections are not fortuitous; fellow monastics or clerics would recognize a second-mode tract phrase at the wrong time of year, or an alleluia phrase in a second-mode tract. Such musical emphasis relates to patristic biblical exegesis. While music has no semantic content, the portions of text emphasized musically can reflect the focus of the exegetical literature.

In this essay, the two second-mode tracts associated with the Good Friday liturgy until the early ninth century provide the focus for an illustrative case study.[4] The themes introduced here are explored at greater length in my forthcoming monograph, *Grammar, Rhetoric and Exegesis in the Second-Mode Tracts*.

The melodic traditions

The Mass Proper chants, a fixed repertoire of texts and melodies sung in the Mass in an annual cycle by musical specialists, are associated with the Roman *Schola cantorum* – the school of singers – which was established sometime before the end of the seventh century.[5] *Domine audiui* and *Qui habitat* were almost certainly attached to Good Friday in Rome and established as second-mode tracts by *c.* 700 CE.

During the 750s, there were close diplomatic relations between the Frankish king, Pippin, and Pope Stephen II. Stephen needed Frankish military help against Lombard invasions of the papal lands, and Pippin, who had usurped the Merovingian throne, sought ecclesiastical legitimacy for his rule. In 754–55 CE, the Pope spent at least six months at the royal abbey of St Denis, near Paris, accompanied by a large entourage, including members of the *Schola cantorum*.[6] The Franks soon started to sing Roman chant, and a *Schola cantorum* on the Roman model was set up at Metz by Bishop Chrodegang before 766 CE. Pippin's son

---

examples of analysis in this vein see Edward Nowacki, 'Text Declamation as a Determinant of Musical Form', *Early Music History* 6 (1986), 193–226; and Emma Hornby, *Gregorian and Old Roman Eighth-Mode Tracts* (Aldershot: Ashgate, 2002), pp. 55–127.

4 In the Frankish empire, *Qui habitat* was replaced on Good Friday before *c.* 850 by a newly composed second-mode tract, *Eripe me*.

5 The dates of establishing the institution and repertoire remain contentious. For two opposing points of view, see James McKinnon, *The Advent Project: The Later-Seventh-Century Creation of the Roman Mass Proper* (Berkeley: University of California Press, 2000); and Andreas Pfisterer, *Cantilena Romana: Untersuchungen zur Überlieferung des gregorianischen Chorals* (Paderborn: Schöningh, 2002).

6 On the papal visit, see Anne Walters Robertson, *The Service Books of the Royal Abbey of Saint Denis* (Oxford: Clarendon Press, 1991), pp. 23–9.

Charlemagne and his advisors attempted to unify the liturgy of the entire empire, including the unification of chant, and they turned to Rome for their models.[7] By *c.* 800 CE all Frankish monasteries and cathedrals were singing basically the same repertoire of *schola* chant, which they considered to be Roman.

The first surviving Frankish manuscripts containing the melodies of the Mass Proper chants date from almost a century later (*c.* 880 CE),[8] and the first complete surviving Roman one was compiled only in 1071 CE.[9] By that time, the chant tradition had diverged into two melodic strands: the Romano-Frankish tradition (familiarly, but inaccurately, known as Gregorian chant) and the Roman tradition (usually known as Old Roman chant). The two traditions generally use the same texts for the same liturgical occasions. The melodic relationship is more variable. In some genres, the two traditions have equivalent melodic outlines, goal tones and melodic density; in others, they have little or nothing in common.[10] The formal structure of the second-mode tracts is basically the same in the two traditions: they have equivalent melodic outlines for each of the four phrase types. It is not possible to say which (if either) dialect is closer to the original. The Old Roman version has more oscillating patterns and tends to move by step; the Gregorian version has more leaps.

7   They seem to have had more success in unifying chant than any other area of the liturgy. 'Throughout Charlemagne's legislation and the Carolingian conciliar decrees, it is only with reference to the chant that the Roman practice is specifically mentioned and ordered to be followed'; Yitzhak Hen, *The Royal Patronage of Liturgy in Frankish Gaul* (Henry Bradshaw Society Subsidia 3; Woodbridge: Boydell and Brewer, 2001), p. 85. This monograph otherwise deconstructs 'the common text-book narrative of the Romanization and unification of the Frankish liturgy under Charlemagne and his successors', p. 151.

8   See Peter Jeffery, 'The Oldest Sources of the *Graduale*: A Preliminary Checklist of MSS Copied before about 900', *Journal of Musicology* 2 (1983), 316–21. See also David Hiley and Janka Szendrei, 'Notation, III, 1: History of Western Notation: Plainchant (iii) Origins and Earliest Examples', in Stanley Sadie and Laura Macy (eds), *Grove Music Online*, <http://www.grovemusic.com> (accessed 30 October 2005).

9   Max Lütolf, *Das Graduale von Santa Cecilia in Trastevere (Cod. Bodmer 74)* (2 vols; Cologny-Genève: Fondation Martin Bodmer, 1987). On earlier examples of Roman notation, see John Boe, 'Music Notation in Archivio San Pietro C. 105 and in the Farfa Breviary, Chigi C.VI.177', *Early Music History* 18 (1999), 1–45.

10   For an example of the former, see Emma Hornby, *Gregorian and Old Roman Eighth-Mode Tracts*. For an example of the latter, see Rebecca Maloy, 'The Offertory Chant: Aspects of Chronology and Transmission' (unpublished doctoral dissertation, Cincinnati University, 2001): and Rebecca Maloy, *Inside the Offertory* (New York: Oxford University Press, forthcoming).

Domine audiui

The text of this tract comes from the canticle in Habakkuk 3.[11] The seventh-century Roman cantors would have been familiar with the Habakkuk commentary by Augustine in *De Civitate Dei* (book 18, chapter 32) and that by Jerome in his commentary on the minor prophets.[12] According to Bede, writing in the same tradition, the canticle 'is mainly a proclamation of the mysteries of the Lord's passion ... it also gives a mystical account of his incarnation, resurrection and ascension into heaven'.[13]

The first place with striking melodic material is 'In medio duorum animalium innotesceris' ('In the middle of two living creatures, you will be known'; Hab. 3.2, Septuagint version).[14] These two living creatures, in the midst of whom Christ shall be recognized, were most often identified as the two thieves at Calvary in patristic and early mediaeval times.[15] This has particular resonance for the Good Friday tract, and this portion of

---

11   The tract is reproduced in full in Appendix 1.

12   Jerome, *Commentarium in Abacuc Prophetam ad Chromatium in Commentarii in prophetas minores*, ed. Marcus Adriaen (CCSL 76A; Turnhout: Brepols, 1970), pp. 618–54. A brief assessment of Jerome on the Habakkuk canticle is given in Éamonn Ó Carragáin, 'The Meeting of Saint Paul and Saint Anthony: Visual and Literary Uses of a Eucharistic Motif', in Gearóid Mac Niocaill and Patrick F. Wallace (eds), *Keimelia: Studies in Medieval Archaeology and History in Memory of Tom Delaney* (Galway: Galway University Press, 1988), pp. 27–9. See also Ó Carragáin, '*"Traditio evangeliorum"* and *"sustentatio"*: The Relevance of Liturgical Ceremonies to the Book of Kells', in Felicity D. O'Mahony (ed.), *The Book of Kells: Proceedings of a Conference at Trinity College, Dublin, 6–9 September 1992* (Aldershot: Scolar Press, 1994), p. 422.

13   Bede, *Bede on Tobit and on the Canticle of Habakkuk* (trans. Seán Connolly; Dublin: Four Courts Press, 1997), p. 65.

14   Éamonn Ó Carragáin has written at length about the resonances this sentence had for mediaeval monks and the role it plays in the iconographic programme of the Ruthwell and Bewcastle crosses. See Ó Carragáin, '*"Traditio evangeliorum"* and *"sustentatio"*', pp. 422–30, for a concentration on the Good Friday-related aspects of 'In medio duorum animalium innotesceris'.

Éamonn Ó Carragáin, 'Christ over the Beasts and the Agnus Dei: Two Multivalent Panels on the Ruthwell and Bewcastle Crosses', in Paul Szarmach (ed.), *Sources of Anglo-Saxon Culture* (Studies in Medieval Culture XX; Kalamazoo: Medieval Institute Publications, Western Michigan University, 1986), pp. 383–90, similarly links the Ruthwell and Bewcastle crosses to the Good Friday liturgy, and particularly to the Habakkuk text. However, Ó Carragáin interprets the tract *Domine audiui* as being a responsory, and this misunderstanding of the performance practice leads him to draw mistaken conclusions about the role of the community in this soloistic chant (p. 387). He also gives a verse division (p. 384) which is not supported by the musical state of the chant. 'In eo' begins a verse rather than ends one; 'in ira' belongs with the second half of the verse rather than the first.

15   Joseph Ziegler, 'Ochs und Esel an der Krippe', *Münchener Theologische Zeitschrift* 3 (1952), p. 401. Various human, animal, inanimate, abstract or angelic forms are interpreted as being the 'two living things' in patristic and mediaeval exegesis. The detail is less important than the fact that the divine and human natures of Christ can be recognized through them. See Ó Carragáin, '*"Traditio evangeliorum"* and *"sustentatio"*', p. 423.

text is highlighted by the music of both the Old Roman and Gregorian versions (see Example 1).[16]

The Gregorian tradition has an open cadence, then a retake of the opening and a normal phrase, followed by a unique phrase with a different tonal space. The Old Roman version also closes the first phrase with an open cadence, and then has a decorated phrase twice in a row, with a high tessitura. The unique Frankish music, the repetition of an Old Roman phrase twice in a row, the avoidance of cadences and the high tessitura all make this portion of text stand out.

It was through the crucifixion that Jesus was recognized as the Messiah, standing between the Old and New Covenants and literally between two thieves. 'In medio duorum animalium innotesceris' is central to patristic explanations of how the canticle prophesies the passion of Christ and the melodic emphasis of this sentence in the Good Friday tract promotes the same message.

A further, additional, interpretation of the sentence's musical emphasis may be proposed, however. The presence of the ox and the ass at the Nativity was an iconographic commonplace from the fourth century onwards,[17] and was usually connected by commentators to Isa. 1.3: 'The ox knows his owner and the ass his master's crib'.[18] The ox and ass were also connected to the Habakkuk text 'In medio duorum animalium innotesceris' in the Apocryphal Gospel of Pseudo-Matthew, dated 550–700 CE, which gave the connection wide textual currency.[19] More generally, the canticle was interpreted by Jerome as prophesying not just the passion but also the incarnation of Christ[20] and the canticle is associated with the Christmas season as well as Passiontide.[21]

---

16 Musical examples are transcribed from *BEN5* (Benevento VI.34, a twelfth-century Beneventan Gradual) and *ORC* (Bodmer 74, an Old Roman Gradual dated 1071). These manuscripts are representative of their respective traditions, but choosing to use their melodies is intended to be illustrative rather than claiming any particular authority for these manuscripts. Ornamental signs in the manuscript are indicated by use of x rather than a round notehead.

17 'The ox and the ass are always present in renderings of the Nativity', Gertrud Schiller, *Iconography of Christian Art* (vol. 1; London: Lund Humphries, 1971), p. 59.

18 Found, for example, in Origen's third-century *Homilies on Luke*. See Ziegler, 'Ochs und Esel an der Krippe', p. 391. The ox was the pure beast (symbolized as the Jewish people, yoked to the law) and the ass was the impure one (symbolized as the heathen, loaded with the sins of idolatry); Schiller, *Iconography*, pp. 650–61.

19 Ziegler, 'Ochs und Esel an der Krippe', p. 388.

20 'Manifestem est autem iuxta Hebraicum quod in aduentu Christi cuncta repleta sint gloria, secundum illud quod in euangelio dicitur: *Gloria in excelsis deo, et super terram pax hominibus bonae voluntatis*. Et alibi: Pacem fecit in caelis et in terra per sanguinem crucis, et sedit in dextera magnitudinis: *Velociter enim currit sermo eius*', Jerome, *Commentarium in Abacuc Prophetam ad Chromatium*, p. 624.

21 It is used as a Matins responsory at the feast of the Circumcision and in the Epiphany Vigil; the related responsory text 'O magnum mysterium' is used on several days at Christmas time; Ziegler, 'Ochs und Esel an der Krippe', p. 385.

Gregorian version (Benevento VI.34)

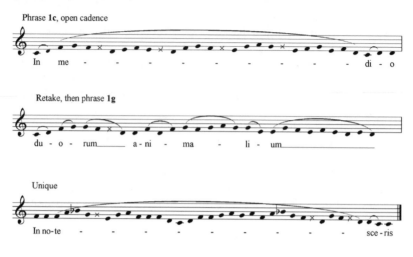

Old Roman version (Bodmer 74)

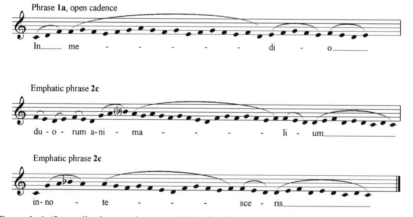

Example 1. 'In medio duorum innotesceris' in the Gregorian and Old Roman traditions

The final verse of the tract *Domine audiui* (Hab. 3.3) confirms that the compilers of this Good Friday chant wanted to remind listeners of Christ's fulfilment of the Habakkuk prophecy in the incarnation as well as the passion (see Example 2).

There is a unique melisma on '(Operuit) celos' in the Gregorian tradition. The Christmas Day alleluia *Dies sanctificatus* has the material

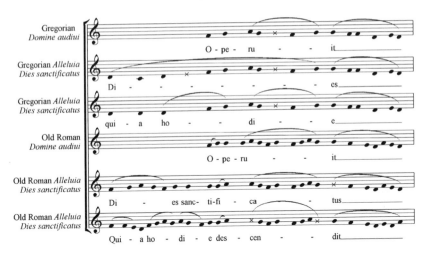

Example 2. 'Operuit celos' compared with the alleluia *Dies sanctificatus*

seen on 'operuit' followed by the 'celos' melisma not once, but twice.[22]
The Old Roman tradition has the equivalent normal phrase on 'operuit'
and then a further normal phrase on 'celos maiestas eius'. The Old Roman

22 Observed by Theodore Karp, *Aspects of Orality and Formularity in Gregorian Chant*
(Evanston: Northwestern University Press, 1988), pp. 64–5. He writes that drawing
conclusions about why this might be so is beyond his brief. *Dies sanctificatus* is one of a
family of interrelated alleluias (pp. 169–79) of which *Dies sanctificatus* is the most prominent;
the melody was originally associated with Feasts between the Nativity and Epiphany (p. 164).

alleluia *Dies sanctificatus* has the 'operuit' phrase followed by the Old Roman equivalent of the 'celos' melisma at the same two points.[23] This suggests very strongly that the Roman equivalent of the 'celos' melisma was used in the eighth-century Roman *Domine audiui*, but that it was replaced by a normal phrase in Rome at some point before the chant was notated.

The alleluia is sung at the third Mass on Christmas Day, one of the most important occasions of the liturgical year. Its text reads: 'Dies sanctificatus illuxit nobis: venite gentes, et adorate Dominum: quia hodie descendit lux magna super terram' ('Holy day, illumine us; come people and adore God, because today a great light descends to earth'). The glory of Christ in the heavens in Habakkuk's prophecy is therefore musically linked with the great light descending to earth from the heavens at the Nativity. Through the non-formulaic musical phrases and inter-genre musical connection, Christ's incarnation is called to mind at the liturgical moment of his crucifixion.

Qui habitat

Until the early ninth century, the second Good Friday tract was *Qui habitat*,[24] which consists of 13 verses of Psalm 90 [91].[25] In the early Middle Ages, *Qui habitat* was sung twice a year; once on Quadragesima Sunday and once on Good Friday.

Psalm 90 [91] is alluded to in Matthew 4:

> [1]Then Jesus was led up by the Spirit into the wilderness to be tempted by the devil. [2]And after fasting forty days and forty nights, he was hungry ... [5]Then the devil took him to the holy city and set him on the pinnacle of the temple [6]and said to him, "If you are the Son of God, throw yourself down, for it is written, 'He will command his angels concerning you' (Ps. 90 [91].11) and 'On their hands they will bear you up, lest you strike your foot against a stone.'" (Ps. 90 [91].12) [7]Jesus said to the devil, "It is written, 'You shall not put the Lord your God to the test.'"[26]

Psalm 90 [91] was connected to the Temptation in mediaeval images and in commentaries.[27] The Temptation was particularly associated with the

---

23 Karp, *Aspects of Orality and Formularity*, pp. 359, 364.

24 The tract is reproduced in full in Appendix 2.

25 Psalm 90 in the Vulgate and Roman Psalters; Psalm 91 in modern English translations.

26 English Standard Version (Wheaton, Ill: Crossway, 2001).

27 Meyer Shapiro, 'The Religious Meaning of the Ruthwell Cross', *Art Bulletin* 26 (1944), p. 233 note 5. See also p. 233 note 7 for a list of Psalters in which this Psalm is illustrated with a picture of the Temptation.

season of Lent, in which the church 'symbolically accompanied Christ into the desert to fast, pray and overcome temptation',[28] and the Gospel reading on Quadragesima Sunday was taken from Matthew 4. Psalm 90 [91] permeates the Quadragesima liturgy, providing the text not only for the tract, but for the introit, gradual, offertory and communion chants as well.[29] The use of Psalm 90 [91] marks Lent more generally as a commemoration of Christ in the desert. The use of the tract *Qui habitat* on Good Friday as well as Quadragesima means that this psalm frames Lent.

Patristic exegesis seems less pertinent to the melodic state of the tract *Qui habitat* than to *Domine audiui*. While the literal historical sense of Psalm 90 [91] is briefly acknowledged in Augustine's commentary on the Psalms ('this psalm is that from which the Devil dared to tempt our Lord Jesus Christ'), Augustine's emphasis is on the moral sense of the text in which we learn how to act by interpreting events in Scripture. He writes, 'Let us therefore attend to it [this psalm], that thus armed, we may be enabled to resist the tempter.'[30] It was in this spirit that Psalm 90 [91] was sung at monastic Compline every day, in preparation against the terrors of the night (v. 6). Every evening, Psalm 90 [91] would have reminded monastics of their kinship with Christ, who also withdrew from the world to do battle with the Devil.

By contrast with Augustine's focus, the tract appears to concentrate on the allegorical (christological) interpretation of Psalm 90 [91] as foretelling and describing Christ's victory over the Devil. The battle between Jesus and the Devil was not limited to the forty days in the desert: the Devil's final gambit is described in Mt. 27.42, where the chief priests, scribes and elders mock Jesus, 'Come down from the cross, and we will believe in you.'

Is the tract *Qui habitat* a Quadragesima chant, adopted into the Good Friday liturgy to frame Lent? Or was it originally a Good Friday chant, marking the passion as the climax of the battle between Christ and the Devil? Chant scholars have rarely ventured an opinion on this matter; when they have, they lean towards Quadragesima being the original context, because the other Mass Proper chants on that day have texts from the same psalm. This may well have been the original assignment of the text, but I shall argue in what follows that the music of the tract *Qui habitat* is particularly appropriate for use on Good Friday.

28 Ó Carragáin, 'Christ over the Beasts', p. 381.

29 McKinnon, *The Advent Project* (pp. 285–6) considers the gradual *Angelis suis* (Ps. 90 [91].11-12) to be a later chant ('it is set to a particularly routine example of the A-2 melody type'), and says that the texts of the introit *Invocabit* (Ps. 90 [91].15-16), offertory *Scapulis suis* (Ps. 90 [91].4-5) and communion *Scapulis suis* (Ps. 90 [91].4-5) also seem to be borrowed from the tract.

30 Augustine, *Commentary on the Psalms* <http://www.ccel.org/fathers2/NPNF1–08/npnf1-08-98.htm#P2350_2286386> (accessed 30 October 2005).

Verse 6 of the tract consists of a list of things which the faithful man will not fear, beginning 'A sagitta volante per diem' ('(you will not have fear) of the arrow which flies by day'; Ps. 90 [91].6). This arrow is consistently interpreted in mediaeval commentary as open temptation to sin.[31] 'A sagitta' uses an emphatic phrase in both traditions; this uses a higher tessitura than usual verse-opening phrases (see Example 3).

'Volante' uses an unusual shape, outside the usual functional phrases, which also appears in the Gregorian version of *Qui habitat* in the tract verse 12 on 'et ego' (Ps. 90 [91].15). This is the beginning of a list of reassurances from God: 'I will hear him, I will protect him, I will deliver him' and so on. The musical connection promotes a particular interpretation of the text in which God promises to protect the faithful man specifically from the (emphasized) arrow of temptation.

The list of things which the faithful man need not fear continues: 'a negotio perambulante in tenebris, a ruina et demonio meridiano' ('[you

Example 3. The flourish on 'a latere' and related phrases

31 R. T. Farrell, 'The Archer and Associated Figures on the Ruthwell Cross – a Reconsideration', in R. T. Farrell (ed.), *Bede and Anglo-Saxon England* (Oxford: British Archaeological Reports, 1978), p. 107.

will not have fear] of the matter that walks in the dark, of ruin and demons at midday'; Ps. 90 [91].6). (See Example 4.)

In the Old Roman tradition, 'a negotio' and 'a ruina' use a rare phrase cadencing on c despite appearing in the second half of the verse, where one would expect a phrase cadencing on f. There is an obvious text cue between the two, and it helps to point out the structure of the list to have the same music on each occasion. The same phrase is used in the tract verse 9 '(ne umquam offendas) ad lapidem (pedem tuum)' ('that you would never hit your foot) on a stone'; Ps. 90 [91].12). In the Gregorian tradition there is a similarly low opening to 'a negotio' and 'a ruina', but there is no cadence on c and the music continues straight into the next phrase. The Gregorian equivalent to the Old Roman c cadence is found in the tract verse 4 on 'et sub pennis eius (sperabis)' ('and under his wings (you will hope)'; Ps. 90 [91].4) and in the tract verse 9, as in the Old Roman tradition, on 'ad lapidem' (Ps. 90 [91].12). The list of terrors in the tract verses 5–6 therefore connects musically to God's reassurances.

The last two verses give God's list of promises to help the faithful man. The psalm text is long, and listeners might be forgiven for having forgotten by this stage that God is making these promises to the faithful man who says to the Lord (in verse 2 of both tract and psalm), 'you are my supporter and my God is my refuge'. The compilers of the chant remind listeners of this: in the Old Roman version, the phrase shape on 'in tribulatione' ('(I am with him) in troubles') in the tract verse 12 (Ps. 90 [91].15) is only otherwise used in verse 2 of this chant on 'I will trust in him [God]' ('sperabo in eum'). (See Example 5, which also shows the usual verse-ending phrase.)

Example 4. 'A negotio' and related phrases

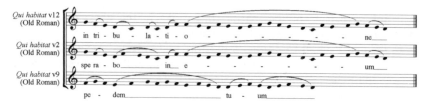

The faithful man does not trust in vain; God will be with him in his troubles. The Gregorian tradition similarly uses the same melody on 'Eripiam eum' ('I will deliver him') in the tract verse 13 (Ps. 90 [91].15) as on 'et refugium meum deus meus' ('my God is my refuge') in verse 2 (see Example 3, above).

The examples discussed so far all illustrate musical ways beyond the formulaic system of tying together a long chant. Key words and ideas are connected musically, which helps the listener to link them in a meditative response. The recurring theme is that God will protect the faithful man in his time of trouble, when he is openly tempted. The Lenten context means that Christ is probably intended to be understood as the faithful man, although the temptation could either be the forty days in the desert or the final temptation of avoiding the passion.

My final example is taken from the Gregorian tradition, but the Old Roman tradition acts in a similar manner. The tract verse 7 begins 'Cadent a latere tuo mille' ('A thousand fall at your side'; Ps. 90 [91].7). 'Tuo mille' has a decorated and emphatic phrase (not shown here). The 'a latere' phrase was already encountered on 'volante' (see Example 3, above): 'A thousand fall at your side' is therefore musically linked to God's protection of Christ from the arrows which fly by day.

'Cadent' has a non-formulaic phrase (see Example 6). The same melody is used on several other occasions. It is used at the end of the tract verse 10 (Ps. 90 [91].13) on 'leonem et draconem' ('(and you will trample) the lion and the dragon') and, in a less closely related form, at the end of verse 6 on '(et demonio) meridiano' ('(you will not be afraid of ...) demons at midday'; Ps. 90 [91].6). The Quadragesima Offertory *Scapulis suis* also uses the same melisma on 'draconem' in its third verse. The lion and dragon are personifications of the Devil, and use of this melody elsewhere therefore brings the Devil to mind.

The 'Cadent' phrase also appears in *De necessitatibus*, the tract sung on the Ember Wednesday after Quadragesima, for the texts 'Deus meus' ('my God'), 'meis' ('(rescue me from) my (fate)') and 'Omnes' ('All (who look to you will not be confounded)').

The phrase also appears at the beginning of the offertory *Anima nostra* ('Our soul (has escaped from the snare of the fowler)'), which is associated

Example 6. The 'Cadent' melisma in the Gregorian tradition

with the feast of Holy Innocents and other martyrs.[32] The text parallels
Qui habitat, verse 3, 'He has freed me from the snare of the hunter'. The
psalm text (Ps. 123 [124]) used for the offertory is interpreted by
Augustine as being about the triumph of the martyr's soul over death: the
snare is the sweetness of earthly life, which God helps martyrs to escape.[33]
The last use of this phrase is in the Easter Day alleluia:[34] '(For Christ, our
Passover Lamb, is) sacrificed'.[35]

The use of the 'Cadent' melisma in various genres and on various
liturgical occasions sets up a nexus of interrelated themes. It calls to mind:
the Devil; a call for God's rescue and an expression of trust in him; the
martyr's escape from the snare of earthly life; and the ultimate sacrifice of
the Passover Lamb. In *Qui habitat* verse 7, the musical cues connect God's
protection of the faithful man from falling to the Devil, to trust in God, to
martyrs, and to the Passover Lamb.

Conclusion

Through non-formulaic musical cross-references, the second-mode tracts
of the Good Friday liturgy chants promote a particular interpretation of
the Good Friday ceremonies. In *Domine audiui* Christ is recognized in the
middle of two living creatures and, as in the Christmas Day alleluia, his
glory fills the sky. He is revealed through his incarnation and his
crucifixion. In *Qui habitat*, God protects the Passover Lamb from the
Devil's temptation.

Appendix 1: Full Text of the Tract Domine Audiui

This text for Habakkuk 3 derives from the Septuagint, unlike most
modern Bible translations. I have therefore translated it literally, and have
included footnotes referencing the standard Septuagint translation by Sir
Lancelot C. E. Brenton.[36] I have not footnoted variants arising from
Brenton's use of archaic forms such as 'thee' or 'shalt'.

32   Karp, *Aspects of Orality and Formularity*, pp. 94–5.
33   Augustine, *Commentary on the Psalms* <http://www.ccel.org/fathers2/NPNF1–08/
npnf1-08-131.htm> (accessed 30 October 2005).
34   Karp, *Aspects of Orality and Formularity*, p. 74.
35   1 Cor. 5.7-8.
36   Lancelot C. L. Brenton, *The Septuagint with Apocrypha: Greek & English* (London:
Samuel Bagster & Sons, 1851), available at http://www.ccel.org/bible/brenton/.

Tract text	Literal translation	Septuagint versification
1. Domine audiui	Lord,[37] I have heard	verse 2
auditum tuum	your voice[38]	
et timui:	and I was afraid	
consideraui	I have considered[39]	
opera tua et expaui	your deeds[40] and was afraid[41]	
2. In medio	In the middle[42]	
duorum	of two[43]	
animalium	living things[44]	
innotesceris	you will be known	
dum appropinquauerintanni	when the years approach[45]	
cognosceris	you will be known[46]	
dum aduenerit tempus	when the time comes[47]	
ostenderis	you will appear[48]	
3. In eo	At that point[49]	
dum conturbata	when [my soul] has been stirred up[50]	
fuerit		
anima mea:	my soul:	
in ira	in anger[51]	
misericordiae	of mercy	
memor eris	you will be mindful[52]	

37 'O Lord' in Brenton.
38 ' your report' in Brenton.
39 'I considered' in Brenton.
40 'works' in Brenton.
41 'amazed' in Brenton.
42 'between' in Brenton.
43 'the two' in Brenton, although there is no definite article in the Greek here. My thanks to Leofranc Holford-Strevens for pointing this out.
44 'living creatures' in Brenton.
45 'draw nigh' in Brenton.
46 'acknowledged' in Brenton.
47 'when the time is come' in Brenton.
48 'be manifested' in Brenton.
49 Not included in Brenton.
50 'when my soul is troubled' in Brenton.
51 'in wrath' in Brenton.
52 'thou wilt remember mercy' in Brenton.

4. Deus	God	verse 3
a libano veniet:	comes from Lebanon:[53]	
et sanctus de monte	and the holy one [comes] from the mountain[54]	
umbroso et condenso	[that is] shady and misty[55]	
5. Operuit	[his glory] covers[56]	
caelos	the heavens	
maiestas eius:	his glory[57]	
et laudis eius	and of his praise	
plena est terra	the earth is[58] full	

Appendix 2: Full Text of the Tract Qui Habitat

Tract text	Literal translation	Roman Psalter versification
1. Qui habitat	He who dwells	verse 1
in adiutorio	with the assistance[59]	
altissimi	of the highest,	
in protectione	in the protection[60]	
dei celi commorabitur	of the Lord of the heavens[61] shall dwell[62]	
2. Dicet domino	He says to the Lord[63]	verse 2
susceptor meus es	"You are my supporter	
et refugium meum deus meus	and my God is my refuge	
sperabo in eum	I will trust in him[64]	

53 'shall come from Thaeman' in Brenton.
54 'and the Holy One shall come from the dark, shady Mount Pharan' in Brenton.
55 'dark, shady' in Brenton.
56 'covered' in Brenton.
57 'his excellence' in Brenton.
58 'was' in Brenton.
59 'shelter' in NEB, ESV, NRSV, NASB; 'secret place' in KJV, NKJV.
60 'under/in the shadow' in ESV, NRSV, NASB, KJV, NKJV, NEB.
61 'the Almighty' in ESV, NRSV, NASB, KJV, NKJV, NEB.
62 'abide' in ESV, NRSV, NASB, KJV, NKJV; 'lodge' in NEB.
63 'I will say to the Lord' in ESV, NRSV, NASB; 'I will say of the Lord' in KJV, NKJV.
64 '"My refuge and my fortress, My God, in whom I trust!"' in ESV, NRSV, NASB; '"He is my refuge and my fortress: my God; in him will I trust"' in KJV, NKJV; 'The Lord is my safe retreat, my God the fastness in which I trust' in NEB.

3. Quoniam ipse	because he himself	verse 3
liberauit me	has freed me	
de laqueo uenantium	from the snare of (the) hunters[65]	
et a uerbo	and from the [rough] word	
aspero	rough"[66]	
4. Scapulis suis	With his shoulders	verse 4
obumbrabit tibi	he will overshadow you[67]	
et sub pennis eius	and under his wings	
sperabis	you will hope[68]	
5. Scuto circumdabit te	[his truth,] will surround you with a shield [69]	verse 5
ueritas eius	his truth	
non timebis	you will not be afraid	
a timore nocturno	of[70] nightly terrors	
6 A sagitta	of the arrow	verse 6
volante per diem	that flies by day	
a negotio perambulante in tenebris	of the matter[71] that walks[72] in the darkness	
a ruina et demonio meridiano	of ruin and demons at midday[73]	

65   The word 'uenantium' is a genitive plural present participle, literally meaning 'of hunters', but translations conventionally use 'of the fowler' (in ESV, NRSV, KJV and NKJV) or, more rarely, 'of the trapper' (in NASB).

66   This clause is not usually translated literally. Rather than 'the rough word', translations use 'the deadly pestilence' (ESV, NRSV, NASB), 'the noisome pestilence' (KJV) or the 'perilous pestilence' (NKJV); NEB instead has 'the raging tempest'.

67   Usually translated as 'He will cover you with his pinions/feathers' ('feathers' in KJV and NKJV).

68   While the KJV has 'you will trust', the other translations are less literal, having 'you will find refuge' or similar.

69   This sentence is not usually translated literally: 'his truth' ('faithfulness' in NASB, ESV, NRSV) 'will be your shield and your rampart/buckler/bulwark'.

70   Here and in the following verse, 'a' literally translates as 'from', but 'of', found also in NASB and NKJV is more idiomatic; ESV and NRSV avoid the preposition by translating as 'you will not fear ...'

71   'pestilence' in the translations.

72   'stalks' in ESV, NRSV, NASB, NEB.

73   The translations instead have 'of the destruction' ('plague' in NEB) 'that wastes/lays waste at noon(day)', reflecting the Gallican Psalter tradition 'ab incurso et demonio meridiano'; where 'incurso' literally translates as an attack or incursion.

7. Cadent	[A thousand] may fall	verse 7
a latere tuo mille	a thousand at your side	
et decem milia	and ten thousand	
a dextris tuis	at your right hand	
tibi autem	but you	
non appropinquabit	it will not come near	
8. Quoniam angelis suis	Because his angels	verse 11
mandauit de te	he has commanded concerning you[74]	
ut custodiant te	that they should protect[75] you	
in omnibus viis tuis	in all your ways	
9. In manibus	In their hands	verse 12
portabunt te	they will carry you[76]	
ne umquam offendas	that you would never hit[77]	
ad lapidem	on[78] a stone	
pedem tuum	your foot	
10. Super aspidem	Upon[79] the snake	verse 13
et basiliscum	and the basilisk[80]	
ambulabis	you will walk[81]	
et conculcabis	and you will trample[82]	
leonem	the lion[83]	
et draconem	and the serpent[84]	

74   All but NEB use future tense here, reflecting the Gallican Psalter tradition, which has the future 'mandabit'.

75   'keep' (KJV, NKJV) or 'guard' ESV, NRSV, NASB, NEB.

76   'they will bear you up' in the translations.

77   'strike' (NEB, KJV, ESV, NRSV) or 'dash' (NKJ, NRSV).

78   'against' in the translations.

79   'on' in ESV and NRSV.

80   All translations have the non-literal 'lion and adder/cobra' in this verse half, except NEB ('asp and cobra').

81   'tread' in the translations.

82   All translations have 'trample under foot' or 'trample down' (NASB).

83   All translations have the non-literal 'young lion' here, except NEB ('snake').

84   'dragon' in KJV.

11. Quoniam in me sperauit	Because he trusted in me[85]	verse 14
liberabo eum	I will free[86] him	
protegam eum	I will protect him[87]	
quoniam cognouit nomen meum	because he knew[88] my name	
12. Inuocavit me	He[89] called on me[90]	verse 15
et ego exaudiam eum	and I will hear[91] him	
cum ipso sum	I am with him[92]	
in tribulatione	in trouble[93]	
13. Eripiam eum	I will deliver[94] him	
et glorificabo eum	and I will glorify[95] him	
Longitudinem	throughout the length	verse 16
dierum adimplebo eum	of his days[96] I will satisfy him	
et ostendam illi	and show him	
salutare meum	my salvation	

85   All translations replace 'hoped in me' with 'has loved me' or similar.

86   'deliver' in all translations.

87   Only in ESV; the other translations have 'I will set him beyond danger' (NEB) or 'I will set him (securely) on high' (KJV, NKJV, NRSV, NASB).

88   'knows' (ESV) or 'has known' (KJV, NKJV, NRSV, NASB).

89   'They'; plural until the end of the Psalm in NRSV.

90   All translations have future (KJV, NKJV, NRSV, NASB) or present tense here (ESV, NEB), reflecting the Gallican Psalter future tense 'clamabit ad me'.

91   'answer' in all translations.

92   future tense in all translations.

93   singular in all translations: 'trouble'.

94   'rescue' in NRSV, NASB, NEB, ESV.

95   'honour' in all translations. The Gallican Psalter has 'et clarificabo eum', literally meaning 'and I will make him famous'.

96   This prepositional phrase is translated as 'with [a] long life' in the translations. The accusative 'longitudinem' signifies a time duration, so that 'throughout the length of his days' is more literal.

References

Andrieu, M.,'Règlement d'Angilramme de Metz (768–791) fixant les honoraires de quelques fonctions liturgiques', *Revue des Sciences Religieuses* 10 (1930), 349–69.

Bede, *Bede on Tobit and on the Canticle of Habakkuk* (trans. Seán Connolly; Dublin: Four Courts Press, 1997).

Boe, John, 'Music Notation in Archivio San Pietro C. 105 and in the Farfa Breviary, Chigi C.VI.177', *Early Music History* 18 (1999), 1–45.

Bower, Calvin, 'The Grammatical Model of Musical Understanding in the Middle Ages', in P. Gallacher and H. Damico (eds), *Hermeneutics and Medieval Cultures* (Albany: State University of New York Press, 1989), pp. 133–45.

Brenton, Lancelot C. L., *The Septuagint with Apocrypha: Greek and English* (London: Samuel Bagster & Sons, 1851), available at <http://www.ccel.org/bible/brenton/>.

Desmond, Karen, '*Sicut in Grammatica*: Analogical Discourse in Chapter 15 of Guido's *Micrologus*', *Journal of Musicology* 16 (1998), 467–93.

Farrell, R. T., 'The Archer and Associated Figures on the Ruthwell Cross – A Reconsideration', in R. T. Farrell (ed.), *Bede and Anglo-Saxon England* (Oxford: British Archaeological Reports, 1978), pp. 96–117.

Hen, Yitzhak, *The Royal Patronage of Liturgy in Frankish Gaul* (Henry Bradshaw Society Subsidia 3; Woodbridge: Boydell and Brewer, 2001).

Hiley, David and Janka Szendrei, 'Notation, III, 1: History of Western Notation: Plainchant (iii) Origins and Earliest Examples', in Stanley Sadie and Laura Macy (eds), *Grove Music Online*, <http://www.grovemusic.com> (accessed 30 October 2005).

Hornby, Emma, *Gregorian and Old Roman Eighth-Mode Tracts* (Aldershot: Ashgate, 2002).

Jeffery, Peter, 'The Oldest Sources of the *Graduale*: A Preliminary Checklist of MSS Copied before about 900', *Journal of Musicology* 2 (1983), 316–21.

Jerome, *Commentarium in Abacuc Prophetam ad Chromatium in Commentarii in prophetas minores* (ed. Marcus Adriaen; CCSL 76A; Turnhout: Brepols, 1970), pp. 618–54.

Kainzbauer, Xavier, 'Der Tractus Tertrardus—eine centologische Untersuchung', *Beiträge zur Gregorianik* 11 (1991), 1–132.

Karp, Theodore, *Aspects of Orality and Formularity in Gregorian Chant* (Evanston: Northwestern University Press, 1988).

Lütolf, Max, *Das Graduale von Santa Cecilia in Trastevere (Cod. Bodmer 74)* (2 vols; Cologny-Genève: Fondation Martin Bodmer, 1987).

Mac Niocaill, Gearóid and Patrick F. Wallace (eds), *Keimelia: Studies in*

Medieval Archaeology and History in Memory of Tom Delaney (Galway: Galway University Press, 1988), pp. 1–58.

Maloy, Rebecca, 'The Offertory Chant: Aspects of Chronology and Transmission' (unpublished doctoral dissertation, Cincinnati University, 2001).

—— *Inside the Offertory* (New York: Oxford University Press, forthcoming).

McKinnon, James, *The Advent Project: The Later-Seventh-Century Creation of the Roman Mass Proper* (Berkeley: University of California Press, 2000).

Nowacki, Edward, 'Text Declamation as a Determinant of Musical Form', *Early Music History* 6 (1986), 193–226.

Ó Carragáin, Éamonn, 'Christ over the Beasts and the Agnus Dei: Two Multivalent Panels on the Ruthwell and Bewcastle Crosses', in Paul Szarmach (ed.), *Sources of Anglo-Saxon Culture* (Studies in Medieval Culture XX; Kalamazoo: Medieval Institute Publications, Western Michigan University, 1986), pp. 377–403.

—— 'The Meeting of Saint Paul and Saint Anthony: Visual and Literary Uses of a Eucharistic Motif', in Gearóid Mac Niocaill and Patrick F. Wallace (eds), *Keimelia: Studies in Medieval Archaeology and History in Memory of Tom Delaney*, pp. 1–58.

—— '*"Traditio evangeliorum"* and *"sustentatio"*: The Relevance of Liturgical Ceremonies to the Book of Kells', in Felicity D. O'Mahony (ed.), *The Book of Kells: Proceedings of a Conference at Trinity College, Dublin, 6–9 September 1992* (Aldershot: Scolar Press, 1994), pp. 398–436.

Pfisterer, Andreas, *Cantilena Romana: Untersuchungen zur Überlieferung des gregorianischen Chorals* (Paderborn: Schöningh, 2002).

Robertson, Anne Walters, *The Service Books of the Royal Abbey of Saint Denis* (Oxford: Clarendon Press, 1991).

Schiller, Gertrud, *Iconography of Christian Art* (vol. 1; London: Lund Humphries, 1971).

Shapiro, Meyer, 'The Religious Meaning of the Ruthwell Cross', *Art Bulletin* 26 (1944), 232–45.

Treitler, Leo and Ritva Jonsson, 'Medieval Music and Language: A Reconsideration of the Relationship', in Ellen Beebe (ed.), *Music and Language* (Studies in the History of Music, vol. 1; New York: Broude, 1983), pp. 1–23.

Ziegler, Joseph, 'Ochs und Esel an der Krippe', *Münchener Theologische Zeitschrift* 3 (1952), 385–402.

Chapter 6

IN PERSONA MARIAE: SINGING THE SONG OF SONGS AS A PASSION COMMENTARY

William T. Flynn

The second vespers service for the Feast of the Compassion of Mary (Friday before Good Friday) is designed to enable the clerical choir to 'see' the passion through Mary's eyes. Playing upon patristic and mediaeval exegesis of the Song of Songs,[1] in which the *sponsa* (bride) was understood in three allegorical personae (the church, the individual soul, and the Virgin Mary), this service produces a performative passion commentary. It developed from devotions that first took similar forms in twelfth-century monastic institutions, and later drew upon popular devotional practices. In this essay, I will first briefly discuss the various influences that formed the service as it is now transmitted in modern chant books, and then describe the service in detail, highlighting its sources in biblical exegesis that helped mediaeval singers interpret it. These same sources can inform a modern reader about its content and intended effect. Along the way, I will consider the different personae a singer was invited to adopt when performing the service, a feature that creates its unusual multiple 'perspectives on the passion'.

In its structure, if not in all of its music, the version of the service published by the abbey of Solesmes is thought to date from the late fifteenth century, when specific feasts focusing on Mary as a sharer in Christ's suffering were first officially promulgated.[2] The sequence *Stabat*

---

1 For an overview of the commentary tradition up to the thirteenth century, see E. Ann Matter, *The Voice of My Beloved: The Song of Songs in Western Medieval Christianity* (Philadelphia: University of Pennsylvania Press, 1990). See also Mary Dove (ed.), *Glossa Ordinaria: Pars 22, In Canticum Canticorum* (*CCCM* 170; Turnhout: Brepols, 1997), pp. 3–70 for detailed information on the gloss tradition.

2 *Liber Usualis* (Tournai: Desclée, 1952), pp. 1422–55. The Cantus database <http://publish.uwo.ca/~cantus/aboutms3.html#augs4304> (accessed 18 April 2006) currently lists only two manuscripts that contain the same antiphon series as the *Liber usualis*. (These are München, Bayerische Staatsbibliothek, Clm 4306, copied in 1501, and Clm 4304, copied in 1519. Both were copied about a century after the first official promulgation of the feast in 1413.) Both manuscripts stem from the monastery of SS. Ulrich and Afra in Augsburg, but

mater dolorosa, assigned to the feast's mass, was suppressed by the Council of Trent, but in 1727, when the service was revived, it was divided into three sections to be sung as the hymn for the prayer offices of the feast.[3] However, in the Middle Ages, the practice of singing the sequence as a substitute for the second vespers hymn was well established, so it is likely that in the late fifteenth century the *Stabat mater* was sung in its entirety at both the mass and the vespers office.[4] Moreover, it is possible that in earlier versions of the service another hymn focusing on Mary's experience of the crucifixion was originally sung at vespers and then later displaced by the *Stabat mater*.

The most striking influence upon this service is the use of biblical exegesis of the Song of Songs to construct the antiphon series. Unlike other late-mediaeval services focusing on the compassion of Mary, the antiphons do not focus directly on the emotions of Mary, but instead the service uses a series of antiphons that is intended to be read allegorically. Throughout the Middle Ages, the erotic love poetry of the Song of Songs, celebrating the betrothal of a regal bride (*sponsa*) and groom (*sponsus*), was read as a description of the love between humanity and God. Specific allegorical readings were employed to draw out various facets of this relationship, the most common of which were: (1) the love of the church (*ecclesia*) and God (developing the Pauline metaphor of the church as Christ's bride in Eph. 5.23); (2) the love of the soul (*anima*) and God; or (3) the love of the Virgin Mary and God.

The Marian reading had initially been developed within the liturgy and, by the seventh century, liturgies that commemorated her birth, purification and assumption used selected verses from the Song of Songs to describe the special favour bestowed upon her.[5] Moreover, in the twelfth century, a few writers produced commentaries on the Song of Songs in which Mary was systematically considered as the *sponsa*. As Matter points out, such commentaries incorporated many features of the earlier traditions into a multivalent commentary in which:

> Mary is totally identified with the female speaker of the Song of Songs and then she is interpreted according to the standard modes of Song of Songs exegesis. According to the allegorical mode, Mary becomes here not only the symbol of the church, but the embodiment of it. On the

---

are generally uncharacteristic of most South German manuscripts and show Italian Franciscan influence. I think, however, that the core of the service (the antiphons and psalmody) may date from as early as the twelfth century.

3   John Caldwell, 'Stabat mater dolorosa', in Laura Macy (ed.), *Grove Music Online* <http://www.grovemusic.com> (accessed 18 April 2006). Cited hereafter as *GMO*.

4   Caldwell, 'Stabat mater', notes that while the melody for this text given in the *Liber Usualis* on p. 1424 dates from the eighteenth century, there is a fifteenth-century melody given for the sequence on p. 1634v.

5   Matter, *Voice of My Beloved*, pp. 151–2.

tropological level, she is also the model of monastic virtues: virginity, humility and obedience.[6]

For this reason, writers and readers of such commentaries were able to keep in play the multiple traditional levels of allegory, using the text not only to honour Mary, but to interpret salvation history through the model of Christ's incarnation, and to model their own lives on the idealized model of Mary.

Although the antiphon series for this service is archaic, the sequence/ hymn *Stabat mater* shows the influence of later mediaeval devotion and poetic technique. It is a fully rhymed poem in accentual verse that first concentrates on Mary's suffering at the cross, and these features place it within the tradition of singing 'complaints of Mary' (*planctus Mariae*). Such songs, written in the voice of Mary, were already found in the twelfth century, but by the end of the thirteenth century were known not only in Latin but also in seven vernaculars.[7] By the mid-fifteenth century, they could be sung as an elaborate rite, sometimes during the Good Friday office itself and usually before a cross set up in the middle of the church.[8] (A similar emphasis can be found in the other late-fifteenth-century antiphon series for the Compassion service, which focuses directly on Mary's emotions, and which is constructed in rhymed hexameter or accentual verse.)[9]

A second and even more prominent influence on the *Stabat mater* was the tradition of meditating on Christ's passion (through contemplating Mary's compassion), in order to produce an affective response. This builds upon a long tradition of meditating on the passion story from the perspective of Jesus' women followers, who, unlike most of the male disciples, did not abandon him at the cross (Mt. 27.55-56; Mk 15.40-41; Lk. 23.55-56) and who play the important part in the Easter story of being the first to find the empty tomb and receive the message of the resurrection (see especially the Easter Day Gospel lection: Mk 16.1-8). For example, in the twelfth century, Abelard produced hymns, sermons and other liturgical materials that masterfully reinterpreted the Easter Triduum liturgy at the Paraclete as an affective 'passover' (*transitus*) from lament to joy, singling out the example of the women disciples as a model for

---

6   Matter, *Voice of My Beloved*, p. 163.

7   John Stevens, 'Planctus', *GMO* (accessed 18 April 2006).

8   John Stevens and Richard Rastall, 'Medieval Drama III, 2, i', *GMO* (accessed 18 April 2006).

9   For a representative selection of the rhymed offices, see Guido Maria Dreves (ed.), *Analecta hymnica medii aevi. Historiae Rhythmicae: Liturgische Reimofficien des Mittelalters* (vol. 24; Leipzig: Reisland, 1896), pp. 122–53.

Heloise's nuns.[10] Indeed, Abelard's so-called moral-influence theory of the atonement gave a theological rationale for creating such devotions, as it tended towards defining the nature of Christian salvation as a continual conversion of one's interior disposition towards Christ, in response to his sacrificial love.

Although the *Stabat mater* was influenced by these traditions, it has a distinctly Marian focus. Not only does its opening reflect upon Mary's suffering at the cross, but its later strophes directly address Mary, asking that she grant the singer a share in Christ's passion, and they suggest that the singer's salvation depends on his affective response. Strophes 17–18 are particularly extreme in their language:

> Fac me plagis vulnerari,   Flammis ne urar succensus,
> Fac me cruce inebriari,   Per te Virgo, sim defensus
> Et cruore Filii.   In die judicii.

(Make me to be wounded by his wounds, / make me drunk on the cross / and the gore of your Son. // Lest I, set on fire, be burned with the flames; / by you, O Virgin, may I be defended / on the day of judgement.)

Thus, the new, locally promulgated, Latin service of the Compassion of Mary in the later Middle Ages was influenced by two well-established monastic practices present especially in the twelfth century: the allegorical interpretation of the Song of Songs and the practice of affective meditation on the passion. These two practices were increasingly focused on reflecting on Mary's role, both as the *sponsa* of the Song of Songs and in the passion story. Perhaps the new Latin service, which eventually was assigned to the Friday before Good Friday, was originally intended to displace the popular Good Friday devotional practices with a more restrained, scholarly and decorous service. However, it is equally probable that this service represents a fifteenth-century updating of an earlier votive service that had twelfth-century monastic roots, whether it arose in central France out of Abelard's theological and liturgical legacy, or in South Germany, where (as will be seen below) the systematic Marian interpretations of the Song of Songs were especially influential.

Like most festal vespers services, the service for the Feast of the Compassion of Mary consists of the standard opening sentences (versicle and response), five antiphons each introducing and following a proper psalm, a truncated Scripture reading, a hymn followed by another short versicle and response, and an antiphon and Gospel canticle (the

---

10   See my 'Letters, Liturgy and Identity: The Use of the Sequence *Epithalamica* at the Paraclete', in Gunilla Iversen and Nicolas Bell (eds), *Sapientia-Eloquentia* (Turnhout: Brepols, June 2008).

Magnificat); the service concludes with prayers, the Lord's prayer, the collect for the day, and a blessing.

The core of the service is the series of antiphons which introduce and conclude their psalms, and the intertextual relationships between them are complex. As will be seen below, the careful selection of the psalms creates the possibility of interpreting them as a progression through the events of the passion.[11] However, the allegorical use of the psalms (most often with reference to Christ) was supplemented by other traditional interpretations of the same psalms, whereby the message of the psalm could equally refer to the spiritual life of the singer (a tropological interpretation) or indeed (with literal or allegorical reference) to Old Testament events or people. The tendency (even in dialectical analysis) was to treat alternate readings of equal authority as complementary to each other rather than as mutually exclusive. Moreover, the variety of interpretations does not stem merely from a fecundity of allegorical imagination, but from the nature of the psalms themselves. They were read not only as allegories or prophecies of Christ (as in the New Testament text itself), but also as prayers of the temple, as prophecies of David about Israel, as the principal prayers of the synagogue and the church, and as the individual prayers of the singer. A set of these basic interpretations destined for a clerical choir can be found in the useful commentary (assembled largely from commentaries by Jerome, Augustine, Cassiodorus, and Bede) by Bruno of Würzburg (c. 1005–45), and in describing the service, I will make reference to his summary of common interpretations.

For the Song of Songs, the commentary by Rupert of Deutz (c. 1075–1129/30 or 1135) is particularly useful for finding how mediaeval exegetes connected the Song of Songs both to Mary and to the passion narrative: it was one of the earliest to develop a systematic reading of the book with Mary as the *sponsa*, and it is perhaps not coincidental that Rupert connects each verse used in this service to the passion. His commentary is mostly conducted in direct devotional address to the Virgin Mary and focuses on Christ's incarnation as its central instance of God's love for humanity.

The multivalency of the quoted Scripture (provided by allegorical exegesis) is an important feature of the service for the Feast of the Compassion of Mary, since it underwrote the practice of singing the words both as one's own and in the personae of the various putative speakers assigned within the text itself (or within traditional interpret-

---

11 A new interest in coordinating 'historical' and 'liturgical' time was a prominent feature of revised liturgies in the twelfth century. For example, Abelard's Triduum hymn cycle provides a hymn for each prayer hour that consists of a description of the events of the passion at those specific hours (many of which are mentioned in the biblical narrative). See Flynn, 'Letters, Liturgy and Identity', June 2008.

ations). The singers of this service were thus aware of a complex set of relationships they might take to the texts they sang.

While allegorical interpretation of Scripture offered a variety of suitable possibilities for the singers, the overall structure of the service suggests that the choir would adopt specific personae at various points, because it has a very strong sense of narrative and dramatic progression. The narrative progression was achieved by arranging the materials in an order that alludes to specific stages of the passion, while the sense of an unfolding drama was created by a careful use of first-person delivery of the texts. Although the singers declaim in the first person in all of the psalms and in many of the antiphons, sometimes the gender of the speaker is intentionally indeterminate, and at other times the singers' 'I' is specifically feminine or masculine. Moreover, the range of these personae is influenced by traditional interpretations that are not reflected in the texts themselves but might be attributed through the singers' memory of them and their association of them with particular speakers. The result is that the singers are sometimes taking on a persona other than their own or adding that persona to their personal 'I'. The purpose of this progression in personae is to create an allegorical dialogue between Mary and Christ, bringing Mary's experience in the passion into progressively clearer focus, after which the singers' own compassionate response to Mary's compassion becomes the focus of the service.

When sung in the context of the overall structure of the service, even the seemingly standard opening sentences, 'God come to my assistance; Lord make haste to help me'[12] (which begin every vespers service), bring liturgical connections to the passion narrative to the fore. They consist of Ps. 69.2-3, which has a proper use in the matins service on Holy Thursday, where it is interpreted as an anticipation of Christ's prayers to the Father in Gethsemane. (It is also sung every Thursday at compline, perhaps in anticipation of the weekly Friday fast commemorating the passion.) Thus the opening sentences set up a reference to a particular time and place in the passion narrative: Holy Thursday, in the middle of the night, before the events of the day. Moreover, the opportunity of connecting Ps. 69 with the passion could encourage the choir to adopt a double persona, singing the words of the psalmist not only as their own prayer for aid, but also in an active anticipation of their communal remembrance of Christ's prayers on Mount Olivet (which would take place on the following liturgical day and night). As pointed out above, neither of these interpretations would have been thought to exclude the other: instead, the continuity (not the distinction) between the two was the goal of such allegorical methods of interpretation.

12   Biblical translations are based on the Douay-Rheims edition and the Latin numbering of the psalms is followed.

The first antiphon, like all the antiphons, consists of a short verbatim quotation from the Song of Songs: 'Vadam ad montem myrrhae, et ad colem thuris' (Cant. 4.6b) ('I will go to the mountain of myrrh, and to the hill of frankincense'). By evoking the metaphor of a journey, it enables the singers to announce the whole purpose of the service: in their own personae, they intend to 'walk' (by performing the service) through the stages or *loci* of the passion traditionally associated with the antiphon. However, since this antiphon is assigned to the *sponsus*, the singers are also allegorically singing *in persona Christi* (reinforcing the ambiguity of persona in the opening sentences). Moreover, since (in the Song of Songs) these words are addressed to the *sponsa*, the choir directly addresses Mary (albeit allegorically) by singing them. This is the line taken in Rupert of Deutz's commentary, where he discusses this verse in the context of vv. 6-7 (which were used in the liturgy for the Feast of the Assumption): the *sponsus* (Christ) explains to the *sponsa* (Mary) that, before she may be acknowledged as *tota pulchra* (all fair) and as having *non maculata* (no blemish) (Cant. 4.7), he (the *sponsus*) must go to the mountain of myrrh (interpreted as Jerusalem, where Jesus will be beaten, crucified and killed) and to the hill of frankincense (interpreted as Christ's resurrection and the consequent worship of him as God, one with the Father and the Spirit).[13]

The psalmody used for this liturgy is a variation on the normal ferial psalmody for Fridays (which is appropriate, since every Friday was considered to be a commemoration of the passion). However, the normal first and second psalms (comprising Ps. 138, sung in two sections) were replaced in this service with Pss. 115 and 119. Although Ps. 138 was interpreted as speaking of both the passion and resurrection, its references are sweeping, and could be taken to cover too much of the narrative. The alternate series beginning with Ps. 115 has a more limited set of references, and its use of future tense throughout means that any references that could be associated with later events in the passion narrative may be read as prophecy or anticipation. Thus it may be read as reminiscent of the events of the Last Supper: the psalmist calls 'every man a liar' (v. 2), takes up 'the chalice of salvation' (v. 4), identifies himself as 'thy servant and the son of thy handmaid' (v. 7), and pays his 'vows in the ... midst of Jerusalem' (v.10). Like the opening versicle and first antiphon, it can be interpreted as continuing *in persona Christi*; however, its traditional associations are broader. Bruno (quoting Cassiodorus) gives the following summary of the argument of Ps. 115: 'Vox martyrum invictorum, qui gloriosam mortem pro Christi nomine sustinuerunt' ('The voice of the unvanquished martyrs, who have sustained a glorious death in Christ's

---

13   R. Haacke (ed.), *Rupertus Tuitiensis Commentaria in Canticum canticorum (de incarnatione domine)* (*CCCM* 26; Turnhout: Brepols, 1974), p. 177. Cited hereafter as Rupert of Deutz, *Commentaria*.

name').[14] Singing this psalm, the choir, adopting its 'I', put themselves in continuity with all who are persecuted in the name of Christ. They remember in a particularly active way (even if common in liturgy), by narrating as if the events that they commemorate actually happened to them personally.

The second antiphon conflates two verses (Cant. 5.10a and 7.5b) from the Song of Songs: 'Dilectus meus candidus et rubicundus: comae capitis ejus sicut purpura regis vincta canalibus' ('My beloved is white and ruddy: the hairs of his head are like purple of the king, bound in channels'). Although sung again in the first person, this 'I' is the feminine 'I' of the *sponsa* singing to her male beloved (*dilectus*). This is an abrupt change of persona, but does not necessarily transgress gender boundaries as dramatically as it might seem. In tropological (moral actionary) exegesis of the Song of Songs, the grammatically feminine soul (*anima*) of any human being was often understood as Christ's bride. Here the ambiguity of persona seems to have been constructed in order for the choir to gain a double perspective. *In persona Mariae*, they sing of her compassion for her son, and in their own personae share in her suffering compassionately. In the context of the Song of Songs, the Daughters of Zion have asked the *sponsa* to describe her beloved, and the description is explained by Rupert using traditional references to Christ: the beloved is white because of his sanctity and ruddy because of his suffering (*passio*).[15] Rupert also connects the conflated portion of the antiphon to the passion: the hair of his head refers to the senses of the heart meditating on the laws of God, and these are royal purple, in commemoration not only of the blood poured out in his passion, but also of the cloth of royal purple put on him when he was mocked.[16] Finally, it is important to note that the tense of the service has now shifted from future to present. The shift in tense suggests that the journey anticipated in the first antiphon has now commenced.

For the most part, the present-tense narration continues in the second psalm (119), but it is (intentionally) not clear who is speaking, as the speaker's gender is not grammatically identified. Since it is a prayer for deliverance it could (at one allegorical level) follow the idea of a temporal remembrance of the events of the passion and be connected to Christ's betrayal and trial before Herod. It mentions crying 'to the Lord in my trouble' (v. 1), prays for deliverance from 'the sharp arrows of the mighty' (v. 4), and stresses the innocence of the sufferer: 'they fought against me without cause' (v. 7). As such a remembrance, the choir would again

---

14   Bruno of Würzburg, *Expositio psalmorum* (*PL* 142, cols 1–530, (col. 420D). Cited hereafter as Bruno, *Expositio*.
15   Rupert of Deutz, *Commentaria*, p. 118.
16   Rupert of Deutz, *Commentaria*, p. 152.

speak *in persona Christi*. However, it could also be the prayer of any person undergoing persecution. For example, Bruno in summarizing its argument applies it to the whole church: 'Ecclesia deprecatur, ut ab iniquo diabolo liberetur: vindictam dicens in futuro judicio super eos venturam, qui pauperes ejus insanis motibus persequuntur' ('The church prays so that she may be delivered from the hostile devil, saying that she will be vindicated in the future judgement over those who persecute the poor from monstrous motives'). As pointed out above, such an ambiguity in identifying the personae most likely underwrites a flexibility in which the multiple possible meanings become part of the point of the performance. Moreover, since the traditional interpretation applies to the whole of the church, a performance *in persona Mariae* as representative of the feminine personified *Ecclesia* might be an alternative emphasis, continuing the persona of the antiphon which precedes and follows the psalm.

The third antiphon consists of a question addressed to the *sponsa*: 'Quo abiit dilectus tuus, o pulcherrima mulierum? quo dilectus tuus declinavit?' (Cant. 5.17) ('Whither is your beloved gone, O thou most beautiful among women? Whither is your beloved turned aside?'). In the Song of Songs, the question is asked by the Daughters of Jerusalem and addressed to the *sponsa*. This verse was often connected with Mary Magdalene's seeking Jesus after his death and resurrection, but Rupert avoids this traditional association, as he must always interpret the *sponsa* as the Virgin Mary. Indeed, Rupert does not directly comment on this verse, but instead comments on the answer the *sponsa* gives to the question in 6.1: 'My beloved has gone down into his garden'. Rupert brings in the association with Christ's death and resurrection by interpreting the garden as a metaphor for heaven, where Christ gathers lilies, i.e. sanctified souls.[17] The traditional associations of this verse disrupt the temporal sequence (i.e. following the passion events) established in the psalmody, but taken at a literal level, the answer to the question might be that the beloved has gone to another garden, the garden of Gethsemane, and has been taken prisoner and is therefore no longer present.

The third psalm (139) reinforces the connection to the sequence of events in the passion. It was sung not only in the Friday office, but also as the second tract on Good Friday, just before the reading of the Johannine passion account; its cry 'Deliver me from the evil man' (v. 1) was therefore closely associated with events of Good Friday, especially the trial before Pilate, which is described in detail in John's account (Jn 18.28–19.16). The psalm speaks of people devising 'iniquities' (v. 2), speaking with sharp 'tongues like a serpent', laying a 'snare' and a 'stumbling block' (v. 5), and refers to 'the head of them compassing me about' (v. 9). The second part

17   Rupert of Deutz, *Commentaria*, p. 131. For the alternative tradition, see Gregory the Great, *Homily* 25 (on Jn 20.11-18), in *PL* 76, cols 1189–1190.

of the psalm (vv. 10–14) prays for God's just intervention and restitution. On the other hand, Bruno's summary of Ps. 139 focuses on the psalmist himself and equates the rejection of the authentic prophecy of the psalmist with hatred of Christ.[18] This suggests that Bruno was thinking of the Johannine portrayal of the Jews in the passion narrative, even though he does not focus on this. For the singers of the service, the triple association of personae would be a common feature of the normal use of the psalm on Fridays.

The fourth antiphon again refers to a male beloved (*dilectus*) and also (like the first antiphon) to myrrh: 'Fasciculus myrrhae dilectus meus mihi, inter ubera mea commorabitur' (Cant. 1.12) ('A bundle of myrrh is my beloved to me; he shall abide between my breasts'). This verse occurs quite early in the Song of Songs, so Rupert's focus is on Mary bearing Christ and giving the infant Jesus her maternal care. Even so he makes connections to the passion narrative, as myrrh always traditionally signifies burial. Rupert interprets the *sponsa's* description of her beloved as a 'bundle of myrrh' who 'will abide between her breasts' as a reference to Simeon's prophecy that 'a sword shall pierce your [Mary's] soul' (Lk. 2.35). Rupert's commentary is particularly dramatic; he concludes with Mary speaking directly to the *sponsus*:[19]

> Cum igitur carne mea taliter progenitum talem filium sinu meo fouerem ulnis gestarem uberibus lactarem et talem eius futuram mortem semper prae oculis haberem et prophetica immo plus quam prophetica mente praeuiderem qualem quantum quam prolixam me putatis materni doloris pertuillise passionem. Hic est quod dico: *fasciculus myrrhae dilectus meus mihi inter ubera mea commorabitur*. O commoratio dulcis quidem sed plena gemitibus inenarrabilibus.

> (Therefore, since I was thus keeping such a first-born son warm with my flesh at my breast, cradled in my arms, fed milk from my breasts, and was holding the manner of his future death always before my eyes, and through a prophetic, indeed more than prophetic, insight, was foreseeing that you would know the kind of passion of maternal sadness I would bear (as intense as it was lengthy), this is what I say: *A bundle of myrrh is my well-beloved to me; he shall abide between my breasts.* O sweet tarrying indeed, but full of unutterable grief.)

As with the second antiphon, the choir sings the fourth antiphon in a feminine persona, whether of their own *animae* or *in persona Mariae*. The highly gendered language of the antiphon text and the ways in which the Marian interpretation highlights the maternal associations are

18 See Bruno, *Expositio*, cols 461C–62D.
19 Rupert of Deutz, *Commentaria*, pp. 31–2.

particularly effective in shifting the focus to the compassion of Mary, i.e. her suffering in compassion with her son.

Bruno again applies the following psalm (140) principally to the psalmist, who prays that his own errors will not make him fall into the webs of sinners.[20] Nevertheless, this psalm's potential allegorical connections to the passion are clear and help explain why it became part of the ferial psalmody for Fridays: the psalmist cries out to the Lord 'hearken to my voice' (v. 1) (perhaps reminding the singers of Jesus' cry quoting Ps. 22, 'My God, my God, why have you forsaken me?'). The text then refers to 'the lifting up of my hands as an evening sacrifice' (v. 2). There are also veiled allusions which could remind the singer of the earthquake: 'when the thickness of the earth is broken up upon the ground' (v. 7) and the resurrection: 'I am alone until I pass-over' (*transeam*) (v. 10).

The fifth antiphon seems to continue the voice of the *sponsa*, and apparently shifts the meaning of the text as it occurs in the Song of Songs from an eroticized love-sickness towards lament: 'Fulcite me floribus, stipate me malis, quia amore langueo' (Cant. 2.5) ('Stay me up with flowers, compass me about with apples, because I languish with love'). However, Rupert's interpretation connects the idea of love-sickness with the passion narrative, attributing the sickness to the absence of the *sponsus* and the *sponsa's* desire for him. He interprets this verse as a meditation on the appropriate comfort given to the *sponsa* through the presence of her beloved, first developing the metaphor of Christ as 'apple', contrasting the bad fruit of Eden with the good fruit of Mary's womb (Christ's humanity) and the good fruit of the Eucharist (Christ's continuing presence to the church). Stating that the *sponsa* languishes because of her beloved's absence (which he relates to Christ's suffering, death, burial, descent into hell, and ascension to heaven), he interprets the continuing presence of Christ to the *sponsa* as being shown by her good works (flowers) and her understanding of the fruit of eternal life (apples).[21]

In the context of the service, the *sponsus's* absence most fully connects to the death of Jesus on the cross, and even Bruno's summary of the traditional interpretation of the following psalm (141) emphasizes this connection:[22]

> Christus ad Patrem clamat, dolos Judaicae persecutiones exponens: liberarique se inferno deprecatur: quoniam omnium sanctorum fides in ejus resurrectione pendebat.
>
> (Christ cries out to the Father, describing the Jews' deceits, their

---

20 See Bruno, *Expositio*, col. 504A.
21 Rupert of Deutz, *Commentaria*, pp. 37–8.
22 See Bruno, *Expositio*, col. 506A.

persecutions: and prays that he may be freed from hell: since the faith of all the saints depends upon this resurrection.)

In the sequence of events established in this service, the potential allusions of Ps. 141 to the death of Jesus on the cross come to the fore: again the psalmist cries out to the Lord (v. 1), this time as his 'spirit fails' him (v. 3). He is abandoned and denied: 'I looked on my right hand and . . . there was no one that would know me' (v. 4). Crying out again (v. 5), the psalmist prays for divine aid:'for my 'persecutors . . . are stronger than I' (v. 6), and commends his soul (*anima*) to God's care: 'Bring my soul out of prison, that I may praise thy name: the just wait for me, until thou reward me' (v. 7). The combination of traditional interpretation and the appropriate echoes of the passion narrative make it likely that this psalm is delivered *in persona Christi*. This makes the shift back to the voice of the *sponsa* (when the antiphon repeats) an effective way of emphasizing the dual suffering of son and mother, with the singers unambiguously taking on the specific personae of each in turn.

The service continues with a short chapter reading from Isa. 53.1-2a: 'Who hath believed our report? And to whom is the arm of the Lord revealed? And he shall grow up as a tender plant before him, and as a root out of a thirsty ground.' It is likely that the rest of this chapter, describing the suffering servant and traditionally understood as a prophecy of Christ's suffering, was to be recalled in memory. The chapter is a third-person description and marks a change in voice for the service, which has been delivered almost entirely in the first person so far.

The change in voice continues for the first four strophes of the sequence *Stabat mater*, with a similar third-person description of the suffering of Mary at the cross:

> (1) The desolate mother was standing next to the cross weeping, while her son was hanging from it. (2) Into her groaning, sad, and sorrowful soul, a sword was thrust. (3) O how sorrowful and afflicted was that blessed mother of the only-begotten; (4) she who was grieving and lamenting, sweet mother, while seeing the torments of her illustrious son.

However, strophes 5–8 shift the focus from Mary's suffering to the singers, who question themselves about what would be an appropriate reaction to their witness of her suffering:

> (5) Who is the man who would not weep if he saw the mother of Christ in so great a humiliation? (6) Who would not be sorrowful to think on the mother of Christ mourning with her son? (7) For sinners of your kind, she sees Jesus in torments and subjected to beatings. (8) She sees her own sweet son dying desolate, as he breathes out his spirit.

Then in strophes 9–18 the singers pray unambiguously in their own personae (for the first time in the service), asking for an active participation in Christ's passion through sharing in Mary's compassion, and they directly address Mary:

> (9) Eya! Mother, fount of love, make me to know the strength of your sorrow, so that I may lament with you. (10) Make my heart burn with love of God, the Christ, so that I may be pleasing to him. (11) Holy mother, do the same, fix the pains of the cross strongly in my heart. (12) Having deigned to suffer so much for me, share the pains of your wounded child with me. (13) Make me cry devoutly with you, make me lament the crucifixion with you, until I come to live with you. (14) I desire to stand with you next to the cross, and to associate myself with you in lament. (15) O most bright Virgin of virgins, do not now be harsh to me: make me lament with you. (16) Grant that I may bear Christ's death, make me a partaker in his passion and recall his wounds. (17) Make me be wounded by his wounds, make me drunk on the cross and the gore of your Son. (18) Lest I, set on fire, be burned with the flames, by you, O Virgin, may I be defended on the day of judgement.

Finally the singers pray directly to Christ, although still invoking the intercession of Mary:

> (19) O Christ, when it may be that I depart from here, grant that I come to the victor's crown through your mother. (20) When my body dies, grant that the glory of paradise be given to my soul.

Even though it is emotional and personal, the text of the *Stabat mater* does not imply that the singers currently feel the affective piety they are praying for. Their inner thoughts are left private, and although the text is designed to move them, it carefully avoids making them claim a piety they may not experience. Thus, even though the service permits the choir to sing in their own personae, it does not become individualized. The following versicle and response underwrites the corporate nature of the service, summarizing the closing thoughts of the *Stabat mater* and changing the language from first person singular to plural: 'Ora pro nobis, Virgo dolorissima. Ut digni efficiamur promissionibus Christi' ('Pray for us, O most sorrowful Virgin, that we be made worthy of Christ's promises').

The next part of the service (antiphon and Gospel canticle) changes back to a third-person description. In this service, not only the canticle, but also the text of the antiphon (*Cum vidisset Jesus*) is taken from a Gospel reading (Jn 19.26-27a): 'When Jesus saw his mother and the disciple whom he loved standing next to the cross, he saith to his mother, "Woman, behold thy son." After that, he saith to the disciple, "Behold thy mother"'. Although the antiphon is delivered in descriptive language, in the third person, it also contains directly quoted speech of Jesus. This gives it the semi-dramatic quality of a passion reading. The narrative places the disciple (allegorically any Christian) into a filial duty towards Mary (allegorically the church) and into her maternal care. Here the gender of the disciple is clearly masculine. There is a final shift into first person for the Gospel canticle (Lk. 1.46-55), Mary's song of rejoicing (*Magnificat anima mea*) at the news that she is to bear Christ. This gives the singers one more opportunity to sing *in persona Mariae*, but the persona has been made more universal and corporate by its identification with the church. Nevertheless, as is the case in the allegorical strategy adopted throughout the service, both of these perspectives are tenable at the same time; the choice of which aspect an individual clerical singer may highlight would in the end depend upon his interior disposition and powers of meditation.

The final prayer concludes the service in this corporate and universalizing tone by invoking not only Mary, but all the 'saints standing by the cross'. Nevertheless, within this context it highlights both the original placement of the Magnificat in the infancy narratives (by referring directly to Simeon's prophecy) and emphasizes the goal of the service – that the singers participate actively in Mary's suffering:

> Deus, in cuius passione, secundum Simeonis prophetiam, dulcissimam animam gloriosae Virginis et Matris Mariae doloris gladius pertransivit, concede propitius: ut qui transfixionem eius et passionem venerando recolimus, gloriosis meritis et precibus omnium Sanctorum cruci fideliter astantium intercedentibus, passionis tuae effectum felicem consequamur.

> (O God, at whose passion, according to Simeon's prophecy, a sword of sorrow thrust through the most sweet soul of the glorious Virgin and mother Mary, graciously grant that we who remember to venerate her piercing and suffering, may, through the glorious merits and prayers of all the Saints standing by the cross faithfully interceding, attain to the happy effect of your passion.)

The service achieves its cumulative effect through its careful manipulation of the singers' personae. Building on the long tradition of allegorical interpretation of the Song of Songs and the later mediaeval tradition of its Marian interpretation, the first part of the service creates a ritual in which the singers re-enact the events of the passion in Mary's persona and in Christ's persona through the allegorical interpretation of the psalm series. The sequence *Stabat mater* then shifts the focus from an allegorical re-enactment of Mary's suffering to a description of her suffering, and this leads to a tropological response to her and to Christ in their own personae. The Gospel antiphon quotes Christ addressing Mary and the beloved disciple from the cross in words also found in ritual readings of the passion on Good Friday. These words are sung before and after Mary's words, the Magnificat, from the infancy narratives of Luke, reversing the relationship between the speakers of the antiphons and psalms from the beginning of the service. What was rehearsed allegorically in the antiphon series is thus displayed through literal quotation, and what was obscured through allegory becomes clear through the Gospel text itself. The final prayer takes up the theme of Simeon's prophecy which had been a refrain throughout the service (in the fourth antiphon's allegorical allusion to it, and in the *Stabat mater*'s reference to it) thus linking through a focus on Mary, the incarnation to the passion narratives. The allegorical, literal and tropological modes of response to the passion narrative can thus be seen to be carefully and artfully manipulated, allowing the singers to move easily from Mary's persona to their own personae, and to experience a biblical narration of her experience (in the Song of Songs) as their own.

References

Abbey of Solesmes, *Liber Usualis* (Tournai: Desclée, 1952).

Bruno of Würzburg, *Expositio psalmorum*, PL 142.

Caldwell, John, 'Stabat mater dolorosa', in L. Macy (ed.), *Grove Music Online* (accessed 18 April 2006) <http://www.grovemusic.com>.

Cantus database <*http://publish.uwo.ca/~cantus/aboutms3.html#augs4304*> (accessed 18 April 2006).

Dove, Mary (ed.), *Glossa Ordinaria: Pars 22, In Canticum Canticorum* (CCCM 170; Turnhout: Brepols, 1997).

Dreves, Guido Maria (ed.), *Analecta hymnica medii aevi. Historiae Rhythmicae: Liturgische Reimofficien des Mittelalters* (vol. 24; Leipzig: Reisland, 1896), pp. 122–53.

Flynn, William. T., 'Letters, Liturgy and Identity: The Use of the Sequence *Epithalamica* at the Paraclete', in Gunilla Iversen and Nicolas Bell (eds), *Sapientia-Eloquentia* (Turnhout: Brepols, forthcoming).

Gregory the Great, *Homily 25*, PL 76.

Grove Music Online <*http://www.grovemusic.com*>.

Haacke, R. (ed.), *Rupertus Tuitiensis Commentaria in Canticum canticorum (de incarnatione domine)* (*CCCM* 26; Brepols: Turnhout, 1974).

Matter, E. Ann, *The Voice of My Beloved: The Song of Songs in Western Medieval Christianity* (Philadelphia: University of Pennsylvania Press, 1990).

Stevens, John, 'Planctus', *Grove Music Online* (accessed 18 April 2006).
Stevens, John and Richard Rastall, 'Medieval Drama III, 2, i', *Grove Music Online* (accessed 18 April 2006).

Chapter 7

EMBLEM AND IRONY: PASSION NARRATIVE IN POST-REFORMATION HYMNODY

J. R. Watson

This essay is concerned with the development of the treatment of the passion story in the English hymn from the seventeenth century to the twentieth century. It is a complex and vivid story. Although until recently hymns have been neglected as a part of the literary 'canon', they offer insights into the perception of the passion that are both popular (in that a great many people read or sing hymns, perhaps more than those who read poetry) and theologically interesting. I have used the words 'emblem' and 'irony' to try to open up the subject in ways that do not oversimplify the hymns of the passion. They are neither 'objective' nor 'subjective', neither discontinuous with the Latin hymns of the pre-Reformation church nor continuous with them. There is both continuity and change.

Emblematically the story is one of continuity. George Herbert's 'The Sacrifice' is evidence of this.[1] It was not a hymn, but influenced many hymn writers, as Herbert's poetry did in general. As Rosemond Tuve has pointed out, 'The Sacrifice' is 'irremediably implicated in its past', most obviously in the *Improperia* or Reproaches of Good Friday, and the responsorial *O vos omnes qui transitis* ('O all ye who passe by, behold and see').[2] Continuity is similarly demonstrated by two of the greatest hymns on the passion, 'O sacred head, sore wounded' and 'Ah, holy Jesu, how hast thou offended'. 'O sacred head' is a translation of Paul Gerhardt's 'O Haupt voll Blut und Wunden', which is a translation of 'Salve caput cruentatum';[3] and 'Ah, holy Jesu' is a translation of Johann Heermann's

---

1 'The Sacrifice', in F. E. Hutchinson (ed.), *The Works of George Herbert* (Oxford: Clarendon Press, 1941), pp. 26–34.

2 Rosemond Tuve, *A Reading of George Herbert* (London: Faber & Faber, 1952), pp. 23–4.

3 Paul Gerhardt's 'O Haupt voll Blut und Wunden' (from Johann Crüger's *Praxis Pietatis Melica,* Frankfurt, 1656) was a translation of a Latin hymn (part of a hymn beginning 'Salve mundi Salutare') at one time attributed to Bernard of Clairvaux (1091–1133). It is now sometimes ascribed to Arnulf von Loewen (1200–51).

'Herzliebster Jesu, was hast du verbrochen', which is based on a Latin meditation of the eleventh century beginning 'Quid commisisti, dulcissime puer, ut judicaveris?'.[4] But in the period under discussion there is also a shift of emphasis. I attribute this to a concern, in the centuries after the Reformation, with individual experience and individual response. It is no longer sufficient to accept the passion narrative as given and interpreted by the church. The driving force of post-Reformation hymns is an interest in the self: the question uppermost in the mind is 'what does this event mean for me, and for my fellow human beings?' Thus the hymns reflect a Protestant concern with grace: in particular, with the extraordinary nature of grace, and the wonder of it.

One way of emphasizing that wonder is to use irony. I began with George Herbert and 'The Sacrifice', because the poem gains much of its force by the contrast between Christ as victim and Christ as God:

> They buffet him, and box him as they list,
> Who grasps the earth and heaven with his fist,
> And never yet, whom he would punish, miss'd:
>   Was ever grief like mine? . . .
>
> The souldiers lead me to the Common Hall;
> There they deride me, they abuse me all:
> Yet for twelve heav'nly legions I could call:
>   Was ever grief like mine?[5]

Here we are both involved in the drama by listening, and distanced from it by being aware of the irony. We hear the voice of the patient and passive Christ, but at the same time we are invited to analyse the situation, because we are reminded of the true nature of the *personae* involved. We are made to face the fact that the suffering figure is in fact the all-powerful, that grace comes through the agency of the divine victim. The point was made again by Henry Hart Milman, Dean of St Paul's in the early nineteenth century, in his Palm Sunday hymn 'Ride on, ride on in majesty', where the angels watch in amazement:

> Ride on! ride on in majesty!
> The wingèd squadrons of the sky
> Look down with sad and wondering eyes
> To see the approaching sacrifice.[6]

---

4   See J. R. Watson (ed.), *An Annotated Anthology of Hymns* (Oxford: Oxford University Press, 2002), p. 72.

5   George Herbert, 'The Sacrifice', lines 129–32, 153–6.

6   Henry Hart Milman, 'Ride on! ride on in majesty!', published in Reginald Heber, *Hymns written and adapted to the Weekly Church Service of the Year* (London, 1827). Text from the *English Hymnal* (London: Oxford University Press, 1906), no. 620.

The angels evidently have their orders not to interfere. Although Christ as God could call for twelve heavenly legions of them, he does not do so, which sharpens awareness of what the actions of Holy Week involve. Those actions deliberately refuse to play the divine card: they insist on limiting the encounters between Christ and his various interlocutors to human interactions. The angels have sad and wondering eyes, because they know what could have been, and consequently what *is*, with all its implications. It is an expression of the kenotic theory, in which Christ 'emptied himself of all but love', to use Charles Wesley's words.[7]

The result is an enhanced awareness of the action of grace. In addition to irony, there is surprise, sometimes in dramatic form. Charles Wesley uses a colloquial opening to produce tension:

> O Love divine! What hast thou done!
> Th' immortal God hath died for me!
> The Father's co-eternal Son
> Bore all my sins upon the tree:
> Th' immortal God for me hath died!
> My Lord, my Love is crucified.[8]

The exclamation 'What hast thou done!' can be an exclamation of wonder, and can be accusatory: God has done something amazing, and also something quite dreadful. It suggests something appalling, as indeed it is: how could such suffering be allowed to happen? The repetition of 'the immortal God', and the reminder that he is 'the Father's co-eternal Son', makes the same point as Herbert, that the crucified one is God. Herbert does it with bitter humour:[9]

> Then they accuse me of great blasphemie,
> That I did thrust into the Deitie,
> Who never thought that any robberie:
>   Was ever grief like mine?

But Christ the victim is not only the all-powerful. He is also the one who has done good, healing the sick and giving sight to the blind:

> Behold, they spit on me in scornfull wise,
> Who by my spittle gave the blind man eies,
> Leaving his blindnesse to mine enemies:
>   Was ever grief like mine?

---

7 From Charles Wesley's 'And can it be that I should gain', in Franz Hildebrandt and Oliver A. Beckerlegge (eds), *The Works of John Wesley. Volume 7: A Collection of Hymns for the use of the People called Methodists* (Oxford: Clarendon Press, 1983), pp. 322–3. This is the modern edition of the 1780 *Collection*, containing many of Charles Wesley's hymns.

8 Hildebrandt and Beckerlegge (eds), *A Collection of Hymns*, p. 114.

9 George Herbert, 'The Sacrifice', lines 61–4, 133–6.

This is the irony exploited thirty years after Herbert by Samuel Crossman, in 'My song is love unknown':[10]

> Why, what hath my Lord done?
>   What makes this rage and spite?
> He made the lame to run,
>   He gave the blind their sight.
>   Sweet injuries!
>   Yet they at these
>   Themselves displease,
>   And 'gainst him rise.

Crossman compresses the irony into the phrase 'sweet injuries!'. His hymn ends by echoing Herbert's 'The Sacrifice', to which it is clearly indebted:

> Here might I stay and sing,
>   No story so divine:
> Never was love, dear King,
>   Never was grief like Thine!

But he also begins the tradition, which is carried on more powerfully by Isaac Watts, of reflecting on his own position in relation to the passion of Christ. He asks two fundamental questions:

> O who am I
>   That for my sake,
> My Lord should take
>   Frail flesh, and die?

'O who am I?' is the cry that emerges from the great tragedies of Western literature, Oedipus's 'I will know who I am' and Lear's 'Who is it that can tell me who I am?' It is related to Crossman's other question, 'What may I say?':

> What may I say?
>   Heav'n was his home;
> But mine the tomb
>   Wherein He lay.

Christ is buried in the tomb of sinning humanity. The 'What may I say?' means not only 'How can I find words?' but also 'What on earth can I say about the responsibility which I have, and share with others, for this situation?' 'What can I say?' is the answer of someone who is accused of a crime and knows himself guilty.

The ironies focus on the figure of love, who is subjected to so much hate

---

10 Samuel Crossman, *The Young Man's Meditation, or some few Sacred Poems upon Select Subjects and Scriptures* (London, 1664). Text from the *Methodist Hymn Book* (London, 1933), no. 144.

– the spitting, the scourging, the crown of thorns, the carrying of the cross, the taunts from the impenitent thief. As Wesley put it, 'My Lord, my Love is crucified'. This is another example of the continuity of the tradition: it goes back to St Ignatius of Antioch and to Origen: 'Meus autem amor crucifixus est'.[11] It leads directly to Isaac Watts, who was a man greatly learned in the traditions and practices of meditation.

Watts knew his Latin poetry, especially the Jesuit Casimire Sarbiewski, known as the 'Christian Horace'. But his immediate inheritance was one of pedestrian metrical psalmody and great devotional poetry. He united the two in a way that transformed them both into a new art. The poetry of Herbert and the hymns of Crossman (notably 'My song is love unknown'), as we have seen, had sharpened an awareness of the fundamental irony inherent in the passion, and with it a series of emotions: horror, guilt, wonder, amazement. Now the intense contemplation of the suffering of Christ drives the beholder back upon him/herself, trying to understand his/her place in it. In Watts's 'When I survey the wondrous Cross',[12] as in Herbert's 'The Sacrifice', the singer is both a spectator of the scene and a part of it. The spectator hears Christ in Herbert's poem; he is a looker-on, a *spectator ab extra*, in Watts's hymn. Both involve the reader in complex processes of participation and analysis.

Watts's hymn has its origins in the emblem tradition. The visual element is strong:

> See from his head, his hands, his feet,
>   Sorrow and love flow mingled down;

It is a verbal equivalent of a seventeenth-century emblem book, with a portrayal of Christ on the cross, with words coming from his wounds. And yet it is too vivid to be just a picture or image. This is a moment at which the speaker clutches his neighbour's arm and says 'See!' From the apparent calm of the opening 'When I survey', the spectator changes with a rapidity that is disconcerting:

> My richest gain I count but loss,
>   And pour contempt on all my pride.

There is a disorientation here, a collapse of the initial stability: from surveying the scene, the spectator has been forced almost instantly to revise all his normal values and expectations. We are back with Crossman and the question 'O who am I?' The spectacle of the suffering Christ has

---

11   See the discussion of St Ignatius's Greek text and Origen's Latin alteration in J. B. Lightfoot, *The Apostolic Fathers* (London, 1885), II. Section I, 222–4.

12   Isaac Watts, *Hymns and Spiritual Songs* (London, 1707) Part III, 'Prepared for the Holy Ordinance of the Lord's Supper', hymn 8.

made Watts reflect that he has nothing to do with normal boasting and the normal world of charming things:

> Forbid it, Lord, that I should boast,
>   Save in the death of Christ my God;
> All the vain things that charm me most,
>   I sacrifice them to his blood.

We shall come across the word 'blood' later. At this point it is both the actual blood that issues from the wounds and also a metonymy for the processes of salvation, the dreadful action itself. The idea of sacrificing all worldly things before this amazing grace echoes the verse in Galatians that is the source of the hymn: 'But God forbid that I should glory, save in the cross of our Lord Jesus Christ, by whom the world is crucified unto me, and I unto the world' (Gal. 6.14). But it is also a recognizably human response, a perception that this event on Calvary requires us to abandon all ordinary values.

The spectator comes to view in what seems initially to be a rather detached way, and suddenly the scene turns nasty – or rather, the scene turns wonderful. From the head, the hands, the feet, comes something that marks the wounds and the pain, but that something, the blood and water, becomes sorrow and love. The beautiful chiasmus of sorrow and love, love and sorrow enacts the meeting of these opposites:

> See from his head, his hands, his feet,
>   Sorrow and love flow mingled down;
> Did e'er such love and sorrow meet,
>   Or thorns compose so rich a crown?

From the specific details of head, hands and feet, we have a sudden transition to love and sorrow. This seems at first like a traditional emblematic figuring, but it is more than that. It intimates something of the very nature of Christ himself. We say of someone that he is 'cold-blooded', or we say that something 'makes my blood boil', for blood is the signifier of character and temperament. Christ's blood is love-blood, sorrow-blood, for these are the constituents of his character: sorrow for the state of the world, and love for humanity. The chiasmus 'sorrow and love ... love and sorrow' means that in the verse we revisit these qualities, and become unsure which is the primary one. At the same time the rhetoric of repetition, so tactfully employed, deepens our realization of what is involved, as the mind comes to sorrow and love, and then comes back to it in the next line.

The sight of the blood, and the awareness of the suffering, is engaged with the thought that this is the act of love:

> His dying crimson, like a robe
>   Spreads o'er his body on the tree:
> Then am I dead to all the globe,
>   And all the globe is dead to me.

This is the chiasmus figure again, taken this time from the second part of Gal. 6.14. It recalls the chiasmus in the previous verse of Watts's hymn, but it also goes back to the sacrifice of all vain things, to the way in which the world is no longer significant in the light of the crucifixion.

In the final verse Watts's spectator reflects that 'Love so amazing, so divine,/Demands my soul, my life, my all'. Once again, there are complex forces at work here. This is a process which 'demands', and this is probably the single most demanding verse in English hymnody. But the subject of the sentence is 'Love', and this radically alters the perception of the exchange. If it is love that demands, then the demand becomes something very different from the demand of any other authority. Indeed, the last line is an assertion of the right to command, but that right is the right of love. And that love is indeed 'amazing'.

The word 'amazing' continues to appear in English hymnody throughout the eighteenth century as the key adjective to describe the love shown on the cross:

> Amazing love! How can it be
> That thou, my God, shouldst die for me?

This is from Charles Wesley's 'And can it be that I should gain', a hymn written shortly after his 'conversion' in 1738.[13] The phrases 'Amazing Love' and 'Amazing Grace' are found in Elizabeth Singer Rowe, Anne Steele, Blackmore, Newton, and in three other places in Watts.[14] The adjective signifies the wonder of the event, and is the chief encouragement to dwell on the crucifixion as the central event in the process of salvation. It is, in John Newton's words, the amazing grace 'that saved a wretch like me'. His co-author in *Olney Hymns* (1779), William Cowper, similarly stressed the importance of the crucifixion, but preferred not to look at it, except obliquely. He presents it in the form of another emblem, that of the fountain of blood drawn from the dying lamb:

> There is a fountain fill'd with blood
>   Drawn from EMMANUEL's veins;
> And sinners, plung'd beneath that flood,
>   Lose all their guilty stains.[15]

---

13 See Hildebrandt and Beckerlegge (eds), *A Collection of Hymns*, pp. 322–3.
14 See the Chadwyck-Healey *English Poetry Database* for these examples.
15 *Olney Hymns* (London, 1779), Book I, hymn lxxix (pp. 98–9).

The emphasis upon 'blood' begins to be very noticeable among evangelical hymn writers at this time. We are, in the words of Rom. 5.9, 'justified by his blood', because 'the blood of Jesus Christ ... cleanseth us from all sin' (1 Jn 1.7). Blood is here a synecdoche for life itself, the divine life that was given up on the cross. But it is also the blood which is drunk at Holy Communion. It takes us into a world in which we drink the blood to give us life. It signifies the blood that sprang from the hands and feet of Christ, and from the spear thrust into his side, but that becomes our saving drink. Charles Wesley describes it in an image which must, like Watts's hymn, have originated in an emblem, or at least in an iconographic representation:

> Then let us sit beneath his cross,
>   And gladly catch the healing stream,
> All things for him account but loss,
>   And give up all our hearts to him;
> Of nothing think or speak beside:
> 'My Lord, my Love is crucified'.[16]

The catching of the healing stream is possible only to those who are close to the cross. F. W. Faber, who knew the Methodist hymn books and the *Olney Hymns*, and who tried to produce an equivalent for Catholics, beckons to them insistently, urging them to come closer:

> O come and mourn with me awhile!
>
> See, Mary calls us to her side;
> Oh come and let us mourn with her;
> Jesus, our Love, is crucified![17]

When they have come, Faber invites them to stand and be washed in the fountain:

> Come, take thy stand beneath the Cross;
>   And let the Blood from out that Side
> Fall gently on thee drop by drop;
>   Jesus, our Love, is crucified.[18]

Faber links Wesley and Cowper. Wesley catches the blood, presumably in order to drink it; Cowper washes his sins white in it. Faber stands where Wesley sat, but he is beneath the fountain, being made clean. Protestant and Catholic writers are both emphasizing the power of the blood and the need for grace.

---

16 This is the final verse of Wesley's 'O Love divine, what hast thou done!', in Hildebrandt and Beckerlegge (eds), *A Collection of Hymns*, p. 115.

17 Frederick William Faber, 'Jesus Crucified', *Hymns* (1849), pp. 81–3.

18 Faber, 'Jesus Crucified', verse 10. *Hymns*, p. 82.

It is that divine response to the need for grace that informs another of Watts's great hymns on the passion of Christ, 'Nature with open volume stands'.[19] The argument of verse 1 is the traditional one of the *liber naturae*: the book of nature shows the glory of God the Creator. As Richard Baxter had written in 'The Resolution':[20]

> The World's thy Book: There I can read
> Thy Power, Wisdom, and thy Love:
> And thence ascend by Faith, and feed
>   Upon the better things above.

Watts uses Baxter's three attributes, but in a different context. His verse 2 claims that God's work as Redeemer surpasses anything that can be found in his work of creation:

> But in the grace that rescued man
>   His brightest form of glory shines;
> Here on the cross, 'tis fairest drawn
>   In precious blood, and crimson lines.

At first the blood and the crimson lines appear, as in 'When I survey', to be the blood trickling down from the wounds; but in the process they 'write' the name of Jesus 'complete'. His action is 'inscribed' by his blood, and it is of a complex kind, so that human beings are hard put to order it in any rational way (the hymn was clearly part of the ongoing debate between reason and faith at the time):

> Here his whole name appears complete;
>   Nor wit can guess, nor reason prove,
> Which of the letters best is writ,
>   The power, the wisdom, or the love.

His whole name appears complete. We expect 'Jesus of Nazareth the King of the Jews' (Jn 19.19), but we get three words – power, wisdom, love – as though the action has now been translated into its true and full meaning. That meaning is threefold, with none of the three elements pre-eminent. Watts then complicates matters even further, taking us deeper into the mystery of the divine figure on the cross:

> Here I behold his inmost heart,
>   Where grace and vengeance strangely join
> Piercing his Son with sharpest smart,
>   To make the purchased pleasures mine.

---

19 *Hymns and Spiritual Songs* (1707), Part III, 'Prepared for the Holy Ordinance of the Lord's Supper', hymn 10.

20 J. R. Watson (ed.), *An Annotated Anthology of Hymns*, p. 102.

O the sweet wonders of that cross,
  Where God the Saviour loved and died!
Her noblest life my spirit draws
  From his dear wounds and bleeding side.

The sacrifice of Christ is God's 'vengeance' for sin, but it is a strange and ironic vengeance because it is also grace. The word 'Piercing' that follows reminds us of the spear, and the pain of the 'sharpest smart', but by a daring opposition they generate pleasures. Those pleasures are dearly bought (purchased), and so the cross becomes a place of sweet wonders. The ironies are complex and all-pervading: the pain generates pleasure, the grace is vengeance, the wonders are sweet, the wounds are dear, the bleeding side gives life to his spirit.

The cross is terrible and yet glorious. Watts ends the hymn in wonder, love and praise:

I would for ever speak his name
  In sounds to mortal ears unknown;
With angels join to praise the Lamb
  And worship at his Father's throne.

The power of these hymns is immense. It comes from the presentation of Christ's suffering as truly terrible, as it is in some Christian art such as the Isenheim Altarpiece (so that realism takes precedence over the emblematic), combined with the awareness that this is the act of amazing grace. The situation, and the perception of it, provide an interplay of responses that sets up complex ironies. Thus Watts begins Hymn 9 in Book II of *Hymns and Spiritual Songs*:[21]

Alas! and did my Saviour bleed?
  And did my sov'reign die?
Would he devote that sacred head
  For such a worm as I?

Thy body slain, sweet Jesus, thine,
  And bath'd in its own blood,
While all expos'd to wrath divine
  The glorious suff'rer stood!

Was it for crimes that I had done
  He groan'd upon the tree?
Amazing pity! Grace unknown!
  And love beyond degree!

---

21 Isaac Watts, *Hymns and Spiritual Songs* (London, 1707), Book II, 'Composed on Divine Subjects', hymn 9.

There are three forces at work here: human sin, divine wrath (the 'vengeance' of 'Nature with open volume stands'), and standing between them as a bearer of human guilt, the suffering Christ. He 'devotes' (dedicates, gives over) his head to this purpose, the head contrasting with the worm underfoot. The process is summed up by the oxymoron 'glorious suff'rer', just as the cross becomes the 'dear cross' in a later verse. Remembering that darkness was upon the earth and that the sun was eclipsed, Watts reflects:

> Thus might I hide my blushing face,
>> While his dear cross appears;
> Dissolve, my heart, in thankfulness,
>> And melt, my eyes, to tears.

The commands ('Dissolve', 'melt') follow the pattern. There is a need to revise all human values in the light of the crucifixion. It is stated magisterially in 'When I survey'. At the same time, the reader or singer of these lines becomes an actor in a drama: he or she puts off the normal self and takes on the role of one weeping with thankfulness. To take part in the dramatic events of the passion is to come closer to them, even become a part of them in the imagination. This is the theme of James Montgomery's participatory 'Go to dark Gethsemane', where the singer is invited to follow Christ through each stage of the awful process:

> Follow to the judgement-hall;
>> View the Lord of Life arraigned.
> O the wormwood and the gall!
>> O the pangs His soul sustained!
> Shun not suffering, shame, or loss:
> Learn of Him to bear the cross.[22]

In these hymns we become human actors in a drama in which one of the characters is divine, a drama that is both human and superhuman. The passion of Christ is applied to the state and condition of sinful human beings: penitent humanity is represented by the 'dying thief' in Cowper's 'There is a fountain filled with blood', who 'rejoiced to see/That fountain in his day' and who is the recipient of mercy, even at the last moment.

In these hymns there is a perpetual sense of a double reading of events, an ironic perception of the emblem, with the cross as terrible and yet also glorious. The adjective most commonly applied to the first state is 'shameful', as it is by Samuel Wesley (John's father):[23]

---

22 James Montgomery, *The Christian Psalmist* (Glasgow, 1825). Text from the *Methodist Hymn Book* (London, 1933), no. 194.

23 Samuel Wesley's hymn was published in John Wesley's first hymn book, *A Collection of Psalms and Hymns* (Charles-town, 1737). Text from the *Methodist Hymn Book* (London, 1933), no. 193.

> Behold the Saviour of mankind
> Nailed to the shameful tree!

Or by Thomas Kelly, in 'The head that once was crowned with thorns', which celebrates 'the joy of all who dwell above' and 'the joy of all below':[24]

> To them the cross, with all its shame,
> With all its grace, is given, ...
>
> The Cross He bore is life and health,
> Though shame and death to Him; ...

The cross is associated with shame, as Christ is treated as a criminal. But in the longer perspective it is seen as sublime, as it is by Sir John Bowring:[25]

> In the Cross of Christ I glory:
> Towering o'er the wrecks of time,
> All the light of sacred story
> Gathers round its head sublime.

A light streams from the cross, which is efficacious in difficult times, when 'it glows with peace and joy', and which makes good times even more wonderful: 'From the cross the radiance streaming/Adds more lustre to the day'.

The cross has become emblematic. It is now a sign that incorporates the salvific event. It takes its place with 'the blood' (the American evangelist, Dwight L. Moody, said that he always preached 'the blood'). It is found earlier than the Romantic period, in Bunyan's *The Pilgrim's Progress* (Part I 1678, Part II 1684) and in the hymns of the evangelical revival. At the foot of the cross, Christian loses his burden from his shoulders. In Toplady's 'Rock of Ages, cleft for me' the cross becomes a lifebelt:[26]

> Nothing in my hand I bring,
> Simply to Thy Cross I cling.

The powerful verb 'cling' has a persistent life in relation to the cross. It occurs in the refrain of George Bennard's 'The Old Rugged Cross':[27]

24 Thomas Kelly, *Hymns on Various Passages of Scripture* (Dublin, 1820). Text from the *Methodist Hymn Book* (London, 1933), no. 244.

25 John Bowring, *Hymns* (1825). Text from the *Methodist Hymn Book* (London, 1933), no. 183.

26 Augustus Montague Toplady, *Psalms and Hymns for Public and Private Worship* (London, 1776). Text from the *Methodist Hymn Book* (London, 1933), no. 498.

27 George Bennard, 'On a hill far away stood an old rugged cross', from Iva D. Vennard, Joseph H. Smith and George Bennard (eds), *Heart and Life Songs* (Chicago, 1915). Text from *The Song Book of the Salvation Army* (London, 1986), no. 124.

> *So I'll cherish the old rugged cross*
> *Till my trophies at last I lay down;*
> *I will cling to the old rugged cross*
> *And exchange it some day for a crown.*

The laying down of the 'trophies' (presumably earthly achievements) is an echo of Isaac Watts's 'My richest gain I count but loss' and 'Then am I dead to all the world'.

The emblems of the cross and the blood are endlessly repeated in the evangelical hymns of the eighteenth and nineteenth centuries. They have become much loved, and are sung almost as mantras in some places. Ira D. Sankey's *Sacred Songs and Solos* contains many examples: one attraction must have been that they linked the salvific action of the crucifixion with the promise of eternal life in paradise.[28] The believer will cling to the cross and exchange it one day for a crown. In 'Beneath the Cross of Jesus/I fain would take my stand' Elizabeth Clephane writes of it as a Jacob's ladder:[29]

> O safe and happy shelter!
>   O refuge tried and sweet!
> O trysting-place where heaven's love
>   And heaven's justice meet!
> As to the exiled patriarch
>   That wondrous dream was given,
> So seems my Saviour's Cross to me
>   A ladder up to heaven.

In these hymns the common phrases are 'precious blood' and 'crimson tide':

> The blood has always precious been,
>   'Tis precious now to me;
> Thro' it alone my soul has rest,
>   From fear and doubt set free.
> *O wondrous is the crimson tide,*
>   *Which from my Saviour flow'd!*
> *And still in heaven my song shall be,*
>   *'The precious, precious blood!'*[30]

Evangelical hymns became very popular, in every sense of that word: they were greatly loved, and they became a part of the people's religious

---

28 Ira D. Sankey, *Sacred Songs and Solos* (London: Marshall, Morgan and Scott, rev. edn, *c.* 1900).

29 Elizabeth Cecilia Clephane, 'Beneath the Cross of Jesus', printed in the magazine *Family Treasury* (1872). Text of this verse from the *English Hymnal*, no. 567.

30 Macleod Wylie, 'The blood has always precious been', in Ira D. Sankey, *Sacred Songs and Solos*, no. 138.

culture. They evidently ministered to a human insecurity and a fear of death in ways that made them very attractive. They did so in verse that was simple and repetitive, the very repetitions reinforcing the simplicity of the message that Christ died for our sins that we might go to heaven. It is not surprising, however, that there was a contrary movement, most evident in the hymns of the Tractarians. Instead of 'At the Cross! At the Cross! Where I first saw the light' and 'Nothing but the blood of Jesus', there is the Oxford Movement's preferred 'Reserve in Communicating Religious Knowledge' (the title of Isaac Williams's Tract 80) as a reaction against evangelical familiarity, especially in relation to the passion story. Reserve avoids the obvious problems posed by certain views of the atonement, such as the notion of substitutionary punishment, found at its most obvious in P. P. Bliss's 'Man of Sorrows! What a name/For the Son of God who came':[31]

> Bearing shame and scoffing rude,
> In my place condemned He stood;
> Sealed my pardon with his Blood:
> Hallelujah! what a Saviour!

This suggests an inheritance from the Calvinism of Watts (though in Watts's case that is tempered by his tender humanity) enthusiastically adopted by evangelical fundamentalism. It is a doctrine which, in the words of John Macquarrie, 'even if it could claim support from the Bible or the history of theology, would still have to be rejected because of the affront which it offers to reason and conscience'.[32]

In opposition to the evangelical reading of the passion story, the nineteenth-century hymn writers offered two things. The first was a return to the ancient hymns of the early church, translated by writers such as John Chandler, Edward Caswall, Richard Mant and John Mason Neale. In the context of the passion story, the most obvious example is the *Stabat mater dolorosa*, translated by Caswall (in the best known of many translations) as 'At the Cross her station keeping'. The return of these hymns, neglected since the Reformation, lies behind the title *Hymns Ancient and Modern*, a title which carries the largest and most complex sub-text in hymnology, because it combined the 'ancient' hymns which satisfied the Anglo-Catholics with the 'modern' hymns of personal experience and reformed doctrine (many of them from Germany).

The second was a decent reticence, shown most remarkably in Newman's 'Praise to the Holiest in the height', where Newman dealt

---

31   Philip Bliss and Ira D. Sankey (eds), *Gospel Hymns No. 2* (1876). Text from the *Methodist Hymn Book* (London, 1933), no. 176.

32   John Macquarrie, *Principles of Christian Theology* (London: SCM, rev. edn, 1977), p. 315.

with the passion by producing what is, in effect, a neatly coded message.[33]
One verse gives the clue, as in a crossword puzzle, and the next verse gives
the answer:

> O generous love! that he who smote
>   In Man for man the foe,
> The double agony in Man
>   For man should undergo;
>
> And in the garden secretly,
>   And on the Cross on high,
> Should teach his brethren, and inspire
>   To suffer and to die.

This occurs in the middle of a careful and very beautiful rendering of 1
Corinthians 15. It draws attention, in the subtlest ways, to the providential workings of the God-Man in response to the Fall, workings which are
the expression not of anger but of generous love.

There are many views of the atonement, and it would require a
theologian, rather than a hymnologist, to deal with them adequately. The
hymns represented in this essay, however, form a distinctive body of
Protestant interpretations, continuing the pre-Reformation tradition of
iconographic representation of the crucifixion and the events that led up to
it, but emphasizing the individual need for grace. Thus Fred Pratt Green's
'Jesus in the olive grove', dating from 1965–67, and later part of a longer
'Hymn for Holy Week', provides quick portrayals of the crucial events:

> Jesus in the olive grove,
> Waiting for a traitor's kiss,
> Rises free from bitterness.
>
> As he wakes his comrades up,
> Torches flicker in the glen:
> Shadows turn to marching men.
>
> In that dawn of blows and lies
> Church and State conspire to kill,
> Hang three rebels on a hill.

Although these verses may remind us of Renaissance altar-pieces, with
panels depicting the unfolding events, they are also cinematic. The hymn
goes on to echo Charles Wesley's ''Tis mystery all! Th'immortal dies':

---

33   John Henry Newman, 'The Dream of Gerontius', published in *The Month* (May–June
1865). Text from the *English Hymnal*, no. 471.

It is God himself who dies!
God in man shall set us free:
God as Man – and only he.[34]

The first line contains the paradox that Wesley, and before him Herbert, was so keen to exploit in various ironic juxtapositions. But these hymns are emblematic in their placing of the cross at the centre of the process, the 'wondrous cross', with its promise of undeserved grace. In the evangelical hymns of the nineteenth century, that need becomes paramount, and can appear self-centred, as the sinner grasps at the cross in order to obtain salvation and a place in heaven; in the hymns of Isaac Watts and Charles Wesley the emphasis is rather on the transformation of the self that takes place through contemplation of the passion. Emblem and irony are allowed to speak, without the distortions of a clamour for individual preservation and salvation. Thus the greatest of all English hymns written on the subject since the Reformation ends not with a comforting assurance but with a demand. It is a demand for self-surrender, but a demand that is made, not by vengeance or anger, but by love:

Love so amazing, so divine
    Demands my soul, my life, my all.

References

Bliss, Philip and Ira D. Sankey (eds), *Gospel Hymns No. 2* (London, 1876).

Bowring, John, *Hymns* (London, 1825).

Clephane, Elizabeth Cecilia, 'Beneath the Cross of Jesus', printed in the magazine *Family Treasury* (1872).

Crossman, Samuel, *The Young Man's Meditation, or some few Sacred Poems upon Select Subjects and Scriptures* (London, 1664).

English Hymnal (London: Oxford University Press, 1906).

Faber, Frederick William, *Hymns* (London: Burns & Oates, 1849).

Green, Fred Pratt, 'Jesus in the Olive Grove', in *The Hymns and Ballads of Fred Pratt Green* (London: Stainer & Bell Ltd, 1982).

Heber, Reginald, *Hymns written and adapted to the Weekly Church Service of the Year* (London, 1827).

Hildebrandt, Franz and Oliver A. Beckerlegge (eds), *The Works of John Wesley. Volume 7: A Collection of Hymns for the use of the People called Methodists* (Oxford: Clarendon Press, 1983).

Hutchinson, F. E. (ed.), 'The Sacrifice', in *The Works of George Herbert* (Oxford: Clarendon Press, 1941), pp. 26–34.

---

34   Lines from 'Jesus in the olive grove' are reproduced from *The Hymns and Ballads of Fred Pratt Green* (1982), by kind permission of Stainer & Bell Ltd, London, England.

Kelly, Thomas, *Hymns on Various Passages of Scripture* (Dublin, 1820).

Lightfoot, J. B., *The Apostolic Fathers* (London, 1885).

Macquarrie, John, *Principles of Christian Theology* (London: SCM Press, rev. edn, 1977).

Methodist Hymn Book (London, 1933).

Montgomery, James, *The Christian Psalmist* (Glasgow, 1825).

Newman, John Henry, 'The Dream of Gerontius', in *The Month* (May–June 1865).

Newton, John and William Cowper, *Olney Hymns* (London, 1779).

Sankey, Ira D., *Sacred Songs and Solos* (London: Marshall, Morgan and Scott, rev. edn, *c.* 1900).

The Song Book of the Salvation Army (London, 1986).

Toplady, Augustus Montague, *Psalms and Hymns for Public and Private Worship* (London, 1776).

Tuve, Rosemond, *A Reading of George Herbert* (London: Faber & Faber, 1952).

Vennard, Iva D., Joseph H. Smith and George Bennard (eds), *Heart and Life Songs* (Chicago, 1915).

Watson, J. R. (ed.), *An Annotated Anthology of Hymns* (Oxford: Oxford University Press, 2002).

Watts, Isaac, *Hymns and Spiritual Songs* (London, 1707).

Wesley, John, *A Collection of Psalms and Hymns* (Charles-town, 1737).

Chapter 8

CHRISTIAN CANNIBALISM AND HUMAN(E) SACRIFICE:
THE PASSION IN THE CONVERSION OF THE AZTECS

Jaime Lara

Unless you eat the flesh of the Son of the Virgin, and drink His
blood, you shall not have life in you. Jn 6.53 (in the Náhuatl
translation by Fray Bernardino de Sahagún, *c.* 1540)

The passion of Christ has been one of the great themes of world art – the
visual, musical, dramatic and literary arts. It has absorbed the religious
imagination of believers and non-believers alike for nearly twenty
centuries, and has been an inexhaustible source of piety and inspiration.
My focus here is on the role of Christ's passion in the religious and
liturgical imagination at the moment when Christianity first met the
peoples of the New World in the sixteenth century, specifically the
indigenous cultures of central Mexico. My approach will be to examine
the material and visual culture as a source text at that missionary moment.

The area we today call Mexico, known then to the Spaniards as New
Spain, is the land of the great civilization of the Mexica. More commonly
known as the Aztecs, they were members of a group of Náhuatl speakers
of the Valley of Mexico, and hence are also known as Nahuas. New Spain
was the first theatre of operations on the American continent for the event
of the Contact – the encounter and collision of peoples, cultural patterns
and world hypotheses.

It is hard for us today to comprehend the worldview of the Aztec
civilization, which reached its apex at the turn of the sixteenth century.
This difficulty was even more acute for the first Europeans who invaded
the Americas; certainly it was a major obstacle to the conquistador
Hernán Cortés and his band of Spanish soldiers who landed at present-
day Veracruz on the very day of the passion, Good Friday, in the year
1519 (Fig. 1). The emissaries of the Aztec emperor Moctezuma were
already on hand, and their first act was to sacrifice several handsome
young slaves and to offer the dissected body parts to the new god, Cortés.
Every Mesoamerican understood that the gods fed on human flesh and

Figure 1. Arrival of Hernán Cortés under a rainbow at Veracruz, like Noah after the deluge. From Fray Bernardino de Sahagún, *Historia general de las cosas de Nueva España* (ed. Paso y Troncoso; Madrid: Fototipia de Hauser y Menet, 1905). (Public domain)

blood and so, logically, this white and bearded god, arriving providentially from the east with the rising sun, must also partake of that most holy rite of human consumption.[1]

While the lay conquistadors made little or no attempt to understand the native religion and practices, the mendicant missionaries certainly tried.[2] The Franciscans, Dominicans and Augustinians began arriving in 1523 in groups of twelve – like the apostles of the primitive Church and the

1 David Carrasco, 'Cosmic Jaws: We Eat the Gods and the Gods Eat Us', *JAAR* 63.3 (1995), 429–63. The early chronicles indicate that Cortés was mistaken to be the divinity Quetzalcoatl who in Mexica belief was a white man who had been banished to the east for opposing human sacrifice, and who would return one day to enact vengeance.

2 The ethnographic studies by friars like Andrés de Olmos, Diego Durán, Bernardino de Sahagún and the like are practically the only sources of information we have about pre-Hispanic practices. They employed native informants and scholars.

Figure 2. The twelve Franciscan apostles. Mural painting, San Miguel de Huejotzingo. (Photo: author)

prophesied disciples of the Last Days[3] (Fig. 2) – and they quickly came to appreciate that, in addition to a comprehension of the many languages, principally Náhuatl, they had to make sense of the bewildering number of deities and seemingly demonic rituals of their potential flock. To the biblically minded friars, the enormous and frightening temples, and the strange iconography, reminded them of the pagan temples of the Canaanites where human sacrifice had been practised in the days of the patriarchs.[4]

The Mexica were an extremely religious people, totally immersed in a sacred cosmos. They were pious polytheists, and foremost among their beliefs was the supposition that the fundamental function of rituals, public and domestic, was to avert catastrophe. There was a sentiment that most ills could be overcome by individual and communal self-assertion. These centred on forms of human sacrifice, or self-inflicted bleeding from the tongue, earlobes, limbs or foreskin, to induce fortunate events to take place and to prevent misfortune from prevailing. Did all this change with the arrival of the new religion of Christ?

3 A final world mission by groups of twelve 'apostles' had been prophesied by Joachim of Fiore in the twelfth century. See Jaime Lara, *City, Temple, Stage: Eschatological Architecture and Liturgical Theatrics in New Spain* (Notre Dame, Ind.: University of Notre Dame Press, 2004), pp. 65–8.

4 Writing at the end of the sixteenth century, Fray Juan de Torquemada, *Monarquía Indiana* (7 vols, Mexico City: Universidad Nacional Autónoma de México, 1983), 3:237 and 331, for example, used Josh. 22.1-20 to explain the Aztec temples.

One needs to remember that the evangelization of the New World coincided with the same years in which Luther, Calvin and others were separating themselves from the Roman Church on important issues like the sacrificial aspect of the Mass and the transubstantiation of the communion elements. Those very doctrines now needed to be instilled and dramatized in the New World among a people quite accustomed to sacred violence and ritual cannibalism. Therefore, among the many tasks confronting the missionaries was the need to rehabilitate the notion of sacrifice for the presentation of Christ's redeeming passion and death on Golgotha, and his real presence as body and blood in the food of the Eucharist.

Further complicating the situation was the belief among the friars that they had stumbled upon the Lost Tribes of Israel who, as everyone knew, would be found near the end of time, just prior to the final battle with the Antichrist and the return of Christ himself for the Last Judgement. Mesoamerican practices like circumcision, ritual priesthood, sacred scriptures, holocaust sacrifices, processions, relics, a liturgical calendar, and the like, seemed to point to some earlier evangelization and a subsequent perversion of Judaeo-Christianity, blamed of course on the presence of Satan in the New World.[5] Coincidentally, the Aztec religion, like mediaeval Christianity, had a strong apocalyptic strain and was expecting a proximate end to world history at the time when the European invaders arrived. In their eschatology, the Mexica understood themselves to be living in the time of the fifth and last solar age. This doomsday scenario of the extinction of the fifth sun would be the definitive end, when the powers of chaos and nothingness would win out.[6]

Meanwhile, like a living body, the fifth age had to be fed if its life were to continue; and its sustenance was human blood. In the temples, human beings were transformed into food for the 'cosmic jaws' of the sun. This act, via a process of divine ingestion, postponed the inevitable cosmic death by starvation. But just as the gods ate human beings so too humans ate the gods in an act of divine reciprocity.[7] This practice was made graphically real in Aztec art and rhetoric. Mesoamericanists agree that the unifying or 'root' metaphors among the Mexica were ones that derived

5   See, for example, Fernando Cervantes, *The Devil in the New World* (New Haven: Yale University Press, 1994), pp. 5–39. Fray Andrés de Olmos, mentioned in footnote 2 above, was a professional exorcist.

6   See Stephen Colston, 'No Longer Will There Be a Mexico', *American Indian Quarterly* 9 (1985), 239–58. Although Mesoamericans believed in a life after death, it was only a temporary state of existence before total annihilation. They had neither a notion of eternity nor of a place of reward and punishment like the Christian belief in heaven and hell.

7   Carrasco, 'Cosmic Jaws', pp. 429–63.

from the sun and, relatedly, from blood. Solar and sanguinal metaphors were so intertwined that it is hard at times to distinguish the two.[8]

The chronicles of eye-witnesses, the data provided by native informants, as well as archaeological remains today, demonstrate that human sacrifice was practised on a massive scale. Human oblations were taken from among the young and beautiful members of society – like lambs, spotless and without blemish – or they were the best of captives taken in holy war. Their selection for this sacred function was considered the highest honour, for in their sacrificial role they were transubstantiated into *ixiptla*, a word that can mean icon, proxy, or impersonator of the gods, and so they themselves became divine. These 'first fruits' of society, as we might call them, received crowns of white feathers and were led intoxicated, dancing their way up the temple-pyramid to the god's house, the *sancta sanctorum*, on top. Four priests threw the victim backward on top of a stone altar, restraining him/her in cross-like fashion, while the high priest and his acolytes opened the chest cavity to extract the heart, sever the arteries, use the blood to anoint the lintel and doorposts of the god's house, and place the heart itself in a sacred stone vessel, a *cuauhxicalli* (literally an 'eagle vessel') understood to transport the heart to the very lips of the solar divinity (Fig. 3).[9] The corpse was then rolled down the temple to the base where other levites waited to dissect and cook choice portions. Only they and the Aztec high nobility were permitted to consume the sacred remains and so prolong their lives by a communion in the deified body.

Other means of sacred oblation involved burning the victim alive as a holocaust offering, or hanging the individual on a scaffold in the manner of a passion play. He became an image or impersonator of the god Xipe Totec when he was shot through with arrows, like the legend of St Sebastian (Fig. 4). The same god was also reminiscent of the martyred apostle, St Bartholomew, who in Christian legend was flayed alive. Here the human offering was flayed and his skin was worn like a garment for several weeks by another young and beautiful human *ixiptla* of Xipe Totec (Fig. 5).[10] As the dead flayed skin gradually fell away, a divine transformation from old to new occurred, suggesting the spring fertility rites of shedding skin and planting seeds. The Mexica also had what appeared to the friars as a satanic parody of the Christian Eucharist. It was a communion meal by the use of a small cake – a sort of 'gingerbread

8   Burr Cartwright Brundage, *The Fifth Sun: Aztec Gods, Aztec World* (Austin: University of Texas, 1979), pp. 37, 222.

9   Leonardo López Luján, *The Offerings of the Temple Mayor of Teochtitlan* (Niwot, Colo.: University of Colorado Press, 1994), p. 283: 'Ministers and the faithful used the blood to anoint the supports, thresholds, and walls of the temples, as well as the rooms and the lips of the sacred images.'

10   Carol Callaway, 'Pre-Columbian and Colonial Mexican Images of the Cross: Christ's Sacrifice and the Fertile Earth', *Journal of Latin American Lore* 16.2 (1990), 199–231.

Figure 3. Images of human sacrifice. From Sahagún, *Historia general de las cosas.* (Public domain)

man' representing the divinity – made from seeds, corn dough and human blood.[11]

After the initial chaos of the first few years, evangelization began in earnest. The friars learned the languages, compiled ethnographic data from the elite native informants, and with their help began translations of the Christian Scriptures, prayers and catechisms. Visual catechisms in pictographs were very successful, and the friars realized that the visual and

11 Diego Durán, *Book of the Gods and Rites and the Ancient Calendar* (trans. and eds F. Horcasitas and D. Heyden; Norman: University of Oklahoma Press, 1977), pp. 94–5.

Figure 4. The arrow sacrifice of the impersonator of Xipe Totec. From *Historia Tolteca-Chicimeca*, mid-sixteenth century. Redrawn from MS mexicain 51–3, Collection Aubin, Bibliothèque Nationale de France.

performative arts were the best means to communicate the new creed.[12] In Fig. 6 we see an engraving from a work on Franciscan missionary practice (1579) in which a friar preaches to the Indian neophytes using pictures of Christ's passion.[13] When native artists learned European ways of creating naturalistic sculptures, they fashioned monumental crucifixes in which the body of Christ was made of corn, a sacred food and a divinity in the Aztec pantheon. In this process, bundles of cornhusks were bound together to form a rough torso and members; then a paste made from the corn pith was overlaid on the bundle, given sculptured form and painted (Fig. 7). The corn made for a large but extremely lightweight image that was ideal

12   See Juan Guillermo Durán, *Monumenta catechetica hispanoamericana: siglos XVI–XVIII* (Buenos Aires: Facultad de Teología de la Pontificia Universidad Católica Argentina, 1984).

13   Diego Valadés, *Rhetorica christiana ad concionandi, et orandi vsum accommodata vtrivsque facultatis exemplis svo loco insertis: quae quidem ex Indorum maxime deprompta sunt historiis. Unde, praeter doctrinam summa quoque delectatio comparabitur* (Perusiae: Petrumiacubum Petrutium, 1579), p. 111.

Figure 5. The impersonator of the god Xipe Totec wearing the flayed skin of a human being at numbers 2, 3 and 7. From Sahagún, *Historia general de las cosas*. (Public domain)

Figure 6. A Franciscan friar preaching with passion pictures. From Diego Valadés, *Rhetorica christiana* (1579). The Latin text reads: 'The master adapts his heavenly gifts to the senses, and waters arid hearts from the font of eloquence.' (Courtesy of the Beinecke Rare Book and Manuscript Library, Yale University)

Figure 7. Crucifix, mid-sixteenth century, with a corpus made of corn paste, Tlaxcala cathedral. (Photo: author)

for carrying in processions.[14] Thus a sacred food, corn, was transubstantiated into a material body, an *ixiptla*-proxy of Christ in his passion.

In addition to the visual metaphors needed to express Christianity, the friars and their native amanuenses searched for verbal metaphors to bridge the divide. When Fray Bernardino de Sahagún translated the Sunday Epistle and Gospel pericopes, he discovered that the biblical

---

14 Xavier Moyssén, *México: Angustia de sus cristos* (Mexico: Instituto Nacional de Antropologíá e Historia, 1967), xxx.

expression 'Son of Man' made no sense in Náhuatl.[15] He therefore changed it to read 'Son of the Virgin'. As we see in the epigraph above, 'Unless you eat of the flesh of the Son of the Virgin . . .', the result was to make Christ's words about theophagy even more carnal. Moreover, the translators felt that they had to use a more commonly understood word for the eucharistic bread, and so they chose 'tortilla'. The Lord's Prayer then translates as 'Give us this day our daily tortilla . . .'; and in the illustrated *Codex Tlaltelolco* (1549) the eucharistic tortilla is displayed in a monstrance wearing a feathered bonnet, a traditional Mexica sign of royalty and divinity (Fig. 8).[16]

It would be a mistake for us to think that the word *tortilla* was used in the prayer merely because it was the Mesoamerican maize equivalent of the wheat bread of the Old World. Corn was also a god in their pantheon and a multi-layered figure of speech for sacrificial eating. As nourishment for human beings, it was the symbolic sustenance for all living entities, and in human sacrifice, people were metaphoric corn for other beings. In fact, the very act of making and kneading the dough, flattening it, and spreading it out (*uemmana* or *tlamana*) was also the metaphoric meaning of the Nahuatl word 'to sacrifice' a human being.[17] Therefore, the use of 'tortilla' in the Lord's Prayer resonated with Nahua-Christians – especially with women who were the tortilla-makers – on a different level than the way 'bread' might resonate with European Christians. It must have reminded them not only of *eating* tortillas and of nourishment, but also of *making* tortillas, and of the fact that a human being could be 'spread out' on an altar in sacrifice like tortilla dough and become ritual food to sustain the life of the world.

For a moment I will address the physical context for preaching the passion of Christ; this is necessary in order to appreciate the cultural and religious convergence that eventually took place in New Spain.

By the mid-sixteenth century, church building began on a grand scale. More than 250 evangelization centres created for the conversion, indoctrination and liturgical life of the natives in central Mexico were all constructed on a similar model. The details are important because they demonstrate that the builders were thinking in both a biblical and a syncretic way. Several of these centres were constructed on top of the partially demolished temple pyramids of the Mexica in an act both of hegemonic dominance and of symbolic replacement. Each of the

---

15   Bernardino de Sahagún, *Evangeliarum, epistolarum et lectionarum Aztecum sive mexicanum* (ed. Bernardinus Biondelli; Milan: Typis Jos. Bernardoni Q. Johannis, 1858).

16   For the use of the word *tortilla* for the communion host see, for example, the doctrinal catechism in the *Egerton MS* 2898, fol. 1, in the British Library. For the feathered eucharistic host, see the *Codex Tlaltelolco* (*c.* 1565) in the Museo de Antropología e Historia, Mexico City.

17   Kay Read, *Time and Sacrifice in the Aztec Cosmos* (Bloomington: Indiana University Press, 1998), pp. 144–5 and 176.

Figure 8. Detail from the *Codex Tlaltelolco* (1549). (With permission of the Biblioteca Nacional de Antropología e Historia, Mexico City)

conversion centres consisted of a walled and battlemented atrium preceding a church, with friary and cloister (Fig. 9). In the atrium is an outdoor apse with altar for the sacrifice of the Mass. Some of these are even elevated above eye-level, reminiscent of the elevated altar and god's house on top of the temple pyramid. In the four corners of the atrium are four diminutive chapels for processional stations, called *posas*, with two doors for entrance and exit. Finally, the conversion centre was completed by a monumental stone cross, erected on a podium at the centre of the atrium. In a recent book, I have been able to determine that the prototype for these complexes was the biblical temple of Jerusalem as seen in the vision of the prophet Ezekiel (chs 40–44). Ezekiel had foreseen a utopian society and a purified temple for pure worship, and these images suited the

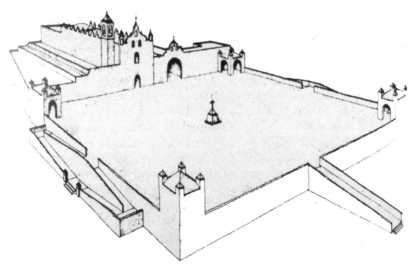

Figure 9. Drawing of the Franciscan catechetical centre at Izamal. From Lara, *City, Temple, Stage.*

utopian and millennial dreams of the mendicant missionaries. Moreover, printed Bibles with these illustrations were plentiful in New Spain.[18]

The New World evangelization centres adapted these buildings for local needs. For example, the church building is divided internally into three sections – the porch, holy place, and holy of holies – in a way similar to the Jerusalem temple-house of Solomon, Ezekiel and Herod. The four *posa* chapels take up the location of the four minor structures in the temple's atrium; while the outdoor altar and the cross on its podium combine to replace the altar of holocausts. It was a well-known mediaeval trope that Christ suffered his passion and died on the 'altar of the cross'.[19] Hence, a biblical model of sacred temple was used to replace the pre-Hispanic temple. But there is evidence that even more daring experiments were conducted in an attempt at cultural and metaphorical elision.

Many of the atrial crosses were mounted on a podium with four corner spikes as if consciously imitating the 'horned' altar of holocausts in Jerusalem. Until this day, Náhuatl speakers call this podium for a cross

18 Lara, *City, Temple, Stage*, pp. 17–34, 126–34. On the utopian ideals of the mendicants, see John Leddy Phelan, *The Millennial Kingdom of the Franciscans in the New World* (Berkeley: University of California Press, 2nd edn, revised, 1970) and Georges Baudot, *Utopía e Historia en México: Los primeros cronistas de la civilización mexicana (1520–1569)* (Madrid: Espasa-Calpe, 1983).

19 Most mediaeval writers, like Prudentius in the *Psychomachia*, used the metaphor of the 'altar of the heart'. It can have liturgical as well as moral meanings. See Christian Gnilka, *Studien zur Psychomachie des Prudentius* (Wiesbaden: Otto Harrassowitz, 1963), pp. 83–128.

momoxtli, the ancient word for an Aztec altar of human sacrifice, suggesting that there was a deliberate syncretism at work. At the Augustinian evangelization centre of Yecapixtla the cross bears the carving of a heart whose arteries have been severed (Fig. 10). While it is true that the heart is a common Augustinian symbol, its location and depiction in this way, on the altar of the cross at the centre of the temple's atrium, points to a new sense of the ancient heart sacrifice. The severed heart appears elsewhere, for example, as a detail sculpted on the processional chapels of the Franciscan centre at Calpan, where the four ventricles are clearly seen (Fig. 11). Since the processions passed in and out of these chapels, with singing and liturgical dancing, it appears that the metaphor has been recycled for a salvific passing through the blood of Christ. The baptismal shell appears to confirm this interpretation, for from his pierced heart flowed blood and water, sacramentally understood as baptism and Eucharist. This conflation of blood and water is confirmed by the pictographic catechisms where the glyph or ideogram for blood and water are always the same: a gash from which drips a sacred liquid.[20]

In days of old an alternative means of human sacrifice had been to impale the victim on a species of cacti that grows in Mexico on the top of hills, and there extract the victim's heart (Fig. 12).[21] It seems quite ingenious then that the designers of an Augustinian mission station at Nonoalco located the cross on a stylized barrel cactus, which, in turn, is seated on an outdoor altar (Fig. 13). An even bolder reuse of the symbols of human sacrifice occurred at the Franciscan centre of Cuernavaca, where a pre-Columbian *cuauhxicalli* box, the very heart receptacle itself, was embedded at the foot of the cross among the four horns of the altar-podium (Fig. 14).

A more subtle reference to blood, and also to sacred sunlight, is found on the crosses that display dark but reflective mirrors where the head of Christ would have been located (Fig. 15). The mirror is obsidian, a black volcanic glass that was so sacred to the Mexica that it was a god in their pantheon. The knives that the high priest employed to open the chest cavity were of sacred obsidian. For that reason it would seem that the use of obsidian would be anathema on a cross or as a Christian altarstone for the sacrifice of the Mass; but it was not.[22] In the experimental days of the evangelization, sunlight and world-maintaining blood were converged

20   See, for example, Carolyn Dean, 'Praying with Pictures: A Reading of the *Libro de Oraciones*', *Journal of Latin American Lore* 15.2 (1989), 211–73, esp. figs 1.12 and 1.15.

21   See the *Codex Boturini* (or *Tira de la Peregrinación*) in the Biblioteca Nacional de Antropología e Historia, Mexico City.

22   George Kubler, 'On the Colonial Extinction of the Motifs of Pre-Columbian Art', in Samuel Lothrop (ed.), *Essays in Pre-Columbian Art and Archeology* (Cambridge, Mass.: Harvard University Press, 1961). Altarstones of obsidian were exported for use in European churches.

Figure 10. Atrial cross with heart and severed aorta on an altar base with four 'horns' at Yecapixtla. (Photo: author)

Figure 11. Detail of a stational chapel in the atrium at San Andrés, Calpan. Decorative pattern with dissected human hearts and conch shells. (Photo: author)

Figure 12. Aztec human sacrifice on cactus plants. Redrawn from the *Codex Boturini*, Biblioteca Nacional de Antropología e Historia, Mexico City.

Figure 13. Atrial cross and altar base at Nonoalco. (Photo: author)

Figure 14. Atrial cross and base with *cuauhxicalli* heart-box (letter 'c') at Cuernavaca. (Photo: author)

into a metaphor that spanned both worldviews and theologies. As the new light of the world and the *Sol Justicia*, Sun of Justice, Jesus Christ in his passion became the solar saviour of the new hybrid society. On one atrial cross at the Dominican conversion centre of Topiltepec, Christ is represented impaled on a scaffold in the guise of Xipe Totec, shot though with arrows (Fig. 16). On the reverse side, a glyph represents the fifth and final sun of Aztec eschatology. It would appear that Christ's passion brings an end to the world as we know it.[23] Indeed, the solar Christ is a common theme in liturgy and music throughout the colonial period.[24]

A collection of Náhuatl hymns, the *Psalmodia Christiana*, was composed *c.* 1550 to be sung to native tunes and rhythms, and danced to in the church atria.[25] One hymn addresses Christ: 'You, you God, you child, you are the sunbeam of your precious Father, you are illumination; come to shed light for us, we who lie in darkness.' When the adolescent Christ converses with the priests and sages in the Jerusalem temple, the text says: 'Indeed, it became sunny, it dawned, it was time, the New Sun,

23   Callaway, 'Pre-Columbian and Colonial Mexican Images', pp. 199–231.

24   Jaime Lara, 'The Sacramented Sun: Solar Eucharistic Worship in Colonial Latin America', in Peter Casarella and Raúl Gómez (eds), *El Cuerpo de Cristo: The Hispanic Presence in the United States Catholic Church* (New York: Crossroad, 1998), pp. 261–91.

25   Bernardino de Sahagún, *Psalmodia christiana, y sermoniario de los sanctos del año en lengua mexicana (Mexico: Pedro Ocharte, 1583)* (trans. Arthur J. O. Anderson; Salt Lake City: University of Utah Press, 1993).

Figure 15. Atrial cross with embedded obsidian mirror at Ciudad Hidalgo. (Photo: author)

Figure 16. Atrial cross with carvings of the Aztec deity Xipe Totec at Topiltepec. (Photo courtesy of Prof. Edward Pepe)

the new illumination came out, came to spread its wings.' When Christ, the solar eagle, offered himself on the sacrificial tree, the text says 'our holy Sun had set, had gone into his house ...'[26] Elsewhere, Christ is referred to as 'the Divine Sun' or the 'Sacramented Sun'. It is no wonder

26 Christ himself becomes a sort of *cuauhxicalli* eagle vessel. See Lara, *City, Temple, Stage*, pp. 174–5.

then that the eucharistic monstrances fabricated in the New World soon took the form of a gold or silver sunburst, a design that was not yet common in sixteenth-century Europe (Fig. 17).

One last example of this convergence of metaphors will suffice. Earlier, I mentioned the corn sculptures of the crucified Christ. Some of these are actually puppets whose battered sacred limbs can be positioned at will to enact the sacred drama (Fig. 18).[27] In an effort to create convincing, lifelike actors, other Christ-puppets used real human hair or even real ribs (Fig. 19). Other images were created to be used on Good Friday for the elaborate theatrical drama of the *Holy Burial*, a ritual that continues today. During the service of the Veneration of the Cross, the corpus is taken down from the cross; the nails are removed from hands and feet. Its arms are hinged and can be folded against its side. This image of the dead Christ is then carried in procession with stops at the four *posa* chapels, to its resting place in a sepulchre-niche (Fig. 20). Liturgical and drama scholars will immediately recognize this action and device as a variation on the mediaeval *Deposition* ceremony and the Easter Sepulchre where the eucharistic host, or the cross, were buried.[28] The sixteenth-century Mexica author, Domingo Chimalpáhin, speaks of these Christ-puppets as *imiquilizyxiptlatzin*, literally, 'buried impersonators of the Christ-God', thus re-employing the ancient Aztec notion of *ixiptla*, image-as-impersonation or proxy.[29]

Conclusions

In this essay I have attempted to present some, but by no means all, of the ways in which the passion of Jesus Christ was appreciated and inculturated in the religious imagination and values of the Aztecs. It appears that the mendicant friars and their Nahua elite purposely selected pre-Hispanic rites and religious artefacts that were not objectively tied to idolatry and that could be given a new, Christian interpretation without too much catechesis. Thus, temples, mirrors, dances, metaphoric expressions – even eucharistic tortillas with feather headdresses – were reworked to accommodate them to the new religion.

---

27 For European precedents, see Gesine and Johannes Taubert, 'Mittelalterliche Kruzifixe mit schwenkbaren Armen', *Zeitschrift des deutschen Vereins für Kunstwissenschaft* 23 (1969), 79–121.

28 Susan Webster, 'Art, Ritual and Confraternities in Sixteenth-Century New Spain', *Anales del Instituto de Investigaciones Estéticas* 70 (1997), 5–43; Idem, 'The Descent from the Cross in Sixteenth-Century New Spain', *The Early Drama, Art, and Music Review* 19.2 (1997), 69–85.

29 Domingo de San Antón Muñón Chimalpáhin Quauhtlehuantzin, *Diario* (trans. Rafael Tena; Mexico: Conaculta, 2000), p. 327.

Figure 17. Typical colonial eucharistic monstrance. (Photo: author)

Figure 18. Processional image of Christ with moveable limbs, Tlaxcala. (Photo: author)

Figure 19. Processional image of Christ with inserted ribs, Guanajuato. (Photo: author)

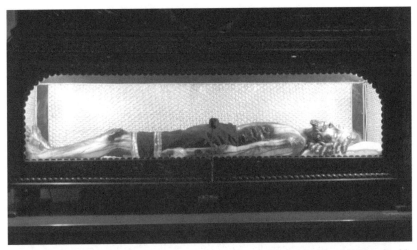

Figure 20. Holy Sepulchre Chapel and casket with 'puppet Christ' for Good Friday, Puebla cathedral. (Photo: author)

While extirpating what the friars considered idolatry and destroying the old temples with their 'demonic' worship, the missionaries, in partnership with the neophytes, erected churches on top of the very same sacred sites, and filled the ritual vacuum with the kinesthetic qualities of the late mediaeval liturgy. Christianity was both literally and metaphorically built up on top of the materials and symbols of the old religion.

By ritual substitution and symbolic equivalency, the friars and neo-Christian natives changed the root metaphor of a civilization from one of continuous sacrificial blood that kept the sun spinning in its orbit, to that of a new sun, the *Sun of Justice*.[30] In the pathos of his passion, Christ's sacred body and blood was humanely sacrificed on the mirror of the cross once and for all, and could now be sacramentally ingested as food. The Aztecs would have instinctually concurred with what the twentieth-century liturgical historian, Aidan Kavanagh, had to say about the need for sacrifice:

> Genesis says that we began in a swamp teeming with life, but that something went vastly wrong one evening at dinner. Apocalypse says that the difficulty was finally resolved into something called the Banquet of the Lamb. [The Letter to the] Hebrews tells how the resolution was accomplished, not in an orchard set in a pleasant countryside but in a butcher shop located at the city's center. The World's story from beginning to end pivots upon this resolution, a resolution the faint of heart, the fastidious, and the squeamish find hard to bear. Suburbia prefers its meat wrapped in plastic, all signs of violence removed so as to

30   Lara, *City, Temple, Stage*, pp. 174–5, 203–4.

reduce the necessity of entering into the dark and murderous transaction with reality which one creature's giving up its life for another entails ... To slay rightly is to transact the inexorable business of life.[31]

Far from merely postponing the inevitable cosmic death by starvation, eating the flesh of this Solar Divinity, the Son of the Virgin (see epigraph), could admit one into an eternal life.

References

Baudot, Georges, *Utopía e Historia en México: Los primeros cronistas de la civilización mexicana (1520–1569)* (Madrid: Espasa-Calpe, 1983).

Brundage, Burr Cartwright, *The Fifth Sun: Aztec Gods, Aztec World* (Austin: University of Texas, 1979).

Callaway, Carol, 'Pre-Columbian and Colonial Mexican Images of the Cross: Christ's Sacrifice and the Fertile Earth', *Journal of Latin American Lore* 16.2 (1990), 199–231.

Carrasco, David, 'Cosmic Jaws: We Eat the Gods and the Gods Eat Us', *JAAR* 63.3 (1995), 429–63.

Cervantes, Fernando, *The Devil in the New World* (New Haven: Yale University Press, 1994).

Colston, Stephen. 'No Longer Will There Be a Mexico', *American Indian Quarterly* 9 (1985), 239–58.

Dean, Carolyn, 'Praying with Pictures: A Reading of the *Libro de Oraciones*', *Journal of Latin American Lore* 15.2 (1989), 211–73.

Durán, Diego, *Book of the God and Rites and the Ancient Calendar* (trans. and ed F. Horcasitas and D. Heyden; Norman: University of Oklahoma Press, 1977).

Durán, Juan Guillermo, *Monumenta catechetica hispanoamericana: siglos XVI-XVIII* (Buenos Aires: Facultad de Teología de la Pontificia Universidad Católica Argentina, 1984).

Gnilka, Christian, *Studien zur Psychomachie des Prudentius* (Wiesbaden: Otto Harrassowitz, 1963).

Kavanagh, Aidan, *On Liturgical Theology* (New York: Pueblo, 1984).

Kubler, George, 'On the Colonial Extinction of the Motifs of Pre-Columbian Art', in Samuel Lothrop (ed.), *Essays in Pre-Columbian Art and Archeology* (Cambridge, Mass.: Harvard University Press, 1961).

Lara, Jaime, *City, Temple, Stage: Eschatological Architecture and Liturgical Theatrics in New Spain* (Notre Dame, Ind.: University of Notre Dame Press, 2004).

—— 'The Sacramented Sun: Solar Eucharistic Worship in Colonial Latin

---

31 Aidan Kavanagh, *On Liturgical Theology* (New York: Pueblo, 1984), pp. 34–5.

America', in Peter Casarella and Raúl Gómez (eds), *El Cuerpo de Cristo: The Hispanic Presence in the United States Catholic Church* (New York: Crossroad, 1998), pp. 261–91.

Luján, Leonardo López, *The Offerings of the Temple Mayor of Teochtitlan* (Niwot, Colo.: University of Colorado Press, 1994)

Moyssén, Xavier, *México: Angustia de sus cristos* (Mexico: Instituto Nacional de Antropologíá e Historia, 1967).

Phelan, John Leddy, *The Millennial Kingdom of the Franciscans in the New World* (Berkeley: University of California Press, 2nd edn, revised, 1970).

Read, Kay, *Evangeliarum, epistolarum et lectionarum Aztecum sive mexicanum* (ed. Bernardinus Biondelli; Milan: Typis Jos. Bernardoni Q. Johannis, 1858).

—— *Historia general de las cosas de Nueva España* (ed. Paso y Troncoso; Madrid: Fototipia de Hauser y Menet, 1905).

de Sahagún, Bernardino, *Psalmodia christiana, y sermoniario de los sanctos del año en lengua mexicana (Mexico: Pedro Ocharte, 1583* (trans. Arthur J. O. Anderson; Salt Lake City: University of Utah Press, 1993).

de San Antón Muñón Chimalpáhin Quauhtlehuantzin, Domingo, *Diario* (trans. Rafael Tena; Mexico: Conacultura, 2000).

—— *Time and Sacrifice in the Aztec Cosmos* (Bloomington: Indiana University Press, 1998).

Taubert, Gesine and Johannes, 'Mittelalterliche Kruzifixe mit schwenkbaren Armen', *Zeitschrift des deutschen Vereins für Kunstwissenschaft* 23 (1969), 79–121.

Torquemada, Fray Juan de, *Monarquia Indiana* (7 vols, Mexico City: Universidad Nacional Autónoma de México, 1983).

Valadés, Diego, *Rhetorica christiana ad concionandi, et orandi vsum accommodata vtrivsque facultatis exemplis svo loco insertis: quae quidem ex Indorum maxime deprompta sunt historiis. Unde, praeter doctrinam summa quoque delectatio comparabitur* (Perusiae: Petrumiacubum Petrutium, 1579).

Webster, Susan, 'Art, Ritual and Confraternities in Sixteenth-Century New Spain', *Anales del Instituto de Investigaciones Estéticas* 70 (1997), 5–43.

—— 'The Descent from the Cross in Sixteenth-Century New Spain', *The Early Drama, Art, and Music Review* 19.2 (1997), 69–85.

Chapter 9

THE MASS AND THE THEATRE: SACRIFICE AND MURDER IN *OTHELLO*

Regina M. Schwartz

Iago: The wine she drinks is made of grapes. (*Othello*, II.i)

There is something unbearable about Iago's triumph in Shakespeare's *Othello*. But where does this sense of the unbearableness of injustice come from? Where does the impossible expectation that it will end, or the corollary belief – that the triumph of evil must mean that the world is out of joint and that eventually it will be righted – come from? What is the source of checks upon naked self-interest, relentless aggrandizement, sheer grasping of power? Does it really come from some rational understanding that our will cannot be done without compromise with the wills of others, some recognition of the necessity of essentially contractual relations, whether unwritten or written? Or is its source some higher desire to make the world a good place, to secure the world through acts of justice? The experience of watching *Othello* induces a particularly painful craving for justice, in part because it is brought into relief against other justices, strict and absolute, retributive and economic, that triumph disastrously over the justice that transcends these values.

In the Bible, justice breaks into the immanent world as Revelation itself: the gift of justice. Among many other philosophers of religion, Levinas and Rosenzweig understand the content of the religions of the book to be not faith in an unseeable divinity or unforeseeable end, but acts of justice in daily life. 'The realm of religion is neither belief, nor dogmatics, but event, passion, and intense activity.'[1] For them, 'Ethics is not simply the corollary of the religious but is, of itself, the element in which religious transcendence receives its original meaning.'[2] But while the source of this justice may be transcendent, justice is also markedly immanent for it only assumes shape in the world of social relations, in and between individuals

1   E. Levinas, 'Franz Rosenzweig, une pensée juive moderne', in Franz Rosensweig *Les Calviers de la Nuit Surveillée*, vol. 1 (Quetigny, France, 1982), p. 74.
2   E. Levinas, *Beyond the Verse: Talmudic Readings and Lectures* (London: Athlone Press, 1994), p. 107.

and communities. When, in Gen. 1.27, man is described as being made in the image of God, this does not mean that man is God-like as possessor of the earth, exercising dominion over it, but man is *imago Dei* in his responsibility for keeping the created order, for tending it, for caring for it. Each act of justice comprises a human partnership in the creation. This biblical understanding of justice veers away from possession of other beings, from dominion over them, and toward respect for the integrity and safety of others: do not kill or steal or even covet what belongs to another.

This theological understanding of ethical life could avoid the modern twin terrors of 'economic' justice and 'strict' justice. In economic justice, beings have a price, are owned and exchanged. The world is reduced to property. In such a worldview, retribution is translated into systematic efforts to assign adequate compensation for injury.[3] Often, when the injury is felt to be immense, these rational efforts collapse, reverting to the raw motive that impels them: vengeance. And in 'strict justice', that vengeance is infected by a dangerous absolute: the crime cannot be paid off, only punished to the very end (execution, genocide, war). But the religious tradition issues cautions. *Genesis Rabbah* draws the conclusion that strict justice is utterly destructive: 'When Abraham addressed his plea to God, "Shall not the Judge of all the earth do justly?" the meaning of his words was, "If You desire the world to continue there cannot be strict justice; if you insist on strict justice, the world cannot endure"' (*Gen. Rab.* 39.6).[4] Jesus recommended turning the other cheek. Neither strict nor retributive, biblical justice is the command to love the neighbour, to engage in acts of goodness.[5] While Paul, on occasion, reduces ancient Israelite justice to mere legalism, to Pharisaism, Jesus typically sees the demand of justice differently. He insists that justice must be fulfilled: 'Do not think that I have come to abolish the law and the prophets; I have come not to abolish them but to fulfil them' (Mt. 5.17). And he sees his own death as the means to achieve the restoration of justice, the forgiveness of sins: 'And he took a cup, and when he had given thanks he gave it to them, saying, "Drink of it, all of you; for this is my blood of the covenant, which is poured out for many for the forgiveness of sins."' (Mt.

---

3   For a further critique of economic justice, see my 'The Price of Justice and Love in *The Merchant of Venice*', in *TriQuarterly* 124 (2006), 225–41.

4   Levinas offers a radical corrective to the procedural justice embraced by so much political theory: 'Justice cannot be reduced to the order it institutes or restores, nor to a system whose rationality commands, without difference, men and gods, revealing itself in human legislation like the structures of space in the theorems of geometricians, a justice that a Montesquieu calls the "logos of Jupiter", recuperating religion within this metaphor, but effacing precisely transcendence' (Levinas, *Beyond the Verse*, p. 107).

5   The classic case of retribution, 'an eye for an eye' is, as all biblical scholars know, the injunction to refuse economic punishment, as it changes the Babylonian law code that demands payment for injury.

26.27-28). In this way, from its biblical institution, the Eucharist was designed to fulfil justice.

One could argue that, in paying for human sin, Christ's death is ultimately economic: a vengeful retribution, an exaction of strict justice by the Father. Anselm's theory of atonement in *Cur Deus Homo* has been read and undoubtedly misread by many Protestant liberal theologians as just that – the execution of strict divine justice. But once humankind has destroyed the image of God, access to it has been lost so completely that they do not even know it. The mark of the unjust is his inability to see himself as such. It is in this context, according to the doctrine of atonement, that God took on humanity – so that mankind could have access to the image of God again as an example, to learn how to restore that image, to act justly and with love for the neighbour. This logic depends upon the ethical acts of men imitating those of Jesus, and the Eastern Fathers wanted to preserve this emphasis upon the example of Christ's goodness against what they perceived as a Western overemphasis on the penal understanding of atonement. They feared that the payment model reduced atonement to 'the status of a simple transaction, enacted more or less entirely on the cross, and intended solely as an appeasement of the Father's wrath against sin ... with its unrelenting concentration of the language of penal suffering and remissions from debt'.[6] But theology suggests instead that nothing can 'pay off' the human failure of rejecting God. Nothing makes it right. As an infinite wrong, it would call for an infinite restitution, and man is only finite. Sin – and, for that matter, salvation – are necessarily outside of any economy. Rather than paying off a debt, the gift of justice has to be given again, and this is achieved by God becoming man, enabling man to imitate God.

If Western religious thought in contexts as various as Genesis and Paul, Anselm and Levinas, persists in imagining humanity grasping for justice, how is that preoccupation felt in cultural formations that are less explicitly theological? How is the impulse to depict justice as 'satisfied' in the Eucharist, if not itself satisfied, then at least addressed? How is the moral frailty of humankind moved toward executing justice and performing acts of goodness? If this impulse moves into culture, into theatre for example, how does the theatre differ from the Mass? On Saturdays, playgoers could watch a revenge tragedy like *The Duchess of Malfi*, or the afflicted conscience of Hamlet tortured by a mission delivered by his father from Purgatory, or the divestiture of divine kingship in *Richard II* or the abandonment of Lear to the raging elements by his own daughters. On Sundays, when plays could not be performed, presumably because they would draw their audience from would-be churchgoers, Shakespeare and

6   D. Bentley Hart, 'A Gift Exceeding Every Debt: An Eastern Orthodox Appreciation of Anselm's *Cur Deus Homo*', *Pro Ecclesia* 7.3 (1998), 333–49, 334.

his contemporaries could attend church, a service made uniform by the Book of Common Prayer, a service that represented one hundred and fifty years of theological conflict and ritual compromise. The theatre made no claims to perform 'work'; the theatre was not trying to effect transformations. The theatre cannot *do* anything to other humans, nor can it *offer* anything to God. But ironically, it was the Reformers' very insistence that in the Mass the sacrifice was only *represented*, and not repeated, that brought the Mass closer to the theatre. After all, it was on stage that representations of events, rather than events themselves, were performed. Perhaps it is helpful to think of the Elizabethan theatre as a space where a community recalled, represented and remembered sacrifice, but did not endure it. And if, in one sense, the Elizabethan theatre competed with the Mass for an audience, in another, deeper sense, it replaced it, becoming the first truly Reformed church.[7]

English Reformation poets lived on the brink of this new world and most embraced, predictably, the Calvinist doctrine of the spiritual – not material – presence of Christ in the Eucharist. But this left them with a persistent nostalgia for that material presence, a nostalgia that reaches just shy of the heresy of transubstantiation. Alongside the explicit theological discourse of the period, the poetry, prose and theatre of the period took up these questions. Despite inveighing against the doctrine of transubstantiation in his prose, John Milton described a whole universe as incessantly and naturally 'transubstantiating' into God in his verse: furthermore, his angel eats not 'seemingly, nor in mist, the common gloss of theologians' but 'with keen dispatch of real hunger, and concoctive heat to transubstantiate' matter into spirit.[8] George Herbert, at the beginning of *The Temple*, composed a visual altar – not a communion table, but an altar – built out of the stones or words of his lyric; this word picture of an altar also forms a capital 'I' – he and the sacrifice become one, and in another lyric, he imagines Communion as literally ingesting the Bible. For

7   See also Michael Davies, 'The Transubstantial Bard: Shakespeare and Catholicism', in D. Burnham and E. Giaccherini (eds), *The Poetics of Transubstantiation: From Theology to Metaphor* (Aldershot: Ashgate, 2005); Clifford Davidson, 'The Anti-Visual Prejudice', in Clifford Davidson and Anne E. Nichols (eds), *Iconoclasm vs Art and Drama* (Kalamazoo, Mich.: Medieval Institute Publications, 1989); Michael O'Connell, 'God's Body: Incarnation, Physical Embodiment and the Fate of Biblical Theatre in the Sixteenth Century', in David Allen and Robert White (eds), *Subjects on the World's Stage* (London: Associated University Presses, 1995); Joel Altman, '"Vile Participation": The Amplification of Violence in the Theatre of Henry V', *Shakespeare Quarterly* 42.1 (1991), 1–32. On the importance of an incarnational aesthetic for concepts of the bodily and materiality in late mediaeval culture, see Miri Rubin, *Corpus Christi: The Eucharist in Late Medieval Culture* (Cambridge: Cambridge University Press, 1991); Sarah Beckwith, *Christ's Body* (New York: Routledge, 1993); and Caroline Walker Bynum, *Holy Feast and Holy Fast* (Berkeley: University of California Press, 1987).

8   John Milton, *Paradise Lost* (Book 5.435–8).

John Donne, the miracle of the Eucharist is the miracle of genuinely combining with the other, soul and body. For him, the longing set in motion by the promise of communion with God is repeated in the longing for consummation with a lover, and he punned endlessly on consume and consummate, communion and common (i.e. promiscuous). I have come to understand these writers as hungry for the mysteries wrought by the sacrament – as their Catholic detractors would have it, condemned to apprehend and desire a dinner that they could not have; but in their work, I have also come to see them concocting their own spiritual food.

With '*sola fides*' as its watchword, much Reformation theology displays a deep distrust of the senses. Faith is 'the substance of things hoped for, the evidence of things unseen' (Heb. 11.1). This invisible truth is both profoundly immanent – the inner Spirit – and transcendent – the God beyond the visible. 'Lies' are very often defined as sensory illusions. When Reformers accused priests of creating illusions that they wanted to be taken as reality, they were accusing them of fraud. For instance, Cranmer complained of the Catholic Mass: 'is not in the ministration of the holy communion an illusion of our sense, if our senses take for bread and wine what whiche is not so indeed?' And even as anti-Catholic propagandists pejoratively referred to the Mass as fraudulent, they inflicted the same charge on the theatre.

Anti-theatrical prejudice found common cause with anti-popery, equating ritual with magic, magic with the theatre, and all of them with lies: 'In Stage Playes for a boy to put on the attyre, the gesture, the passions of a woman; for a meane person to take upon him the title of a Prince with counterfeit porte, and traine, is by outward signes to shewe themselves otherwise than they are, and so within the compasse of a lye.'[9] This pseudo-Platonic equation of lies with the senses and truth with the invisible is fraught with difficulties. A less debased understanding of the sacramental, one less dependent upon crude binary distinctions between the visible and invisible, would issue in very different valuations: the Mass could provide access to truth and the theatre could be a storehouse of truths. Indeed, even Reformers understood the sacraments as the 'seal' of faith, and the most common Renaissance theory of drama was that it offered an image of actual life: 'the purpose of playing ... was and is to hold as 'twere a mirror up to nature.'[10]

An accumulating body of criticism has also been willing to think synoptically and fruitfully about religious ritual and the theatre, sensitive not only to the ritual origins of drama in ancient Greek religions and the

9   Stephen Gosson, *Plays Confuted in Five Actions* (1582) facsimile edn (New York: Johnson Reprint Corp., 1972), sigs C5, G6–G7.

10   This derives from Donatus on comedy where it is attributed to Cicero ('commoediam esse Cicero ait imitationem vitae, speculum consuetudinis, imaginem veritatis').

miracle and morality plays of mediaeval Catholicism, but also to the complex relation between the Elizabethan stage and the English Reformation. Two poles have emerged in these speculations, stressing either that theatre is virtually a religious ritual – 'for Shakespeare, the carnal spectacles of the theatre are better than demystifying: they are sacramental'[11] – or that ritual is mere theatre – 'theatrical seduction . . . is the essence of the church'.[12]

According to Stephen Greenblatt, in order to demystify the Catholic practice of exorcism definitively, Samuel Harsnett felt the need to demonstrate not only why the ritual was empty but also why it was effective, 'why a few miserable shifts could produce the experience of horror and wonder [in an exorcism] . . . He needs an explanatory model, at once metaphor and analytical tool, by which all beholders will see fraud where they once saw God'. Harsnett finds that explanatory model in theatre, an arena that readily acknowledges its magical mechanisms, admitting arts of illusion as such. In theatre he discovers magic, not miracles: divine justice does not prevail, sin is not redeemed. Greenblatt writes that in Lear, the 'forlorn hope of an impossible redemption persists,

---

11   Jeffrey Knapp, 'Preachers and Players in Shakespeare's England', *Representations* 44 (1993), p. 33. Knapp continues: 'Following those Protestants who instead treated the petty materiality of the wafer as proof that the eucharist represented Christ, Henry V suggests that the carnal spectacles of the theatre sacramentally highlight, rather than obscure, the operations of the spirit precisely because those spectacles are so conspicuously inadequate to the tales of *Non nobis* and *Te Deum* (4.8.121) they represent' (p. 33). In a similar vein, Stephen Greenblatt spoke of the 'emptying out' of ritual as the enabling condition of the 'craving' set in motion by theatre for effective ritual (Greenblatt, *Shakespearean Negotiations* [Berkeley: University of California Press, 1988], pp. 126–7). Louis Montrose writes of a transfer of the functions of rites of passage from ritual to the theatre in 'The Purpose of Playing: Reflections on Shakespearean Anthropology', *Helios* 7 (1980), 51–74. Historians concur: 'If the opportunity for popular participation in public rituals was . . . largely removed, that especial meaning which sacred ceremonies and popular rites had periodically conferred on the citizens' tangible environment also fell victim to the new 'secular' order' (Charles Phythian-Adams, 'Ceremony and the Citizen: The Communal Year at Coventry 1450–1550', in P. Clark and P. Slack (eds), *Crisis and Order in English Towns 1500–1700* [London: Routledge and Kegan Paul, 1972]). See also C. L. Barbar, *Creating Elizabethan Tragedy* (Chicago: University of Chicago Press, 1988) which, with Montrose, argues that the theatre compensates for affective losses wrought by the elimination of ritual in Protestantism. The account needs nuancing as ritual was not eliminated, but altered and given altered significance.

12   *A Declaration of Egregious Popish Impostures*, where Harsnett identifies exorcism with the theatre, quoted in Stephen Greenblatt, *Shakespearean Negotiations*, p. 112. See Christopher Hodgkins, 'Plays Out of Season: Puritanism, Antitheatricalism, and Parliament's 1642 Closing of the Theaters', in Daniel W. Doerksen and Christopher Hodgkins (eds), *Centered on the Word: Literature, Scripture, and the Tudor-Stuart Middle Way* (Newark: University of Delaware Press, 2004); Margot Heinemann, *Puritanism and Theatre* (Cambridge: Cambridge University Press, 1980); Jonas Barish, *The Anti-Theatrical Prejudice* (Berkeley: University of California Press, 1981).

drained of its institutional and doctrinal significance, empty and vain ...
but like the dream of exorcism eradicable'.[13] This leads him to the
conclusion that, at best, theatre generates expectations that are disappointed. But where Greenblatt speaks of disappointed expectations in
tones of lament, I celebrate the remarkable expectation itself, so that
precisely where he is discouraged, I locate hope. The very frustration of
redemption is the way theatre performs its moral vision. And this craving
for redemption is not a sign that religion is 'emptied'; this craving is itself
religious.

To see ritual as 'emptied out' because it no longer performs magic is to
presume, rather unsympathetically, that magic is the function of ritual,
and that religion is, in turn, reducible to practices claiming to be magical.
Greenblatt knows better, and surely in finding religion so 'emptied' in
Shakespeare, Greenblatt has not unwittingly accepted the terms set by
propagandists, reducing religion to '*mere* ritual', ritual to magic, and
magic to fraud. Because it was the work of propaganda to equate ritual
with theatre and both with lies, we might do well, for all of their affinities,
to regard the equation as deeply suspect.

Ritual is not 'mere theatre', in the sense of false, nor for its part does
theatre, however deep its affinity to religion, claim the function of a
sacrament.[14] While principals may dress in elaborate costumes and
perform ceremonial-like acts, clearly religious ritual makes different
ontological claims from the theatre. A priest is not a character
'personated' by a 'player' (the Renaissance terms for acting and
actor)[15]; rather, he is the authorized and sanctified vicar of God. Ritual
summons the holy, *mysterium tremendum*, and its acts are neither
imitations of life nor imitations of imitations, but acts that enable the
sacred to be manifest and transcendence to erupt into immanence. The
effect of such acts on the audience – and they are not an audience, but

---

13   *Shakespearean Negotiations*, p. 125.

14   Critics can be given to the same equation of ritual and theatre, but for different
reasons: for Julia Houston, Cranmer's innovations in the 1552 Book of Common Prayer had
the effect of transforming the sacrament precisely into theatre: 'Transubstantiation and the
Sign: Cranmer's Drama of the Lord's Supper', *Journal of Medieval and Renaissance Studies*
24 (1994), 113–30. On theological 'participation' and its relation to theatre, see the brilliant
essay by Anthony Dawson, 'Performance and Participation' in Anthony Dawson and Paul
Yachnin, *The Culture of Playgoing in Shakespeare's England* (Cambridge: Cambridge
University Press, 2001), pp. 11–37. He argues that the theatre both encourages and
undermines the understanding of bodily participation. See also Rajiva Verma, *Myth, Ritual
and Shakespeare* (New Delhi: Spantech Publishers, 1990).

15   Andrew Gurr, *The Shakespearean Stage 1574–1642* (Cambridge: Cambridge
University Press, 1970).

participants – is to be conclusively altered.[16] The acts performed by the priest are not intended to inspire pity or strike terror, as Aristotle said tragedy does, or to delight or instruct, as Horace said poetry must, but to change the world.

And what is theatre? If we were to heed anti-theatrical prejudice, we would learn that the theatre is a seething cauldron of disease, depravity and debauchery, an immoral realm where 'players' threaten the serious business of assuming real social roles. '[The theatres] maintain idlenes in such persons as have no vocation and draw apprentices and other servauntes from theire ordinary workes and all sortes of people from the resort unto sermons and other Christian exercises, to the great hindrance of traides and prophanation of religion established by her highnes within this Realm.'[17] But if we were to tune our ears to the defenders of the theatre, we would hear that, for them, the relation of the world of theatre to the world of reality is a more deeply considered one, and the relation of the drama to ethics – including drama's moral accountability – is equally serious. Hamlet understands the play as the very instrument that allows us to discern morality: 'the play's the thing wherein I'll catch the conscience of the king'. Hamlet is not sure whether he should trust his senses or the restless purgatorial ghost (the very existence of purgatory was subjected to doubt), but he does trust *conscience*. Moreover, he trusts the play's ability to exhibit that arbiter. Then too, the notion of redemption is not an empty one to Hamlet: indeed, it is his aching need for justice, for redeeming the crime, that drives the play. If the theatre could not fulfil the religious craving for justice, it could and did express that craving with stunning eloquence. Whether or not it was 'the purpose of playing', it was the power of performance.

If by the late Middle Ages the traditional church rites had, for some, begun to lose some of their former power, one reason was that these rites were perceived to be on a collision course with ethics.[18] Whether the

---

16 Some critics are quite sensitive to the distinction:

> Playgoing is a little like churchgoing. It is a public act for private ends. It is a private act performed publicly. It is intimate and individual. It is impersonal and communal. It brings us nearer to the apprehension of our own godhood while at the same time it reinforces awareness of the transitory properties of our flesh. Yet likeness is not identity. Playgoing is a surrender to illusion while churchgoing is a ritual embodiment of a higher truth. Through churchgoing we hope to step from one truth to *the* truth. Playgoing holds out the possibility that we can slip through fancy to a lookout upon truth.

(Bernard Beckerman, 'Shakespearean Playgoing Then and Now', in Sidney Homan (ed.), *Shakespeare's More Than Words Can Witness: Essays on Visual and Nonverbal Enactment in the Plays* [Lewisburg, Pa: Bucknell University Press, 1986], p. 142).

17 Montrose, 'The Purpose of Playing', p. 58.

18 Miri Rubin, *Corpus Christi: The Eucharist in Late Medieval Culture* (New York: Cambridge University Press, 1991).

strains of Protestantism indebted to Luther stressed that only faith grounds morality through Christ's merit, or with Calvin emphasized the discipline of the church, or like Zwingli focused on communal responsibility, all inveighed against the perceived 'abuses' of clergy and liturgy – not with secular scepticism, but with the fury of moral indignation. The theatre also addressed this felt need for a moral order, differently, but perhaps as effectively as the church. At precisely the time when the theatre was under attack for fostering immorality, and the rituals of Catholicism were under scrutiny for their 'falsity and hollowness', the theatre was reaching its apex: the old Senecan version of revenge tragedy flowered into Elizabethan moral tragedy, that is, into a tragedy of injustice. When I understand Shakespeare as 'religious', then, it is not because his actors satisfied or did not satisfy longings for magic acts, but because he repeatedly addressed, in his way, the problem that the sacrament also addressed in its way: justice.

When sacraments figured among the important resources he called upon from the stage business of life, Shakespeare turned them to an ethical purpose. For his audience, a spotted handkerchief would allude not only to a marriage bed, to virginity and fidelity, but also to a spotted altar-cloth, ocular proof of Christ's miraculous gift of his broken and bleeding body in the Eucharist. Such cloths were relics in Catholic Europe, testimonies to the miracle of the bleeding host. Through lenses that empty it of this sacramental significance, the spotted cloth in *Othello* becomes a heathenish cloth in which magic, not God, was woven. But that reading does not suffice: for the handkerchief *also* becomes ocular 'proof' of a betrayal that never occurred, a piece of false testimony used wrongfully to indict the innocent. So if the reference to the religious ritual has been 'emptied out', Shakespeare has re-filled it. If Shakespeare has 'given up on religion', as C. L. Barbar depicts him, surely he has not given up on justice. It is the imaginary that has such a deep hold on his plays that they scarcely can make sense without it. How otherwise could we understand Lear as suffering? Hamlet as tormented? Macbeth as guilt-ridden? Emptied of its sacral significance, sacrifice is meaningless killing, but Shakespeare does not have meaningless deaths in his tragedy. Like the spotted handkerchief, they are not just emptied, but re-filled – with moral outrage.

Sacrifice and Murder

Much of the Reformation was spent negotiating two different meanings of death, as murder and as sacrifice. Whether a death is viewed as a murder or an act of sacrifice depends entirely on how it is culturally framed, but in both cases, its definition is at the service of some idea of justice. Death framed as a sacrifice is most often understood as a gift to a deity, as appeasing his ire for our wrongdoing. 'Sacrifice' compensates, pays back, pays off, recompenses, redeems. When the gift offered is pure, chaste, unadulterated, without sin, it compensates for the impure, tainted, adulterated, sinful nature of man. Divine justice is understood to be satisfied by this retribution: 'Die he or justice must', as Milton's God puts it in *Paradise Lost*. Sacrifice is substitutive and metonymic: the individual dies for the community, on behalf of the community, as Christ dies for mankind. Murder is framed very differently: far from *satisfying* the demands of justice, murder *violates* them, and its object is not heroically embracing or stoically accepting destruction; it is an unwilling victim. In murder, the emphasis shifts away from the community to the individual, whose death does not satisfy collective justice, but whose murder threatens collective peace. Hence, a specific retributive justice comes into play: not the substitutive redemption offered by sacrifice, but the collective apparatus of the law. In that system, murder does not satisfy justice; it cries out for satisfaction.

During the Reformation, as reinterpretations of the ritual of the Eucharist occurred, the relation between sacrifice and murder, as well as their relation to justice, was also revisited. When Reformers altered participating in the material godhead through transubstantiation to only *representing* God, merit was conferred on undeserving man by Christ's sacrifice 'as if' the communicant were also sacrificed; merit was imputed to man for something he did not suffer. In the process, the satisfaction of justice and gift of mercy were radically redefined. For Luther, the church and its priesthood have no agency in the economy of grace. 'Once the Mass has been overthrown, I say we'll have overthrown the whole of Popedom.' Luther insisted that the Lord's Supper was only a promise and a testament. 'God does not deal, nor has he dealt with man in any other way than by the word of his promise. So too we can never have dealing with God in any other way than by faith in that word of promise.' Distinguishing the Catholic Mass from the Reformed Holy Supper, Calvin explained that, 'here is as much difference between this sacrifice and the sacrament as there is between giving and receiving. And such is the most miserable ungratefulness of man that where he ought to have recognized and given thanks for the abundance of God's bounty, he makes God in this his debtor!'[19] Thomas Cranmer opens his 'Defence of the True and Catholic Doctrine of the Sacrament' (1550) with a preface in which he takes pains to distinguish the reformed (i.e. original and true) understanding of the Eucharist from the (he thinks) misguided direction it had taken in Rome:

19   John Calvin, *Institution of the Christian Religion* (1536 edition; New York: John Knox Press, 1975), p. 160.

Our Saviour Christ Jesus according to the will of his eternal Father ...
made a sacrifice and oblation of his own body upon the cross, which
was a full redemption, satisfaction, and propitiation, for the sins of the
whole world ... [H]e hath ordained a perpetual memory of his said
sacrifice, daily to be used in the Church to his perpetual laud and praise
... But the Romish Antichrist, to deface this great benefit of Christ,
hath taught that his sacrifice upon the cross is not sufficient hereunto,
without another sacrifice devised by him, and made by the priest, or else
without indulgences, beads, pardons, pilgrimages, and such other pelfry,
to supply Christ's imperfection: and that Christian people cannot apply
to themselves the benefits of Christ's passion, but that the same is in the
distribution of the Bishop of Rome ...

His response to this assessment is not subtle: 'O heinous blasphemy ... O
wicked abomination ... O pride intolerable ... For he that taketh upon
him to supply that thing, which he pretendeth to be unperfect in Christ,
must needs make himself above Christ, and so very Antichrist.'[20] Only
God could perform a sacrifice. Men perform a murder. If priests were
accused of presuming to act as sacrificer, offering Christ at the altar, for
its part, Catholicism never claimed that the priest was the sacred
executioner, only that he was the means through which Christ repeated
his sacrifice of himself. But Reformers, eager to reduce the power of the
priesthood, claimed that the agency of the priest was, at best, irrelevant; at
worst, idolatrous, for man could not offer God – only God could offer
himself.

To underscore the point, Cranmer returns to what he deems this
greatest of offences at the beginning of Book V of his *Defence*: it is not
transubstantiation nor is it a failure to embrace double predestination, it is
presuming to repeat the sacrifice. 'The greatest blasphemy and injury that
can be against Christ, and yet universally used through the popish
kingdom, is this, that the priests make their Mass a sacrifice propitiary, to
remit the sins as well of themselves as of others, both quick and dead, to
whom they apply the same.'[21] Cranmer claimed that the doctrines of the
Defence were reflected in the 1549 Book of Common Prayer and we can
discern that even as it went through its contested emendations and
revisions over the language of the real presence, this much – that the
sacrifice occurred once and is now only commemorated in the Lord's
Supper – remained unchanged: there are no offertory prayers; the Secret
Prayers, offering-prayers that refer to the *munus*, *oblatio*, *sacrificium*,
hostia and *mysterium* have been eliminated. This distinction between
divine and priestly agency was reflected in the careful wording of the Book

20   *The Work of Thomas Cranmer* (vol. 2; Appleford: Sutton Courtenay Press, 1964),
pp. 55–6.
21   *The Work of Thomas Cranmer*, p. 215.

of Common Prayer (1559): 'And although we be unworthy through our manifold sins to offer unto thee any Sacrifice: yet we beseech thee to accept this our bounden duty and service, not weighing our merits but pardoning our offences ... Amen.'[22] Reading the sacramental logic unsympathetically produced a contradiction unknown to the Roman church: if the act is repeated, then the original must be incomplete, and conversely, if the original were complete, any repetition becomes superfluous.

This harsh emphasis on remembrance alone was somewhat softened, as became evident in the sacred treatment of the wine and bread. John Jewel's understanding of the Eucharist was close to Cranmer's with the exception of his regard for the elements; the bread and the wine needed to be set aside, consecrated, in order to fulfil their sacramental function: 'We affirm that bread and wine are holy and heavenly mysteries of the body and blood of Christ, and that *by them* Christ himself, being the true bread of eternal life, is so presently given unto us that by faith we verily receive his body and blood.'[23] Richard Hooker's 'real receptionist' understanding of the Eucharist enunciated in his *Ecclesiastical Polity* kept the sacramental emphasis on participation: 'The fruit of the Eucharist is the participation in the body and blood of Christ.'[24] 'This bread hath in it more than the substance which our eyes behold, this cup hallowed with solemn benediction availeth ... what these elements are in themselves it skilleth not, it is enough that to me which take them they are the body and blood of Christ.'[25] After the accession of James I (provoking the Millenary Petition, and the Hampton Court Conference which ultimately issued in the King James Bible and the Canons of 1604), church doctrine inched closer to asserting the vital importance of the bread and wine – almost, but not quite as an offering of sacrifice – reflected in the felt need to legislate, without precedent, the consecration not only of the bread and wine, but if that supply is supplemented, even of the added bread and wine (canon 21). For all of the Reformers' rhetoric against the 'grievous error' of making an offering, by 1604 they had rejected it in doctrine far more definitively than in ritual. Nonetheless, that same year, the stage could offer a clearer – more or less satisfying? – sacrifice, of Desdemona, whose name includes the *daimon* of sacrifice.

Reformers were not only disturbed by the problem of agency in

22   Marion J. Hatchett, *The Eucharistic Liturgies of Historic Prayer Books: Historic Rites Arranged for Contemporary Celebration* (Sewanee, Tenn.: St. Luke's Journal of Theology, 1984), p. 36.

23   J. E. Booty, *John Jewel as Apologist of the Church of England* (London: SPCK, 1963), p. 33. Emphasis added.

24   Richard Hooker, *Ecclesiastical Polity* (London: Everyman, 1907), Book V, chapter lvii, section 6, 322–3.

25   Hooker, *Ecclesiastical Polity*, Book V, chapter lxvii, section 12, pp. 330–1.

sacrifice; they were also clearly uncomfortable with its materiality, preferring to speak of spiritual eating and drinking instead of the literal body and blood of God: 'Take and eat this, in remembrance that Christ died for thee, and feed on him in thy heart by faith, with thanksgiving.'[26] When they denied the material body in the Mass, to substitute a seal of the promise of faith, they were implicitly putting the meaning of death – as sacrifice – at risk. Foreseeing the problem, Calvin was careful to claim that the sacrament's meaning depends wholly on the body of God having been sacrificed: 'It must be carefully noted that the most conspicuous, indeed almost the whole power of the sacrament resides in these words, "which is given for you" ... "which is shed for you". For otherwise it would be of no avail that the body and blood of the Lord should be administered, had they not once for all been *sacrificed* for our redemption and salvation.'[27] His anxiety is palpable. For with the sacrifice remembered rather than repeated, how can justice be effectively satisfied? What is remembered is the suffering of Christ, the suffering of a victim, but the question still presses: is this a murder victim or a sacrificial offering?

Othello *and Justice*

I discern a crisis over the distinction between sacrifice and murder in *Othello*, and I will glean allusions to the sacrifice of the Eucharist from the play, not to assert that Shakespeare is more or less Catholic or Protestant,[28] nor to establish his position on the controversy that raged

26 Hooker, *Ecclesiastical Polity*, Book V, p. 35. Susan Zimmerman's *The Early Modern Corpse and Shakespeare's Theatre* (Edinburgh: Edinburgh University Press, 2005) includes an excellent discussion of the Reformers' aversion to the materiality of mediaeval religious thought. See especially chapter 2, 'Body Imaging and Religious Reform: The Corpse as Idol', pp. 24–89.

27 *Inst.* IV, 17.3, emphasis added. Calvin joined in with vehemence against the Catholic Mass, attacking the 'mass-Doctors who purport to be the agent of grace instead of Christ: while they have fashioned themselves a god after the decision of their own lust, they have forsaken the living God. Indeed they have worshipped the gifts instead of the giver. In this there is a double transgression, for both the honour taken from God has been transferred to the creature [cf. Rom. 1.25], and he himself also has been dishonoured in the defilement and the profanation of his gift, when his holy sacrament is made a hateful idol.'

28 With the stakes high that England's 'national poet' does or does not represent England's national religion, the discussion of his greater or lesser sympathy to Catholicism is of considerable interest. See Peter Milward, *Shakespeare's Religious Background* (Bloomington: Indiana University Press, 1973); Richard Wilson, *Secret Shakespeare: Studies in Theatre, Religion, and Resistance* (Manchester: Manchester University Press, 2004); Arthur Marotti, *Religious Ideology and Cultural Fantasy: Catholic and anti-Catholic Discourse in Early Modern England* (Notre Dame, Ind.: Notre Dame University Press, 2005); Arthur Marotti (ed.), *Catholicism and anti-Catholicism in Early Modern Early Texts* (New

in his day over the Eucharist, but to demonstrate that *Othello* is a play that evokes longing for justice; longing, that is, for some antidote to the rhetoric of devils and hell that fills the stage; some redressing of the fiendish rituals of murderous vows, blasphemous oaths, and monstrous births of plots engendered by hell and night, invocations of whores and sorcerers, and the triumph of a deadly design that unravels as relentlessly as a providential one, but is so antithetical to providence that it springs from one who inverts the divine name, turning the tetragrammaton of Exodus 3, 'I am who I am', into 'I am not what I am', thereby setting sin loose upon the world. In a play where the tempter embraces divinity as surely as Milton's Satan does – 'divinity of hell ... So I will turn her virtue into pitch, and out of her own goodness make the net that shall enmesh them all'; 'If then his Providence/ Out of our evil seek to bring forth good,/ Our labour must be to pervert that end,/ And out of good still to find means of evil' (*Paradise Lost* I: 162–5) – it seems especially terrible that the other shoe does not fall, that infernal ends are not frustrated to bring good out of evil. Desdemona has precisely that intention. When Emilia has just described to her a world in which wrongdoing issues in wrongdoing – 'the ills we do their ills instruct us so' – Desdemona objects, 'God me such usage send, Not to pick bad from bad, but by bad mend!' Mend, amend, make amends, redemption: Desdemona has articulated her intent to turn evil to good with stunning emphasis at the end of Act IV, but that is just before, disturbingly enough, we see evil triumph and Desdemona undone.

Shakespeare challenges us to rethink these differences between a sacrifice and a murder. In his tragedies, acts of violence seem to hint toward redemption, but it is not clear that Desdemona's death redeems. Can we see her death as a sacrifice? A remission of sins? A benefit to others? A satisfaction of the demands of retributive justice? Othello himself wants to stage it that way. The murderous Othello stages his

---

York: Macmillan, 1999). Historical re-examinations of the nature and extent of the Reformation have altered the assumption that the religious landscape quickly and decisively converted to Protestant ritual and doctrine. See Eamon Duffy, *The Stripping of the Altars: Traditional Religion in England 1400–1580* (New Haven: Yale University Press, 1992); John Bossy, *The English Catholic Community 1570–1850* (London: Darton, Longman and Todd, 1975); and Christopher Haigh, *English Reformations: Religion, Politics, and Society under the Tudors* (Oxford: Clarendon, 1993). Arthur Marotti has concluded that the categories of Catholic and Protestant are too rough-hewn to describe the beliefs and practices of those in Shakespeare's audience who constitute a 'great muddled middle in English Christianity' ('Shakespeare and Catholicism', in Richard Dutton, Alison Findlay and Richard Wilson (eds), *Theatre and Religion: Lancastrian Shakespeare* [Manchester: Manchester University Press, 2003], p. 222). See also Debora K. Shuger, *Habits of Thought in the English Renaissance: Religion, Politics and the Dominant Culture* (Berkeley: University of California Press, 1990), and *The Renaissance Bible: Scholarship, Sacrifice, and Subjectivity* (Berkeley: University of California Press, 1994).

'sacrifice' of Desdemona like a priest at the altar and, before he kills her, delivers the injunction to confess derived from the communion service: 'If you bethink yourself of any crime,/ Unreconciled as yet to heaven and grace,/ Solicit for it straight.' He tries to stage a ritual death. It is marked by prayers:

> Oth. I would not kill thy unprepared spirit,
>   No, heaven forfend, I would not kill thy soul.
> Des. Talk you of killing?
> Oth. Ay, I do.
> Des. Then Lord have mercy on me.
> Oth. Amen, with all my heart!

And, in the role of priest, he would extract her confession:

> Oth. Therefore confess thee freely of thy sin
>   For to deny each article with oath
>   Cannot remove, nor shake the strong conceit
>   That I do groan withal: thou art to die.
> Des. Then Lord have mercy on me.
> Oth. I say, Amen.

But this is a perverse priest, for the final prayer that would assure Desdemona's redemption is silenced by Othello:

> Des. Kill me tomorrow, let me live to-night ...
>   But half an hour,
>   but while I say one prayer.
> Oth. Tis too late.

Othello's carefully orchestrated sacrifice quickly turns into a vengeful murder, as even he admits.

> Oth. O perjur'd woman, thou dost stone thy heart
>   And makest me call what I intend to do
>   A murder, which I had thought a sacrifice.

(V.ii)

He has come to her as a divine executor of justice ('vengeance is mine,' saith the Lord); 'it is the cause' says Othello, bearing the terrible mission of strict justice and retribution, 'else she'll betray more men'. The performative confusion of Desdemona crying out to the Lord and Emilia crying 'My Lord' seems to lure Othello himself into ontological confusion about his divine mission: 'I that am cruel, am yet merciful', he pronounces like an Old Testament deity who punishes the hardened heart, but also like the New Testament father who demands the life of his Son. But wait: he is murdering all the while, stifling Desdemona's breath *even as* he invokes mercy. Is this sacrifice or murder? If sacrifice, it should redeem and indeed Othello alludes to the eclipse and earthquake that marked

Christ's death. But none happen. He expects to see cloven hoofs on the devil Iago – but has to admit it is only a myth. And so his pretensions to being divine judge soon collapse and he assumes another role: the betrayer of divinity. No longer God the Father demanding retribution for sin, Othello becomes the Judas who betrays his master.[29]

Amidst his confused assertions of justice, Othello virtually confesses that he has sold her:

> nay, had she been true,
> If heaven would make me such another world
> Of one entire and perfect chrysolite,
> I'd not have sold her for it.

Like Judas, Othello brought false evidence against the blessed one, and like Judas, he kissed before he killed (Mk 14.44-46, cf. 14.55-56). False

---

29   For studies of Shakespeare's Protestantism, see the important studies by Huston Diehl, *Staging Reform, Reforming the Stage: Protestantism and Popular Theater in Early Modern England* (Ithaca: Cornell University Press, 1997) and Donna Hamilton, *Shakespeare and the Politics of Protestant England* (Lexington: University Press of Kentucky, 1992).

The discourse on Shakespeare and religion is extensive; among other works, it includes Roland Mushat Frye, *Shakespeare and Christian Doctrine* (Princeton: Princeton University Press, 1963); Herbert Coursen, Jr, *Christian Ritual and the World of Shakespeare's Tragedies* (Lewisburg: Buckell University Press, 1976); Roy Battenhouse (ed.), *Shakespeare's Christian Dimension: An Anthology of Commentary* (Bloomington: Indiana University Press, 1994); Francis Dolan, *Whores of Babylon: Catholicism, Gender, and Seventeenth-century Print Culture* (Ithaca: Cornell University Press, 1999); Judy Kronenfeld, *King Lear and the Naked Truth: Rethinking the Language of Religion and Resistance* (Durham, N.C.: Duke University Press, 1998); Debora K. Shuger, 'Subversive Fathers and Suffering Subjects: Shakespeare and Christianity', in Donna Hamilton and Richard Strier (eds), *Religion, Literature and Politics in Post-Reformation England, 1540–1688* (Cambridge: Cambridge University Press, 1996), pp. 46–69; Lowell Galligher, *Medusa's Gaze: Casuistry and Conscience in the Renaissance* (Stanford: Stanford University Press, 1991); Dennis Taylor and David Beauregard (eds), *Shakespeare and the Culture of Christianity in Early Modern England* (New York: Fordham University Press, 2003); Maurice Hunt, *Shakespeare's Religious Allusiveness: Its Play and Tolerance* (Aldershot: Ashgate, 2004).

For considerations of religion and *Othello*, see Eric Griffin, 'Un-sainting James: Or Othello and the "Spanish Spirits" of Shakespeare's Globe', *Representations* 62 (Spring 1998), 58–99; Huston Diehl's chapter on *Othello* (pp. 125–55); Robert Watson, 'Othello as Protestant Propaganda', in Claire McEchern and Debora Shuger (eds), *Religion and Culture in Renaissance England* (Cambridge: Cambridge University Press, 1997), pp. 234–57; Richard Mallette, 'Blasphemous Preacher: Iago and the Reformation', pp. 382–414; and Paula McQuade, 'Love and Lies: Marital Truth-Telling, Catholic Casuistry, and Othello' in Dennis Taylor and David Beauregard (eds), *Shakespeare and the Culture of Christianity in Early Modern England* (New York: Fordham University Press, 2003), p. 415–38; excerpts from David L. Jeffrey and Patrick Grant, Joan Ozark Holmer, and Roy Battenhouse in *Shakespeare's Christian Dimension*, ed. Battenhouse, pp. 415–29.

Discussions of the importance of the sacrament for drama include David Lee Miller, 'Witness as Theater in Shakespeare', in *Dreams of the Burning Child* (New York: Cornell University Press, 2003).

evidence violates justice but Othello's court of justice does not hesitate to admit it.

In the communion service in the Book of Common Prayer, after the recital of the Lord's Prayer, it calls for the rehearsal of the ten commandments, with the communicant praying that each of the sins he has committed be forgiven and that grace help him ward off transgression in the future. It is little wonder that *Othello* incites hunger for some vision of redemption, for in it each of the commandments is broken. The name of the Lord is used in vain repeatedly; 's'blood' (Christ's blood) is the first word out of Iago's cursing mouth; and 'zounds' (Christ's wounds) and 'by the mass' are blasphemous invocations of the sacrifice. The sabbath day is not kept holy – it sees a brawl; a father is not honoured – his daughter flees him in the night and disobeys him; what belongs to the neighbour is coveted – Iago covets Cassio's position; false witness is made – Iago uses the handkerchief; and murder is committed: all of the 'thou shalt nots' are violated. The only command of the decalogue that is conspicuously not broken is adultery, and it becomes, in this perverse covenant with a God who-is-not-what-he-is, the provocation of wrath. Othello succumbs to a perversion of the violence of monotheism: 'For I am a jealous God, you shall have none but me.'[30]

With this old covenant broken, we may well long for a new one, one written on the heart, like that of the prophets, not like the one broken when Israel disobeyed the law, but a Logos incarnated. And the breaking of the old law given in blood may well demand a new gift given in blood, a sacrifice, like that of Jesus. These allusions hover tantalizingly around Desdemona who does her part in tempting us into seeing her own death as a sacrifice. She calls out in her moment of death, 'O Lord Lord Lord' as Christ had called out 'Eli Eli'. And she withstands her version of the temptation offered to Christ in the wilderness, the gift of all the kingdoms of the world: 'all this dominion will I give to you and the glory that goes with it'. Just as Jesus need only do homage to Satan to gain the whole world, so in Emilia's test, Desdemona could have the whole world for one infelicity.

> Des.   Wouldst thou do such a deed, for all the world?
> Emil. Why, would not you?
> Des.   No, by this heavenly light!
> Emil. Nor I neither, by this heavenly light. I might do it as well in the
>   dark.
> Des.   Wouldst thou do such a thing for all the world?
> Emil. The world is a huge thing, 'tis a great price, For a small vice.
> Des.   Good troth, I think thou wouldst not.

---

30 Further discussion of this possessive violence is in my *The Curse of Cain: The Violent Legacy of Monotheism* (Chicago: University of Chicago Press, 1999).

Emil.   By my troth, I think I should, and undo't when I had done it;
marry, I would not do such a thing for a joint-ring; nor for
measures of lawn, nor for gowns, or petticoats, nor caps, nor
any such exhibition; but for the whole world? Why, who would
not make her husband a cuckold, to make him a monarch? I
should venture purgatory for it.

Des.   Beshrew me, if I would do such a wrong for the whole world.

(IV.iii)

The communion service begins with the recitation of the Lord's Prayer,
seeking out its eucharistic significance: 'give us this day our daily bread
and forgive us our trespasses as we forgive those who trespass against us.
And lead us not into temptation and deliver us from evil . . .' Desdemona
is not led to temptation, and her dying words suggest that she forgives
Othello's trespass: 'Commend me to my kind Lord, O farewell!' But is she
delivered from evil or to evil? She is the soul of purity who kneels and
prays before her murder. Her prayer is drawn from the general confession
of the communion service of the Book of Common Prayer: 'We [ac]
knowledge and bewail our manifold sinnes and wickedness, which we
from time to time most grievously have committed, by thoughts, word,
and deeds, against thy divine majestie.'

Des.   Here I kneel:
If e'er my will did trespass 'gainst his love
Either in discourse of thought or actual deed,
Comfort forswear me.

(IV.ii)

How can Desdemona's death be figured as a redemptive sacrifice when
Othello so resembles a perverse priest or even a sorcerer at a black mass?
At the opening of the play, he is arraigned and tried in what is virtually a
witch-trial scene, 'I therefore apprehend and do attach thee,/ For an
abuser of the world, a practiser/ Of arts inhibited and out of warrant' (I.
ii), one whose foul charms, drugs or minerals, have bound her in his
chains of magic. But his acquittal by the Venetian Senate in this scene
does not put an end to the suggestion of dark arts in this play. He calls
Desdemona to the same court, demanding ocular proof of her fidelity –
the spotted handkerchief he had given to her: but 'ocular proof' was the
technical term in witch trials for the mark on the body of the witch, the
'witch's teat', as it was so misogynistically called. To demand ocular proof
is to demand evidence of sorcery. From at least one of the perspectives
that reigns in the play, that of Iago, she is indicted. According to Iago,
Brabantio and Roderigo, she *has* had sexual congress with the devil.

According to historians' accounts of witchcraft beliefs, the devil himself
presided at the sorcerer's mass as a big black-bearded man, or as a

stinking goat or occasionally as a great toad, and an infernal Eucharist took place at the witch's sabbath where the blood of the devil is drunk instead of the blood of God. In that context, Cassio drinks a cup that holds the devil in it at an infernal marriage celebration: 'O thou invisible spirit of wine, if thou hast no name to be known by, let us call thee devil!' This seems compatible with a Reformer's version of the Mass as the work of the devil, a Black Mass, in their rejection of transubstantiation for the invisible spirit. Cassio will even invoke transubstantiation, not upwards, of man into god, but downward, of man into beast. 'I remember a mass of things', he laments with remorse – and we can be sure the pun on mass was not lost to the audience – 'but none distinctly, a quarrel but nothing wherefore. O God, that men should put an enemy in their mouths, to steal away their brains; that we should with joy, revel, pleasure, and applause, transform ourselves into beasts! ... To be now a sensible man, by and by a fool, and presently a beast! Every unordinate cup is unblessed and the ingredience is the devil' (II.iii). This is the Eucharist from hell.

By means of all these perversions and inversions – all the while calling to mind doctrinal Christian solutions even as they are withheld – Shakespeare is teasing us over and over with the possibility of redemption: an aborted Mass ministered by a demented priest, a communion cup turned into a vessel of drunken disorderliness and bestiality, a prayer ('Lord, have mercy on me') that is really a plea for life from the hands of a murderer, a vow that is really a curse, a sacrifice that is really a murder, a death that does not make the earth quake or the sun stand still, a light that, once put out, will not rekindle. Shakespeare even assigns the most explicit articulation in the play of that yearning for salvation to a drunk: 'there are souls that are saved and those that are not, may my soul be saved', slurs Cassio. Again, Shakespeare is only teasing us with the idea of redemption, for Cassio's high but drunken talk of salvation reduces to ludicrous pettiness:

> *Cassio.* For mine own part, no offense to the general, nor any man of
>   quality, I hope to be saved.
> *Iago.* And so do I Lieutenant.
> *Cassio.* Ay, but by your leave, not before me; the lieutenant is to be
>   saved before the ancient.
>
>   (II.iii)

This tease about the idea of redemption is sustained from the beginning of the play to the end: an 'old black ram' – it was a ram caught in the thicket that substituted for the sacrifice of Isaac, the typological prefiguration of the sacrifice of Christ – 'tupping your white Ewe', the Lamb of God. But is there a sacrifice? Othello takes by the 'throat the circumcised dog' – circumcision, the mark of the old covenant, 'and smote him thus' with the sign of the new covenant? That is, is Othello's suicide a sacrifice? Does it offer, in his self-murder of the self-defined infidel/idolater a restoration of justice, one confirmed by the legal restitution of order? Or rather, are we left aching for justice in the face of the triumph of evil? I would argue that this unmet craving for justice, so carefully incited and sustained throughout the play, is both the source of the play's tragedy and its 'conscience', pointing beyond the terrors of plot and experience to another vision of human possibility.

All of this is certainly not to say that Othello is merely a Christian allegory; of course it plumbs the depths of all-too-human passions (as do powerful religious myths, for that matter). Nor would I want to suggest, despite the frequent dating of the play to 1604, the very year Convocation was assembled to further emend the Prayer Book in a period fraught with controversy over the Eucharist, that the play became Shakespeare's covert expression of what had been censured on the stage – his stand on the religious controversy. The evidence is conflicting: on the one hand, a deranged Othello imagines himself a priest at a sacrifice as he performs a murder; on the other, an innocent victim, falsely accused but faithful to the last, cries out to the Lord at her death by a deranged killer, invoking prayers that did precede the Anglican communion service but do not save or redeem her.[31] These do not add up tidily either to an argument that Shakespeare is critiquing or that he is embracing the doctrine of the sacrifice of the Mass. Rather, in a play preoccupied with the problem of evil and the problem of justice, I discern Shakespeare needing to invoke the Mass – not only the Catholic Mass, but also its infernal parody – because it addressed the problem of justice so forcefully with its promise of the remission of sins through the sacrifice.[32]

Surely something profound was lost when Reformers attenuated the sacrifice of the Eucharist, or, to be more precise, turned it into a commemoration of a sacrifice rather than a re-enactment, a commemoration of a moment in the distant past rather than a sacrifice that occurs at the very moment when the communicant ingests the host, a moment when suffering is redeemed, a mysterious moment when our depravity is absolved. Gabriel Biel was one of the most widely read authorities on the Mass at the time of the Reformation – seven editions of his *Exposition of the Sacred Canon of the Mass* were printed between 1488 and 1547; even Luther said it was the best Catholics possessed on the subject – and he summarizes well what was at stake in the loss: 'In this sacrifice there is the commemoration of and calling on that unique and perfect sacrifice by

31   Shakespearean allusions to assassins taking the sacrament prior to their crime include *Henry VI* 4.2.28; *Richard III* 1.4.191; *King John* 5.2.6, and *Richard II* 5.2.97-9.

32   This inadequacy was felt by the radical Reformers themselves, figures like Menno who needed to solve the problem through a God-man whose heavenly, rather than earthly flesh, offered man the chance to be perfected through communion with that flesh.

which heaven was opened, grace is given, through which alone our works can be meritorious, through which alone all the sins of men are remitted, and heavenly glory, lost by our sin, is restored ...' (Lectio LVII, lit. D).[33]

For most of Christian history, the work of redemption is able to occur during the Mass because it is theologically grounded in a ritual temporality which is not simply or strictly linear: the sacrifice of Christ was both then and now. Although Christ was offered but once in the natural appearance of his flesh, nevertheless he is offered daily on the altar, veiled under the appearances of bread and wine. This offering of him does not, of course, entail any suffering, for Christ is not wounded, does not suffer and die each day, a distinction that came to be known as the bloody and unbloody sacrifices of the Lord. As Biel summarizes, consecration and reception of the Eucharist is called a sacrifice and an oblation both to commemorate and to re-enact: 'first, because it represents that true sacrifice and holy immolation made once upon the cross, and is its memorial; secondly, because it is a *cause* through which similar *effects* are produced'.

Having dispelled the *opus operatum*, the Reformers threatened to dispel the sacramental organ of salvation, the means for incarnating Christ within each communicant to effect his redemption. How frail the mantra of their movement, 'faith', must have felt before the power of the sacrifice of the God-man that had successfully satisfied justice from the time of the Gospels to Luther.[34] With the English Church's reluctance to offer sacramental deterrence and remission of sins – that is, sacramental justice – the scene shifted to the theatre where justice was taken on imaginatively. With the change from sacrifice to remembrance, from transformation to representation, the church had left less the power of ritual than (ironically, given its opposition to theatre) the catharsis of spectacle. When communion offers a memory of a past and a promise of a future event but no redemption in the present, then redemption becomes the object of longing – in memory and in hope. Not only because Reformers foregrounded representation were they unwittingly closer to the theatre they so severely critiqued, but also because the theatre too evinced the moral outrage – the longing for justice rather than its satisfaction – that

33   Gabriel Biel, *Expositio sacri canonis missae* (*c.* 1488) Brescia edn, 1576.

34   Herbert Coursen, Jr's Introduction to his *Christian Ritual and the World of Shakespeare's Tragedies* (Lewisburg: Buckell University Press, 1976) includes a fine discussion of the importance of Communion to the Elizabethan: 'It is in the receiving of the sacraments and not in the consecration of the elements that the fusion of Christ and communicant, blood and wine occurs ... It is more important, says Hooker, to "meditate with silence what we have by the sacrament, and less to dispute the matter how"', pp. 5–6. He concludes that 'the 1559 Prayer Book's confirmation of the individual's role in Communion was bound to affect, if not determine, the drama that emerged in the late sixteenth and early seventeenth centuries'; p. 8.

became the deep structure of the Reformed ritual. On the one hand, the theatre can invite its audience to long for a grace it cannot give through a faith it cannot confer. On the other hand, when the wine only signifies blood and does not become the blood, the church's communion risks the slippery slope toward disillusionment: 'the wine she drinks is made of grapes'. And if there is no wine that is blood – not even Desdemona's – then perhaps there is no redemption, and this may well be the matter for tragedy and tears, after all, and not for the transformations of religious ritual.

That the theatre should flower during the chill of Protestantism's heyday is no mystery. With bodies strewn all over the stage, the theatre became a truly Protestant church, where a community convened and remembered sacrifice – without the *operatum* of the church – and where each individual was challenged privately to try to distinguish sacrifice from murder, *the* question for faith, and to crave for justice no longer satisfied by the sacrament. Othello's distorted oath, 'My life upon her faith' hauntingly suggests theatre's distinct performative symbiosis of sacrifice and faith in a world that craves for both, for either, for anything but 'what you know you know' as an answer to why our demi-devils ensnare our souls.

References

Altman, Joel, ' "Vile Participation": The Amplification of Violence in the Theatre of Henry V', *Shakespeare Quarterly* 42.1 (1991), 1–32.

Barbar, C. L., *Creating Elizabethan Tragedy* (Chicago: University of Chicago Press, 1988).

Barish, Jonas, *The Anti-Theatrical Prejudice* (Berkeley: University of California Press, 1981).

Battenhouse, Roy (ed.), *Shakespeare's Christian Dimension: An Anthology of Commentary* (Bloomington: Indiana University Press, 1994).

Beckerman, Bernard, 'Shakespearean Playgoing Then and Now', in Sidney Homan (ed.), *Shakespeare's More Than Words Can Witness: Essays on Visual and Nonverbal Enactment in the Plays* (Lewisburg, Pa: Bucknell University Press, 1986).

Beckwith, Sarah, *Christ's Body* (New York: Routledge, 1993).

Biel, Gabriel, *Expositio sacri canonis missae* (*c.* 1488) Brescia edn, 1576.

Booty, John E., *John Jewel as Apologist of the Church of England* (London: SPCK, 1963).

Bossy, John, *The English Catholic Community 1570–1850* (London: Darton, Longman and Todd, 1975).

Bynum, Caroline Walker, *Holy Feast and Holy Fast* (Berkeley: University of California Press, 1987).

Calvin, John, *Institution of the Christian Religion* (1536 edition) (New York: John Knox Press, 1975).

Coursen, Herbert Jr, *Christian Ritual and the World of Shakespeare's Tragedies* (Lewisburg: Bucknell University Press, 1976).

Cranmer, Thomas, 'A Defence of the True and Catholic Doctrine of the Sacrament' (1550), in Gervase E. Duffield (ed.), *The Work of Thomas Cranmer* (vol. 2; Appleford: Sutton Courtenay Press, 1964).

Davidson, Clifford, 'The Anti-Visual Prejudice', in Clifford Davidson and Anne E. Nichols (eds), *Iconoclasm vs Art and Drama* (Kalamazoo, Michigan: Medieval Institute Publications, 1988).

Davies, Michael, 'The Transubstantial Bard: Shakespeare and Catholicism', in Burnham and Giaccherini (eds), *The Poetics of Transubstantiation: From Theology to Metaphor* (Aldershot: Ashgate, 2005).

Dawson, Anthony, 'Performance and Participation', in Anthony Dawson and Paul Yachnin, *The Culture of Playgoing in Shakespeare's England* (Cambridge: Cambridge University Press, 2001), pp. 11–37.

Diehl, Huston, *Staging Reform, Reforming the Stage: Protestantism and Popular Theater in Early Modern England* (Ithaca: Cornell University Press, 1997).

Dolan, Francis, *Whores of Babylon: Catholicism, Gender, and Seventeenth-century Print Culture* (Ithaca: Cornell University Press, 1999).

Duffy, Eamon, *The Stripping of the Altars:Traditional Religion in England 1400–1580* (New Haven: Yale University Press, 1992).

Frye, Roland Mushat, *Shakespeare and Christian Doctrine* (Princeton: Princeton University Press, 1963).

Galligher, Lowell, *Medusa's Gaze: Casuistry and Conscience in the Renaissance* (Stanford: Stanford University Press, 1991).

Gosson, Stephen, *Plays Confuted in Five Actions* (1582) facsimile edn (New York: Johnson Reprint Corp., 1972), sigs C5, G6–G7.

Greenblatt, Stephen, *Shakespearean Negotiations* (Berkeley: University of California Press, 1988).

Griffin, Eric, 'Un-sainting James: Or Othello and the "Spanish Spirits" of Shakespeare's Globe', *Representations* 62 (1998), 58–99.

Gurr, Andrew, *The Shakespearean Stage 1574–1642* (Cambridge: Cambridge University Press, 1970).

Haigh, Christopher, *English Reformations: Religion, Politics, and Society under the Tudors* (Oxford: Clarendon, 1993).

Hamilton, Donna, *Shakespeare and the Politics of Protestant England* (Lexington: University Press of Kentucky, 1992).

Hart, D. Bentley, 'A Gift Exceeding Every Debt: An Eastern Orthodox Appreciation of Anselm's *Cur Deus Homo*', *Pro Ecclesia* 7.3 (1998), 333–49.

Hatchett, Marion J., *The Eucharistic Liturgies of Historic Prayer Books:*

Historic Rites Arranged for Contemporary Celebration (Sewanee, Tenn.: St. Luke's Journal of Theology, 1984).

Heinemann, Margot, *Puritanism and Theatre* (Cambridge: Cambridge University Press, 1980).

Hodgkins, Christopher, 'Plays Out of Season: Puritanism, Antitheatricalism, and Parliament's 1642 Closing of the Theaters', in Daniel W. Doerksen and Christopher Hodgkins (eds), *Centered on the Word: Literature, Scripture, and the Tudor-Stuart Middle Way* (Newark: University of Delaware Press, 2004).

Hooker, Richard, *Ecclesiastical Polity*, V (London: Everyman, 1907).

Houston, Julia, 'Transubstantiation and the Sign: Cranmer's Drama of the Lord's Supper', *Journal of Medieval and Renaissance Studies 24* (1994), pp. 113–30.

Hunt, Maurice, *Shakespeare's Religious Allusiveness: Its Play and Tolerance* (Aldershot: Ashgate, 2004).

Jeffrey, David L., Patrick Grant, Joan Ozark Holmer and Roy Battenhouse, in *Shakespeare's Christian Dimension,* ed. Battenhouse, pp. 415–29.

Knapp, Jeffrey, 'Preachers and Players in Shakespeare's England', *Representations* 44 (1993), 29–59.

Kronenfeld, Judy, *King Lear and the Naked Truth: Rethinking the Language of Religion and Resistance* (Durham, NC:Duke University Press, 1998]

Levinas, E., 'Franz Rosenzweig, une pensée juive moderne', in Franz Rosenzweig *Les Cahiers de la Nuit Surveillée*, vol. 1 (Quetigny, France, 1982).

—— *Beyond the Verse: Talmudic Readings and Lectures* (London: Athlone Press, 1994).

Mallette, Richard, 'Blasphemous Preacher: Iago and the Reformation', in Dennis Taylor and David Beauregard (eds), *Shakespeare and the Culture of Christianity in Early Modern England* (New York: Fordham University Press, 2003), pp. 382–414.

Marotti, Arthur (ed.), *Catholicism and anti-Catholicism in Early Modern Early Texts* (New York: Macmillan, 1999).

Marotti, Arthur, 'Shakespeare and Catholicism', in Richard Dutton, Alison Findlay and Richard Wilson (eds), *Theatre and Religion: Lancastrian Shakespeare* (Manchester: Manchester University Press, 2003), pp. 218–41.

—— *Religious Ideology and Cultural Fantasy: Catholic and anti-Catholic Discourse in Early Modern England* (Notre Dame, Ind.: Notre Dame University Press, 2005).

McQuade, Paula, 'Love and Lies: Marital Truth-Telling, Catholic Casuistry, and Othello', in Dennis Taylor and David Beauregard (eds), *Shakespeare and the Culture of Christianity in Early Modern England* pp. 415–38.

Miller, David Lee, 'Witness as Theater in Shakespeare', in *Dreams of the Burning Child: Sacrificial Sons and the Father's Witness* (Ithaca: Cornell University Press, 2003).

Milward, Peter, *Shakespeare's Religious Background* (Bloomington: Indiana University Press, 1973).

Montrose, Louis, 'The Purpose of Playing: Reflections on Shakespearean Anthropology', *Helios* 7 (1980), 51–74.

O'Connell, Michael, 'God's Body: Incarnation, Physical Embodiment and the Fate of Biblical Theatre in the Sixteenth Century', in David Allen and Robert White (eds), *Subjects on the World's Stage* (London: Associated University Presses, 1995).

Phythian-Adams, Charles, 'Ceremony and the Citizen: The Communal Year at Coventry 1450–1550', in P. Clark and P. Slack (eds), *Crisis and Order in English Towns 1500–1700* (London: Routledge and Kegan Paul, 1972).

Rubin, Miri, *Corpus Christi: The Eucharist in Late Medieval Culture* (Cambridge: Cambridge University Press, 1991).

Schwartz, Regina, *The Curse of Cain: The Violent Legacy of Monotheism* (Chicago: University of Chicago Press, 1999).

——, 'The Price of Justice and Love in *The Merchant of Venice*', in *TriQuarterly* 124 (2006), 225–41.

Shuger, Debora K., *Habits of Thought in the English Renaissance: Religion, Politics and the Dominant Culture* (Berkeley: University of California Press, 1990).

—— *The Renaissance Bible: Scholarship, Sacrifice, and Subjectivity* (Berkeley: University of California Press, 1994).

—— 'Subversive Fathers and Suffering Subjects: Shakespeare and Christianity', in Donna Hamilton and Richard Strier (eds), *Religion, Literature and Politics in Post-Reformation England, 1540–1688* (Cambridge: Cambridge University Press, 1996), pp. 46–69.

Taylor, Dennis and David Beauregard (eds), *Shakespeare and the Culture of Christianity in Early Modern England* (New York: Fordham University Press, 2003).

Verma, Rajiva, *Myth, Ritual and Shakespeare* (New Delhi: Spantech Publishers, 1990).

Watson, Robert, 'Othello as Protestant Propaganda', in Claire McEchern and Debora Shuger (eds), *Religion and Culture in Renaissance England* (Cambridge: Cambridge University Press, 1997), pp. 234–57.

Wilson, Richard, *Secret Shakespeare: Studies in Theatre, Religion, and Resistance* (Manchester: Manchester University Press, 2004).

Zimmerman, Susan, *The Early Modern Corpse and Shakespeare's Theatre* (Edinburgh: Edinburgh University Press, 2005).

Chapter 10

BAD FRIDAY

Sara Maitland

I have a bit of a problem with this story. It's not really like some of the other stories about my somewhat tiresome guardian angel.

For one thing it happened in the night.

Oddly enough – well it does seem odd to me – my guardian angel does not often appear in the night. As a matter of fact, I strongly suspect that this is because she has such a pathetic imagination. She can't cope with dreams, and is confined to the daily. You read in the Bible of truly wonderful dreams; like Jacob's ladder or Joseph putting his brothers in their place by boasting about their measly little sheaves of corn bowing down to his great big fat one.

I think a few dreams would be fun, and a much better way of getting spiritual guidance because you could chat for hours with your friends about interpretations and Freud and sex and things. But do I dream? No, I don't. All I get are her clichés, and her interfering pettiness, and her tedious scruples.

Of course, she doesn't agree. She says the reason I don't get dreams is because I sleep so soundly, for which – in her opinion – I ought to be grateful. I find this terribly unromantic, but it's true: frankly the minute I turn the light out I slump asleep and practically never wake up again until the alarm clock rings. But you might well think a half-way competent angel would be able to deal with such a minor impediment. It makes you wonder. If I were God the very least I'd do is check that all the guardian angels had *some* creative flair, and ones like mine who are so totally prosaic and mundane would be kept in heaven, well out of the way of delicate and aspiring souls.

Anyway, all this is pretty irrelevant because as it happens this story did take place in the night. At twelve minutes past three to be precise. The very worst imaginable time to be woken up by an angel with a slightly common accent manifesting herself all of a sudden, and saying 'I've just popped in to say goodbye.'

'Go away,' I muttered. In my own defence I must stress that I was nine-tenths asleep. Then I remembered with a horrid jerk that I had said much the same thing to my daughter one night when she was ten years old and had been woken up two hours later by my very angry oldest son reporting that she was retching and shivering and swallowing her pain in the bathroom, and telling him not to wake me or I would be cross. She had acute appendicitis; and had been wheeled into surgery still apologizing for having disturbed me.

(By the way, in fairness since I am always complaining about Angel, I should mention that she was completely marvellous that night, and came with us all the way in the ambulance and did try to comfort me, and reassure me that I could go on being a mother. Unlike usual, she didn't rub my face in guilt. I refused her consolation thought – I knew all about my inadequacy and awfulness on that occasion.)

So with that unfortunate precedent looming in my consciousness I sat up and said 'Sorry, Angel, I was asleep. Is it something important?'

'I just popped in to say goodbye.'

'Can't that wait?' I asked peevishly.

'You are always telling me you want divine revelations in the cold small hours of the night,' she said. If anyone else had used that tone to me I would have thought they were being a bit sarcastic, but Angel is too dense for such subtleties.

'I don't see your departure exactly as a spiritual revelation,' I muttered. And then it hit me. Her departure. She couldn't leave me, not just like that. I hadn't been *that* nasty to her; it was just that we disagreed about quite a lot of things. Surely angels could accept and tolerate difference? Surely she wouldn't be that small-minded? What did she expect, slavish obedience or something? Not that I minded of course; if she wanted to desert her God-given duties that was up to her; it was none of my business. It was just the principle of the thing.

'Angel . . .' I began.

'You know we always take this Friday off,' she said.

She always did too. Regular as clockwork. 'Fine,' I said, ignoring a great surge of relief and happiness, 'I don't see why you had to wake me up for that. Did you think I'd forget or something? See you Easter Day.'

There was a pause. Then she said, with what sounded like an unusual degree of diffidence, 'I thought I'd better remind you about fasting.'

'Fasting! For Good Friday!' I exclaimed. 'Oh don't be so antiquated. No one does that any more.'

She didn't argue with me, there was just one of her long silences.

'I'm not,' I said boldly, 'into all that body-hating, masochistic, mediaeval stuff. Do you fast in heaven?'

Her silence continued. I waited hopefully. For once, I thought, I had her where I wanted her. In the wrong. After a bit I heard her sniffle; the poor thing was probably embarrassed. I felt a moment of compassion, but, thinking about all the times she had forced me to apologize, I clung to my moment of triumph.

'Well,' I said, after I thought she had been silent for long enough, 'do you fast in heaven?'

The silence went on a bit longer. It was almost beginning to feel awkward; then she said, quite suddenly and almost crossly for her, 'Well we can't, can we? We don't eat. We don't feel hunger.'

But the odd thing was that she didn't sound the least bit pleased with herself – either for her minor victory over me, or for this abundant proof of the superiority of angels.

We fell into silence again. It went on for a long time. I thought she had finished harassing me and would dematerialize herself in her own good time, so I lay down again and tried to go back to sleep. She was still there, hovering in my left cortex as only angels can. Now and again she made a funny snuffly sound, as though she had a cold; but when someone has just reminded you, and in a rather disagreeable tone, that they don't experience hunger, you can't very well offer them a handkerchief and tell them to blow their nose.

It was all very annoying. I felt more and more obstinate. She could stay or go in her own good time, but I was not going to initiate another conversation. It was three o'clock in the morning, for goodness sake, and no time for a busy woman to be having to deal with sulky angels. And in passing I would like to say that no human being, not even the adolescent male, can sulk as efficiently and thoroughly as your average angel. All I wanted was to go back to sleep.

The snuffling however did not diminish. On the contrary. Then I realized that she was crying. I mean really crying. It was a bit embarrassing actually, like the first time a grown-up man cries those terrible awkward male tears onto you; you know it's a sort of compliment, you have an inkling of how much they need to do it, and, at the same time, you just wish they wouldn't, because they are so bad at it. Angel's tears made me squirm a bit; I nearly asked her how it was that angels could cry when they couldn't eat, and then decided that would not be very kind. But I really did feel quite strongly that it was an angel's role to comfort, not to be comforted, so I let her get on with it for a bit.

In the end it got to me; that irrepressible maternal instinct – or since I'm a feminist perhaps I should say human instinct – that simply prevents you from letting a person, or I suppose an angel for that matter, cry. I wasn't best pleased about it.

'Oh for heaven's sake, Angel,' I said, when I could bear it no longer, 'whatever's the matter now?'

But she didn't reply. She just went on crying. It was really getting on my nerves. I said 'All right then, if it means that much to you I will fast today.'

You might think that this generosity of spirit would cheer anyone up, but it didn't work with her.

'Please.' I could hear myself begging. When I think of all the times that she has felt free to interrupt me and demand that I talk to her about whatever idiotic banality she chooses. And now she was refusing me the same privilege. It wasn't fair. That sounded a bit childish, so I changed my mind. It was outrageous!

'You're behaving like a teenager,' I said; I tried to say it firmly rather than angrily. Three teenage children in one household is quite enough, without having to put up with a teenaged spiritual force that skulked about somewhere slightly above my top vertebra. Once my daughter locked herself in the bathroom and howled for three hours, and when she finally came out she demanded cinnamon toast and refused point blank ever to say what the matter was. I was not going through that again, especially not with a blasted angel about whom I could not even have the dubious satisfaction of murmuring 'boy-friend-trouble' with the world-weariness of middle age.

'Angel,' I said, 'don't be such a baby.' But when babies cry you can comfort them. You can kiss them and cuddle them; you can wrap them warm and safe against you, petting their pink, flushed faces. You can find their favourite teddy bear, its face already worn bald with the receiving of love and the giving of furry comfort. You cannot do any of these things, or anything like them, with an angel. Grey matter may be soft and warm, but cuddly it is not. I reached through my mind and spirit for tenderness and comfort and found my hands empty. It was very frustrating.

The crying went on and on. I had tried emotional bribery and I had tried emotional blackmail. There was nothing left except love. And, given the difficulties of our relationship, and the degree to which I felt irritated by her, it was not an easy thing to offer.

'Angel,' I said, as carefully as I knew how. 'I love you. When you came to say goodbye I had forgotten about the Friday bank holiday or whatever you call it in heaven, and I thought you were leaving me permanently. I was sad. I didn't even know I was sad, but I was. I was sad because I love you. And because I need you. But honestly I would rather you left me if that made you happier than have you stay like this.'

I felt a complete idiot when I said this. There are many things you find yourself doing as you get older which your optimistic young self would never have known how to dream of, but very high on that list for me comes sitting up in bed at four in the morning, in a flannel nightie, trying to tell *anyone*, let alone a weeping and unresponsive citizen of heaven, that you love her.

But it worked. Not magically or instantaneously or anything, but the solid flow of desolate tears turned back into the infuriating adenoidal snuffles, and then into the hiccups of a sob-exhausted toddler.

Finally she said, 'It's worse than you know.'

'What is?' I asked, relieved that we were getting somewhere, but weary with the strain.

'I'm jealous.'

'Jealous!' I exclaimed, startled. 'Jealous?' I inquired, in an attempt at non-judgemental open-minded interest.

There was a bit more snuffling, and then finally she said 'I'm jealous of *you*.'

'Me?' I said tentatively, though really I meant 'What on earth are you talking about?'

'Yes you. I'm jealous of you because you can get hungry. Because you can get hurt, I mean physically hurt; because you can have pain, and suffering, and agony.'

'But that's not nice. I mean, those things aren't nice. They're horrid. Why does that make you jealous?'

'Because you can be with Him today and we can't. We just can't. We tried and tried and we couldn't understand. After the Last Supper he went away from us. We thought we could rescue him and he wouldn't let us. Then we thought at least we could comfort him, and we couldn't. That peasant woman could; she may be the Queen of Heaven now, but then she was just a middle-aged woman from the sticks, but she could comfort him, and her half-daft fisherman friend and that red-headed whore from Magdala; they could comfort him because they could understand. And we, the first-born of the creation, the spinners of the seven spheres, the messengers of the Holy Spirit, the powers and dominions, cherubim and seraphim, angels and archangels; we could do nothing. He didn't need us. We could not go where he had gone. We could not understand. That's why we all take the day off; not for a holiday but because we know we're useless.

They scourged him and we could not feel it. They crowned him with thorns and it didn't hurt us. They banged those nails through his hands and we wept for his humiliation, but we could not go where he had gone when he went into the pain-place, whatever that is. He gave you the glory, the privilege of going where he went, into the body in all its beauty and holiness, into the pain and the pleasure of the flesh. He loves you more than he loves us. And you have taken that privilege, that gift, that joy so lightly that you don't even care enough to fast once a year. *Of course I'm jealous!*'

She began to cry again. So did I, as a matter of fact. We wept together and we could not comfort each other.

'We don't call it Good Friday,' she gulped after a while, 'we call it Bad Friday.'

'Angel,' I said, 'I really will fast today. I'll fast for me and I'll fast for you.' This time the generosity of spirit was slightly more authentic.

'Thank you,' she said.

It was nearly dawn, grey light was coming through the curtains. She got ready to depart. I began to think about how impressed my children would be when they saw I wasn't eating, not even the hot cross buns. It might even reconvert my middle son who was trying out existentialism at that moment. I might even become a great ascetic saint pretty soon, known for the rigours of my life and for my charity to lesser mortals.

Angel put a stop to that; she paused in her soft descent through my cranial cavity, and murmured, 'Watch it, sister; we haven't even started on hair shirts and flagellation yet, and they're tough.' But she was grinning a shy, happy little grin.

'Peace be with you,' she said as usual, 'and see you on Sunday.'

Nancy A. Macky

Despite its gruesome reality, for over a millennium Christ's crucifixion has fascinated artists of all media – music, poetry, story, painting, sculpture, textiles, even jewellery. What was to the Romans a shaming public spectacle meant to deter political threats has, instead, been to centuries of Christians a focal point of faith and mystery. Using different Gospel versions of Christ's passion week blended with St Paul's theological interpretations, artists have explored this mystery with their imaginations and talents.

From their explorations, we can find in these essays varied visions of basic questions: Who was at each event in Christ's last week? From the Gospel stories, how can their attitudes be conveyed? Jensen asks how body positions – head, eyes, arms, torso – affect emotional reactions. How are we to react to a God/Man synthesis, as Hawkins probes? Christ's body on the cross – was it muscular? Emaciated? Distorted? Covered? Exposed? Beautiful? Were his eyes open, and if so, looking where? Paintings, drawings and sculptures present possibilities.

Those at the foot of the cross – at what were they gazing: Christ? Each other? Their gambling? Heaven? How did their gestures convey their attitudes?

How did the setting contribute to the mood: ground (flat, undulating, blurred, tortured); sky (bright, dark, cloudy, threatening, blank); vegetation (benign, scarce, abundant, menacing)? While Christ's body in all physical media is unquestionably the focus, artists obviously brought their own interpretations, using line, light, colour, texture and shadow to explore these questions.

Obviously from these essays, we see that all artists examine Christ's passion with more than clinical or voyeuristic intentions. Observers, listeners, readers, are invited to share the artist's *response* to Christ's suffering and death, as Luz and the other essayists confirm. Musical depictions first demand performers' commitment in learning and presenting lyrics and melodies that require them to present themselves as actors in the drama, either as solo character or reacting chorus. This, in turn, invites listeners to respond to the story as modulated by voice and orchestration. Even the kind of music that composers select affects how broadly the passion can be interpreted, as Flynn and Hornby remind us. Issues raised by Christ's death echo in several other genres, notably story and drama, Maitland and Schwartz point out.

But all artistic presentations call for response, even advocating action suggested by the political or cultural milieu where the artist places the scene. Several show parallels in contemporaneous political turmoil, as Gorringe contends. Other cultures adapted the passion story into their ancient traditions to make it meaningful, as Lara reveals. Most often, these essays explore possible responses: sorrow, sympathy, empathy, gratitude, compassion, consolation, hope, transformation. As Watson concludes, 'There is a need to revise all human values in the light of the crucifixion.'

Index of References